New Priorities in the Curriculum

LOUISE M. BERMAN
University of Maryland

CHARLES E. MERRILL PUBLISHING COMPANY
COLUMBUS, OHIO
A Bell & Howell Company

Merrill's

INTERNATIONAL SERIES IN EDUCATION

Under the Editorship of the Late
KIMBALL WILES
University of Florida

International Standard Book Number: 0-675-09612-X

Library of Congress Catalog Card Number: 68-28703

4   5   6   7   8   9   10   —   74   73

PRINTED IN THE UNITED STATES OF AMERICA

To my
MOTHER AND FATHER

Preface

A person's life is an ever-changing blend of peak experiences of the past, demanding circumstances of the moment, and hopes and expectations of the future. To the degree that the person can make sense out of his swirl of contacts, memories, and aspirations, to the same degree will he live a meaningful and satisfying life. Fortunate indeed is the person who has learned to resolve conflict with a reasonable degree of competence and to establish priorities so that he can place the impact of the moments into perspective.

Curriculum workers, being faced with an unwieldy set of challenges because of the newness, imprecision, and complexity of the curriculum field, have a tremendous task. To resolve the dilemmas caused by conflicts in a person's own ideologies and the persistent shifts in curriculum emphases calls for mental agility and physical stamina beyond what many persons normally possess. Yet, the educator, anxious to make a difference in the lives of those for whom he is responsible, must be engaged in a constant search for priorities. If he fails to see his job as the quest for the significant and important, his life will be bombarded by detail which he will be unable to place into any type of construct or to arrange in a hierarchical order.

This writer's search for priorities in the curriculum is the theme of this book. Among the chronic hopeful educators who believe that school learning could and should make a difference in the lives of children and youth, the writer has decided upon the major suggested curriculum emphases after considerable sifting through alternative concepts.

Because persons are called upon to make so many adjustments in life for which they have not been adequately prepared, it appears that the intent and the substance of the curriculum should be geared in such a way that it has two major characteristics: (1) Its major concern is with the ongoingness rather than the staticism of life; (2) the substance of the curriculum is related to human processes such as perceiving, knowing, and organizing; and the program is so designed that children and youth not only experience but also study these functions in a systematic way.

The purpose of the book is to sketch in broad outline what some of the components of the curriculum ought to be, if the development of a process-oriented person is seen as a critical goal of the school. In moving toward a curriculum construct, one has the problem of resolving certain seemingly contradictory elements. For example, the stimulus for a construct should invite serious thought but also playfulness with ideas. The ideas should be persuasive, but they should also lend themselves to be stated as hypotheses for testing. The construct should contain some tried ideas but also some fresh ones. It should be open enough to include relevant concepts from many disciplines but also bounded so that priorities are established within the curriculum.

Before proceeding further into this book, the curriculum worker should be aware that the new priorities suggested are sketched only in very broad strokes. The detail is yet to be filled in. Furthermore, persons expecting to find the traditional school subjects such as mathematics, science, or social studies treated with any degree of adequacy will be disappointed. Although the author acknowledges the potential value of these traditional school subjects, she takes the position that a school program which places priority upon the skills and content described in Chapters Three through Ten is more appropriate for today's children and youth. It should be noted, however, that many of the inquiry-based approaches to the academic disciplines are subsumed under the topic of "Knowing," Chapter Six.

In writing a work of this nature an author is indebted to many sources. I am particularly grateful to those persons or groups who triggered my thinking, which was later followed up by more systematic study. The well-turned phrases of authors in a variety of fields, the penetrating question of an astute student, the support of a tentatively formulated idea by a thoughtful class, the wise comment by a passer-by—these are the jabs that stimulated the book.

I am indebted to several persons for their thoughtful assistance along the way. To the late Mrs. Lorraine Schudson, Milwaukee, Wisconsin, I am grateful for her enthusiasm and help in locating sources during the initial writing stages. Miss Kathy Goodman, of Milwaukee and Jackson College, Tufts University, was particularly helpful during the final stages in editing, obtaining clearances, and typing the final draft. Without the sustained interest and encouragement of the administrative personnel of Charles E. .Merrill Publishing Company during some very busy years, I doubt that this book or its forthcoming companion volume on educational leadership would have come into being.

Cynthia Korfmann, Production Editor, and other members of Merrill's staff, were also most cooperative and helpful in the final preparation of the manuscript.

Shortly before his death, Kimball Wiles, Dean of the College of Education, University of Florida, and Editor of Merrill's International Series in Education, read and commented upon the entire manuscript. He was enthusiastically supportive during the writing of the book. Those who knew him will miss his great energy and vibrant personality.

For permission to quote from their publications I am grateful to the following publishers and persons:

Alfred A. Knopf, Inc.

American Association for Higher Education, NEA

American Association of Colleges for Teacher Education, NEA

American Journal of Psychoanalysis

Appleton-Century-Crofts, Division of Meredith Publishing Company

Donald G. Arnstine

Association for Supervision and Curriculum Development, NEA

D. E. Berlyne

The British Journal of Educational Psychology

Harry S. Broudy

Cambridge University Press

Charles E. Merrill Publishing Company

Columbia University Press

David McKay Co., Inc.

Doubleday & Company, Inc.

Education Development Center

The Educational Forum, Kappa Delta Pi, An Honor Society in Education

Educational Theory

ETC: A Review of General Semantics, International Society for General Semantics

The Free Press of Glencoe

The Futurist, The World Future Society

H. B. Gelatt

Ginn & Company

George Braziller, Inc.

Harper & Row, Publishers

Harvard University Press

William G. Hollister, M.D.

Holt, Rinehart & Winston, Inc.

Houghton Mifflin Company

John Wiley & Sons, Inc.

Journal of Applied Behavioral Science, National Training Laboratories, NEA

Journal of Counselling Psychology, American Psychological Association

Journal of Creative Behavior

Journal of Existential Psychiatry, now *Journal of Existentialism*

McGraw-Hill Book Company

Mentor Books

The Philosophical Library, John Wiley & Sons, Inc., Science Editions

Prentice-Hall, Inc.

Random House, Inc.

James Raths

Saul Bass & Associates

What appears on the pages that follow is a broad conception of what I feel are some major priorities that need new emphasis in the curriculum. The impact of the book can be measured, however, only in the thinking and changed practices which may result from the consideration of new priorities in the curriculum.

Louise M. Berman

Washington, D. C.

April, 1968

Contents

144—Creating and Perceiving; Creating and Discovery; Creating and Error; Creating and Psychological Support; Creating and an Internal Locus of Evaluation; Creating and Ideas; Capturing the Process of Creating. *Creating and the School of the Future*, 150. *Hypotheses for Testing*, 151.

10 **VALUING: ENCHANTMENT WITH THE ETHICAL**   155

Valuing: The Need for Renewed Attention to the Ethical, 156. *Valuing as Enchantment with the Ethical: Major Concepts*, 160—Contributions of Raths and Krathwohl to the Understanding of Valuing; Attributes of Valuing. *Guidelines for Dealing with Valuing: One Viewpoint*, 165—Development of Personal Integrity; Recognition of the Ongoingness of Human Nature; Respect for the Internalized Self of Others; Self-Growth Through Self-Giving; Respect for the Various Fields of Human Endeavor; Interest in the Communication Process; Attention to the Individuality of the Person; Examined and Explicit Biases; The Establishment of Priorities. *Valuing and School Practices*, 169—Clarifying Values; Changing Values; Creating Values. *Valuing and the School of the Future*, 173. *Hypotheses for Testing*, 175.

PART 3

Toward New Programs

11 **ORGANIZING THE CURRICULUM FOR NEW EMPHASES**   179

Organizing Schemes, 180—Blending Process and Traditional Subjects; Process, Content, and Methodology; Combining One Process and the Traditional Subjects; Emphasis on Individual Process; Interrelatedness of Processes; One Process Pervasive. *Considerations in Organizing the Curriculum*, 188—Criteria for Developing an Organizing Construct; Grouping of Students; Use of Materials; The Use of Time. *Epilogue*, 191.

APPENDIX   193

BIBLIOGRAPHY   197

INDEX   240

PART 1

Needed: New Priorities

TOWARD PROCESS-ORIENTED PERSONS

1

Schooling, to be effective, must be concerned with man's tangle with himself in his rendezvous in time and space. Whether or not today's child ever reaches other planets, he often perceives himself as visiting not only the four corners of earth, but also the moon and celestial bodies beyond. Young people have been introduced in such a way to the tools, questions, and answers of the scientist that their knowledge and understanding of what lies beyond this earth may be more detailed and systematic than the knowledge and wisdom they need to live aright with their fellowmen. The scope of material from which the school might select in educating today's children and youth is so vast that new priorities must be established in conceptualizing what and how the school will teach, or the educational enterprise stands to lose. What is important for children to know must be taught sharply and clearly. Questions must be broader and possible solutions stated in forms that invite testing.

A conceptualization of the curriculum must encompass several ingredients. A few are mentioned. First, it must be based upon an adequate view of man—a conception that is broad enough to account for a wide range of behaviors. Second, the curriculum should provide among its activities those which are designed to give children and youth the opportunity to develop the competencies designated in the view of man. Third, the curriculum must establish its points of emphasis or priority. Without such emphases the curriculum becomes bland and does not provide for means of dealing with problems of conflicting interests.

Although attention is directed in this book toward a way of viewing the person and planning educational experiences for him, hopefully the dimensions of man's humanness which we have chosen to explore lend themselves to fruitful reflection and further probing. An attempt has been made to focus upon the aspects of man's self which make him an ongoing system of energy capable of movement in a variety of directions. The task of education is to aid the person in harnessing his energies in such a way that he is able continuously to bring his new insights into line with a view he is developing about himself. His idealized and his actual self are in constant movement. Furthermore, the assumption is made that man is responsible for his own mental and physical health and has the obligation to help foster the human community where each person is concerned for the other.

In the search for a group of concepts which would help in the understanding of man, four assumptions were made. These assumptions led to the notion of the "process" aspects of the person, a concept explored later in some detail.

EDUCATION AND PERSONS IN PROCESS: BASIC ASSUMPTIONS

First, persons who are to live adequately within a world in which physical distances are becoming less remote because of newer modes of transportation must learn the principle of *spatial transcendence*. Persons who can transcend space are comfortable in various types of surroundings whether like or unlike those to which they are accustomed. In addition, persons are able to become contributors to the settings in which they find themselves.

Second, because many persons have more demands made upon

their time than can possibly be fulfilled, and others do not realize the opportunities that might be possible to them, the principle of *intentional temporality* is critical for maximum effectiveness. By intentional temporality is meant the development of an awareness of time and its utilization to further carefully designed and considered ends.

Third, if persons are to transcend space and make intentional the use of the moments, they must each develop *integrity of selfhood,* a self which faces the eventualities of each situation with honesty and feelings of inward rightness.

Fourth, if persons are to behave as integrated wholes, then *thinking-feeling cohesion* is essential. To dichotomize the cognitive and the affective promotes a way of conceptualizing about persons which is not always fruitful in view of the grossness and overlapping nature of each of the concepts.

Each of these assumptions is now described in more detail.

Spatial Transcendence

Shortly, in addition to learning to live on this planet, many persons will be learning to adapt to life outside the earth. The space race obviously has many implications for the lives of today's children and youth, for some of them may be the builders of new worlds on new planets.

If the notion is accepted that transiency and mobility rather than permanency and stability will characterize the lives of many of tomorrow's adults, then today's children should be given experiences which permit them to learn to accommodate to a wide variety of circumstances and situations. Learning to relate to others at a personal and satisfying level is necessary if the individual is to feel comfortable in various kinds of settings. Spatial transcendence means that individuals learn to see similarities as well as differences in others. It means that individuals learn to assume responsibility for the improvement rather than the deterioration of the spaces in which they find themselves.

In addition to planning for those children and youth who may be involved in situations which require ease in accommodating to new kinds of space, school programs should include experiences which help the individual see the possibilities inherent in a space in which one might remain over a period of time. Consider the astronauts who live for weeks in a small capsule, or individuals who live in the same dwelling and community from birth to death. In actuality it is the internalized view of space that makes the difference in how a person handles himself, whatever the nature of the space. Mobility, as contrasted with stability, is an internalized concept. Our concern is that persons accept their settings with grace and responsibility.

Intentional Temporality

If educators were to stop and ponder the brief life span each individual has in relation to the continuity of time, perhaps extremely serious consideration would be given to the insuring of optimal use of time during school programs—and during life. In addition, persons would be left with the feeling that time must not sneak. It must march! The use of time would be intentional, not haphazard. Insofar as possible the individual would plan for his own use of it. He would ponder the potential outcomes of an anticipated act in terms of whether carrying through a possible plan is the wisest course of action.

An important purpose of the school is to help students bring to the level of awareness the meaning and significance of time. As children come to understand the "ordering of events," "the classification of events," and "the measurement of time,"[1] they can apply some ethical purpose to these temporal operations. Students can then learn to evaluate the use of time, to change their course in order to use time more in line with their intent, and to feel comfortable with decisions about the use of time.

Our concern is not that persons learn to live tightly scheduled lives nor that schools plan rigid programs. Rather our concern is that "lived time" or "psychological time" be differentiated from "physical time,"[2] or time as measured by the clock. Piaget says that "psychological time is the time of work accomplished in relation to the speed of the activity in progress or motor activity."[3] He later points out that an interesting task seems to take a shorter period of time than a boring one. A person attacks a task wholeheartedly when it is of interest to him. "On the other hand, boredom, disinterest, disassociation can cause visible diminution of strength, or in other words, a shutting off of energy."[4] Our concern is that persons be satisfied with the way

---

[1] Jean Piaget, "Time Perception in Children," trans. by Betty M. Montgomery, in *The Voices of Time,* ed. J. T. Fraser (New York: George Braziller, Inc., 1966), pp. 202–216, pp. 214–215.
[2] Terms from Piaget, *Ibid.,* p. 211.
[3] *Ibid.,* pp. 211–212.
[4] *Ibid.,* p. 212.

they use internalized or psychological time. Time is destructible, and we lack means to re-create it.

Time might take on more meaning if more attention were given to the realities of birth, life, and death. The hesitancy to deal with man as a being occupying a very minute space on the continuum of time precludes adequate attention to his abrupt entrance into and departure from the world.

On the one hand he [the teacher] must stress the values of life; on the other, the vital function of death. The problem becomes all the more complicated when we realize that for youth, death is really a paradox in time and place. As a natural phenomenon, it dwells too far in the future to be of serious momentary consideration; as an ever-present lure to live life to its full, it is accepted by many as the price one may have to pay for extracting the last measure of life's delight.[5]

If time is seen as important, "it is the *justification* for life that becomes the ideal we must defend, and not simply the enjoyment of it. A life unjustified becomes a useless experience . . ."[6] Education in which the meaning of life and death is given consideration will deal constructively with the dimension of time and its purposeful use.

Intentionality in the use of the temporal means that periods are provided for thinking, touching, wondering, applying, dreaming, loving, working, and the multitudinous other kinds of activities of which human beings are capable. The primary difference between what is being proposed and what actually happens in the lives of many persons is that the *person knowingly* plans for as wide a realm of activity as seems appropriate to him. Teachers, parents, and other adults early let children in on decision making relating to the use of their own time.

If individuals are to consider time in their thinking and planning, then a balance needs to be found between two important elements: activity and meditation. Activity permits the intake, analysis, and evaluation of experiences and ideas. Meditation permits the synthesizing and establishing of priorities among competing ideas and forces. It enables man to be honest with himself and to develop the inner resources necessary for the tasks persons must accomplish in today's

---

[5] George F. Kneller, *Existentialism and Education* (New York: Science Editions, John Wiley & Sons, Inc., 1958, 1964), p. 111.
[6] *Ibid.*, p. 112.

world. That which has been considered in solitude is often of more worth than that which has not been subjected to reflective thought.

Intentional temporality is important if the moment of *now* is to count and successive moments of now are to add up to something of worth to the individual. Hammerskjöld says,

> The present moment is significant, not as the bridge between past and present, but by reason of its contents, contents which can fill our emptiness and become ours, if we are capable of receiving them.[7]

Again, on the same point he says,

> It is *now*, in this very moment, that I can and must pay for all that I have received. The past and its load of debt are balanced against the present. And on the future I have no claim.[8]

Integrity of Selfhood

Closely related to the worth of internalized moments is the necessity of individual integrity mentioned earlier. The literature of existentialism has made us aware of man's aloneness, his uniqueness, and his potential for developing the individual self. Biographies of great men stress their uniqueness and their greatness, often growing out of contemplative solitude. The development of individual selfhood means that the person garners the courage and resources to live comfortably within his own skin. He realizes that although conflict of necessity accompanies choice making, he must accommodate to conflict if he is to become the kind of person he wishes to be. Otherwise, he will constantly be trying to fit into the skin of another. Persons lose much of their individuality by engaging in such a process.

The individual requires freedom if he is to develop in a manner peculiar to himself. The more restraints, impositions, and limitations, the greater the possibility that the person will either have to search for ways to break out of the wall that has been built around him or devise ways of adapting and conforming rather than exercising initiative and responsibility.

Growth of selfhood demands that constraining forces and controls be established within a society, for man's interdependence demands

---

[7] From *Markings,* by Dag Hammarskjöld, p. 62. © Copyright 1964 by Alfred A. Knopf, Inc., and Faber and Faber Ltd. Reprinted by permission of the publishers.
[8] *Ibid.,* p. 57.

such protection. It is essential, however, to keep restraints at the level where individual creativity and integrity are fostered, and lifeless conformity or active rebellion is deterred.

How children and youth can develop and maintain integrity is a critical consideration for school programs. The term *group* takes on a different hue if individual integrity is highly prized. The concept has meaning only when it is seen as an aggregate of individuals relating to others at various levels of intimacy. Obviously persons come to share understandings, realities, questions, and problems as they interact, but only that group which prizes individual uniqueness and selfhood above group solidarity is making room for the primacy of the individual. The critical norm is the right to responsible individuality.

Thinking-Feeling Cohesion

Although the literature tends to deal with thinking and feeling as separate strands within man, in actuality thinking and feeling are usually transpiring simultaneously. One may be more easily observed, however, at a given point in time than the other. The young child anticipating his birthday presents may be so excited that his thought processes are not operating as sharply as when he is concentrating on a game designed to stimulate certain of the logical processes. Nonetheless, under both sets of circumstances some thinking and some feeling are transpiring.

Thinking takes place when a person is attempting to fill in gaps in knowledge. Russell says, "Thinking is a process rather than a fixed state. It involves a sequence of ideas moving from some beginning through some sort of pattern of relationships, to some goal or conclusion."[9] Thinking can go on deliberately or semi-deliberately. As persons become increasingly aware of thought processes such as analysing, generalizing, imagining, redefining, predicting, judging, and developing fluency, they can intentionally select the mode of thinking that seems most appropriate to the situation at hand. At times, to imagine or to think of new and fresh ideas is important. At other times, to pattern ideas or to arrange them in some satisfying order is critical to the project being undertaken. In short, thinking has many faces, and it is critical that the individual know its aspects and be able to utilize them intelligently.[10]

---

[9] David Russell, *Children's Thinking* (Waltham, Mass.: Blaisdell Publishing Company, a Division of Ginn and Company, 1956), p. 27.

[10] The bibliography accompanying this chapter lists several references which focus upon the thinking process.

Feeling has been defined in a variety of ways. Some define it as passion, but Shirk, in an analysis of Spinoza's work, says,

> "Passion" literally means that the agent is passive; his emotions are not self-generated and therefore push and coerce him into activity. He *suffers* them in the old sense of that term. Passive emotion occurs when the mind is responsive to outside stimuli which can arouse desire and aversion simply because the reasons why one is so aroused are not understood; the causes for our being so moved are not clear. The mind in the grip of passive emotion is in bondage to its ignorance. It wants but it knows not what or why it wants. It yearns and craves, but the basis of this unruly desire is not comprehended.[11]

Again, defining feeling as containing many unknown elements, Buytendijk says,

> Feeling is a mode of replying to a situation and transforming it as a projected new work, in which unknown qualities are categorically experienced. There are as many feelings as there are situations and the situation is created by the mode in which I have accepted it, *i.e.*, by my chosen projection. Of course this projection is not the result of my reasoning and my choice is not arbitrary. I choose my emotional attitude on the same unreflective, non-considering . . . mode of consciousness as I choose my words in speaking or writing.[12]

Feelings contain a response to a situation, selected, but not in an intentional manner. More simply stated, Combs and Snygg say, "Feelings are perceptions of ourselves, of the situations in which we are involved, and the interrelationship of these two" (italics removed).[13]

The feeling qualities of the individual cause him to reexamine, internalize, and remodel the ideas of others until they have meaning for him.

---

[11] Evelyn Shirk, *The Ethical Dimension: An Approach to the Philosophy of Values and Valuing* (New York: Appleton-Century-Crofts, Division of Meredith Publishing Company, 1965), p. 258.

[12] F. J. J. Buytendijk, "The Phenomenological Approach to the Problem of Feelings and Emotions," in *Feelings and Emotions*, ed. Martin L. Reymert (New York: McGraw-Hill Book Company, 1950). Also in *Psychoanalysis and Existential Philosophy*, ed. Hendrik M. Ruitenbeek (New York: E. P. Dutton & Co., Inc., 1962), p. 160.

[13] Arthur W. Combs and Donald Snygg, *Individual Behavior: A Perceptual Approach to Behavior*, Revised Edition (New York: Harper & Brothers, Publishers, 1959), p. 232.

But feeling cannot adequately be described without seeing it as closely interrelated with mind. Perhaps the title of Langer's book *Mind: An Essay on Human Feeling*[14] indicates the interrelatedness of the emotional and the intellectual aspects of life. This viewpoint is reflected in the pages that follow.

MAN: A PROCESS-ORIENTED BEING

Any carefully designed conception of curriculum must be based upon some basic assumptions about man. The search by this author for a view of man led to a description of him as a process-oriented being. Process orientation, as used in this book, means that a person has within his personality elements of dynamism, motion, and responsibility which enable him to live as an adequate and a contributing member of the world of which he is part.

It is our assumption that all persons are process-oriented to some degree and can become more so through planned experiences. Furthermore, it is our assumption that it is "good" for persons to have some degree of process orientation. What are some of the characteristics of such persons?

These persons are ongoing, growing, developing beings. They may achieve stability under certain circumstances, but inertness, staticism, unthinking behavior, or rigidity seldom characterize them. Because of insatiable curiosity and searching, at times tension and a mild state of disequilibrium may be prerequisite to new insights, new ways of organizing, new dreams, hopes, or visions. Highly process-oriented persons do not stagnate under the debris of nonessential or nonmeaningful aspects of life. They see purposes to the degree of change and movement they plan for themselves.

Process-oriented persons have broad rather than narrow or restricted fields of vision. They utilize a wide range of intellectual skills such as comparing, analyzing, elaborating, and evaluating in solving problems.

They can be compared to generators as opposed to parasites, to reconcilers of conflict rather than avoiders of conflict. Process-oriented persons are interested in the possible rather than the probable. They are often spontaneous as opposed to deliberate. When

---

[14] Susanne Langer, *Mind: An Essay on Human Feeling*, Vol. I (Baltimore: The Johns Hopkins Press, 1967).

challenged to carry out worthwhile tasks they are zealous, extravagant, and fervent at times as opposed to being continuously moderate.

They tend toward internal integrity rather than outward conformity, toward friendliness to difference and newness as opposed to hostility to the unknown. They pace their activity in a variety of ways rather than in one way.

Their mistakes arise from the premature rather than the after-the-fact sharing of ideas, from errors of commission rather than omission, from overestimation rather than underestimation. When a mistake has been made, persons with a high degree of process-orientation tend toward bravery rather than cowardice. They are more likely to anticipate rather than regret; they possess more foresight than hindsight and live in terms of prospect rather than retrospect.

Process-oriented persons are concerned with the moral and ethical. They are interested in the past as it relates to the present and future. Their energies are not dissipated into a variety of areas, rather they are channeled to promoting causes which are identified as worthwhile or to bringing about constructive changes within fields of knowledge, institutions, or persons. In the attempt to be change agents, such persons have acquired judgmental skills and the capacity to resolve conflict both within themselves and the situations of which they are a part.

In summary, process-orientation characterizes persons who are able to handle themselves and the situations of which they are a part with adequacy and ease. Such persons are the contributors to as well as the recipients of society's resources.

All educational institutions, particularly the school, should give high priority to fostering process-concepts in today's children and youth, if personal adequacy and individual responsibility are among the major goals of school programs.

THE INGREDIENTS OF PROCESS

Process skills are those which have an element of ongoingness about them. Their relevancy and applicability to a wide range of situations mean that learning of them involves two dimensions: (1) the opportunity to experience the use of the skill in a wide variety of contexts, and (2) the chance to verbalize the meaning of the skill so an interplay can exist between the logical and the intuitive. In other words, although process skills are ordinarily called into play spontaneously, the individual should have the tools at his command to go back and analyze what may have transpired through more or less intuitive judgment. By so doing, the person can behave in different or possibly more adequate ways in future situations which are somewhat similar.

Customarily, school curricula have given heavier emphasis to what already has happened than to what is to come. By emphasizing process skills, persons have the opportunity to plan for the future rather than merely to reflect upon the past. Persons and school programs need to be future-oriented because of the tremendously stepped-up pace of today's and tomorrow's world. It is necessary to get at the essence of human living and understanding.

In the pages which follow, eight process skills are discussed which should be emphasized in school programs. The reader will note that several of these skills are already receiving much attention. In some instances a different type of treatment is proposed. In no case is a comprehensive discussion given of the skill. The reader will also note overlap and big gaps which are not probed. In addition, many related skills which merit attention in a book of this type are intentionally ignored.

Our purpose is simply to open up the possibility of the development of process-oriented persons within our schools. The processes discussed in this work are noted below.

Perceiving

Central to one's actions is a mode of perceiving. One must have impressions, ideas, concepts out of which to add to one's own knowledge and life and from which to make sense from the past. That the ways of perceiving are basic to other processes is an underlying assumption; hence, the attention to this process.

Communicating

What one perceives can be made meaningful to the self and others only as effective modes of sharing one's own thoughts and ideas are found. Communication must go beyond the mere dictionary meaning of words to the subtleties of the nondiscursive, the nonverbal, the emotion-laden messages. Intense study of this valuable human process is necessary if man is to utilize his aloneness, uniqueness, and means of relating to others in ways which are satisfying to himself and others.

Loving

A cursory glance at current literature indicates the distorted notions man has of his affiliations with others. Even so, we have failed oftentimes to take constructive steps to help him understand the satisfactions that can come from relating to others in mutually satisfying ways. Love has many forms; the school can help children and youth understand its dynamics, ingredients, and pitfalls.

Decision Making

Human beings daily are called upon to make decisions, with consequences of varying degree. Although decision making can be likened to the problem solving process in many regards, it is unique in that meaningful decisions can and often should be made in an intuitive manner. It is to the intuitive in decision making that special attention is given.

Knowing

To make wise decisions, to love intensely, to communicate clearly demands knowledge. Yet the traditional method of the teacher selecting facts which children need to learn will not lead us ahead in helping children see the intrigue and excitement in the knowing process. Teaching how to know rather than teaching the known has been a practice in some schools and is a necessity in a process-oriented curriculum.

Patterning

If one is to have increased responsibility for his own knowing, then he needs to have at his command skills for organizing material new and old into coherent patterns. The individual must develop an awareness of how men organize. Such an awareness helps the person to have a place onto which to hang new learnings. It also helps him realize when old hooks are no longer adequate for the material with which he is dealing.

Creating

Because society needs increasing numbers of generative individuals and fewer parasitic ones, all individuals need to understand some of the intricacies of the creative process. As the individual develops an understanding of the process, he can better know when to accept the wisdom and knowledge of others and when to shape his own ideas into something new which may be either for himself or for the outside world. The development of creativity cannot be left to chance. It can be the heritage of all to some degree.

Valuing

To be a process-oriented person may not necessarily lead to good either for one's self or for others unless the person prizes the excitement which the ethical can play in adding unity and cohesion to life. Without the desire to seek priorities among competing goods, a person will fail to utilize other process-oriented skills to make his unique contributions. School programs desiring process-oriented persons should provide opportunities for students to become involved in value-laden situations.

Each of the chapters attempts to do several things. First, the need for the process is discussed. The process is then briefly discussed in terms of some of its basic components. Then attention is given to making broad concepts practical in the teaching situation. Last, broad hypotheses for testing are developed.

THE EMERGING
EDUCATIONAL SCENE

2

Education cannot afford to be pedantic. It must be imbued with freshness and vitality, or our educational system, as we know it, cannot survive.

Several factors are breathing newness into the educational enterprise. These must be taken into account as curriculum is planned. A few are noted.

INFLUENCES UPON CURRICULUM PLANNING

New Learning Materials

Many new instructional materials have two characteristics not common to materials developed prior to 1960. First, the materials are self-instructing. The child can work at them without the constant supervision of the teacher. Second, the materials are self-correcting.

The child has immediate access to the "rightness" of his responses in terms of knowledge which is common to the culture.

The presence and availability of such materials have implications for education, for children and youth can now learn much more rapidly critical elements of the culture. On the other hand, the child has less chance for playing with ideas—an opportunity which should be his if he is to add to as well as absorb the culture. Many of our learning materials are strong in helping children learn to implement but weak in providing the setting to innovate.

Changing Classroom Personnel

The concept of one teacher to a classroom of children or youth is receding into the background as schools seek to instruct the young.[1] Although many theories of grouping teachers for instruction call for persons competent in professional expertise, some theories are attempting to place in the classroom persons whose formal educational background is minimal. The range of competence among persons working with children calls for new definitions of teaching. New uses of personnel also necessitate new modes of preparing persons for their particular tasks within the classroom.

More Precise Looks at Teaching

Although teaching has been studied with more or less precision for decades, current methods for achieving feedback enable a new look at this critical educative act. Instruments for recording teachers' verbal behavior enable the study of what has been said. Teachers then can change with awareness their behavior.[2] Videotapes, tape recorders, and eight or sixteen millimeter movie cameras provide feedback on nonverbal as well as verbal behavior. The opportunity for specificity in feedback should enable teachers to make their contacts with children and youth increasingly significant.

Many Fields Represented in Curriculum Development

Increasingly, various groups of persons are entering the arena of developing educational programs for children. The increased activity

---

[1] The National Commission on Teacher Education and Professional Standards of the National Education Association is studying the trends toward utilization of a variety of personnel in the classroom.

[2] For a summary of frameworks for studying the verbal behavior of teachers see Louise M. Berman and Mary Lou Usery, *Personalized Supervision: Sources and Insights* (Washington, D. C.: Association for Supervision and Curriculum Development, NEA, 1966), pp. 5–18.

of academic scholars, private industry, and the government is clearly evident.

As a variety of persons get together to plan school programs, it appears that different roles are emerging for persons interested in curriculum development. Deriving insights from social scientists, theologians, dramatists, poets, and other students of the human condition, the first group will concentrate on developing statements of alternative ways of viewing man. A second group of persons will be concerned about developing instructional materials, materials that are aesthetically attractive and sharp in their viewpoints. A third group, curriculum theorists, will be concerned with deriving new insights for the curriculum field and building bridges from theoretical considerations to practice. A fourth group are those developing school programs for children and youth—principals, assistant superintendents in charge of instruction, curriculum coordinators, and teachers.[3]

Increased Flexibility in Scheduling

Recent years have seen a trend toward ungrading the elementary school, toward modular scheduling at the secondary level, and toward increasing time for independent study. Lengthening the time for study through after school tutorial sessions is common in some areas. The increased numbers of persons available to work with children and youth, through the use of auxiliary personnel, make possible creative arrangements for schooling which have hardly been tapped, especially in areas of economic deprivation.

Rapid Transmittal of Information

Because of the highly developed modes of public communication now available, newly tapped or acquired information can be rapidly transmitted. The receiving of information by persons demands a reorganization of previous concepts in order to accommodate the new. This factor has highly significant implications for the curriculum, for it places much responsibility upon the school to develop the kinds of persons that can reorganize their own thinking to make personal sense out of the many impressions they regularly perceive.

------

[3] For further discussion of personnel responsible for curriculum development see Louise Berman, "New Curriculum Designs for Children," in *The New Elementary School*, ed. Alexander Frazier (Washington, D. C.: Association for Supervision and Curriculum Development, NEA, 1968).

Artificial Tampering with Psychical Processes

No longer does man need to accept his natural endowments as those with which he must live. Available to man are artificial means which enable a person to change his view of the world. Drugs which temporarily accelerate and expand psychical processes, such as LSD, are used by some youth and adults, particularly in the middle class, with the intent of opening up new vistas of seeing and feeling not experienced before. Depressants, causing the world to lose its vividness, have long been used by adults and youth. The increasing amount of tampering with perceptual and subsequent decision making functions has significant implications for today's children and youth. If society fails to deal with the problem of man's intervention in the ongoingness of his psychical processes, societal controls may need to become radically different, for man loses the opportunities he has for individual responsibility, control, and freedom.

Changing Sex Patterns[4]

The "pill" for women and long hair for men are indications of changing sex patterns far more pervasive than may appear on the surface. Women are being emancipated from the fear of childbearing as a result of sexual relationships, and men are being released from fear of displaying feminine characteristics, such as tenderness, sensitivity, and sorrow. Increasing similarities in appearance and temperament cause an uneasiness on the part of many as to what the consequences will be. In any event, the school needs to examine its concepts of the roles of men and women in our society and design curriculum which takes into account the trend toward revamped sex roles.

These and other factors suggest that new priorities must be established in the curriculum. We are caught in a bind, however. Because the school is one of the slowest of the social institutions to change, some educators are stumped by the problem of how to bring fruitful new findings and insights into the schools. The task is one of using existing constructs in dealing with new material. Educators must work with old terms to explain new or reorganized ideas. Hence a need for definition exists.

---

[4] For a provocative article on this topic see Marshall McLuhan and George B. Leonard, "The Future of Sex," *Look*, XXXI (July 25, 1967), 56–63.

THE MEANING OF CURRICULUM: ONE VIEW

Through the years the term curriculum has taken on many meanings. Because in this book we are concerned with process, we need to insure that the term "curriculum" is appropriate for the type of schooling with which we are concerned.

The view of curriculum which we are proposing has several ingredients.

Purpose

One ingredient relates to purpose. The assumption is that children and youth engage in schooling for reasons which those responsible for them deem important. Those aspects of schooling, therefore, which have been deliberately planned comprise the curriculum. That is *not* to say that children and youth cannot be included in the designing or selecting of experiences, but rather that overall goals would have made provision for such participation by children.

Time

Another component of our view is related to the use of time. With many learning materials being self-instructional, with the use of auxiliary personnel, and with the potential for extended use of school facilities, the curriculum need not be planned only for the school day as it is currently conceived. In some communities the day might be extended to include some meals, a late afternoon program, or evening tutorial sessions. The possibilities are unlimited.

Curriculum Stages

A third ingredient involves stages in time which comprise the curriculum. The first stage is the "pre-active" and "includes such things as preparing lesson plans, arranging furniture and equipment within a room, . . . studying test reports, reading sections of a textbook, thinking about the aberrant behavior of a student. . . ."[5] The second stage is the "interactive"[6] or actual on-the-spot teaching

---

[5] Philip W. Jackson, "The Way Teaching Is," in *The Way Teaching Is,* Report of the Seminar on Teaching (Washington, D.C.: Association for Supervision and Curriculum Development and the Center for the Study of Instruction, NEA, 1966), pp. 7–27, p. 12.

[6] *Ibid.*, p. 13.

stage. Here we are concerned with the materials, language, and gestures teachers use to help them carry out immediate objectives in their work with children. On-the-spot decisions of teachers influence the shaping of the curriculum in this stage. The third stage is the evaluative and involves analysis of children's work, verbatim accounts of classroom incidents, tape recordings, and videotapes of what transpired in the classroom setting. This third stage then leads back toward the first stage, the curriculum thus being spiral.

Other Terms and Curriculum

If the curriculum is viewed as involving stages, then other difficult-to-define terms can be seen in relationship to curriculum. For example, terms such as *schooling, teaching,* and *instruction* have relational kinds of definitions.

Schooling: all the experiences which children have within the school, including those that are planned for them by the school. Schooling is broader than curriculum in that only *planned* experiences for children are included in the curriculum.

Teaching: an act on the part of the teacher designed to mediate between the pupil and that portion of the environment which is to be learned. Teaching takes place in the present moment. It is concerned with the execution of goals which may have been determined by the teacher alone, the teacher and the child, or the child alone. Goals may be clearly stated, held with some degree of awareness, or not brought to the level of consciousness. Teaching includes the total arena of human behavior which sets the stage for pupil learning.

Instruction: an act somewhat synonymous with teaching but which involves a more methodical, structured presentation of what is to be learned. Instruction may occur through the interaction of a child with another person or with materials. Implicit in the act of instructing is a greater emphasis upon the logical development of content than in the act of teaching.[7]

---

[7] For further discussion of the above terms see Elliott W. Eisner, "Instruction, Teaching, and Learning: An Attempt at Differentiation," *The Elementary School Journal,* LXV (December, 1964), 115–119. Reprinted in *Professional Reprints in Education,* No. 8610 (Columbus: Charles E. Merrill Publishing Company).

James B. Macdonald and Robert R. Leeper, eds., *Theories of Instruction* (Washington, D. C.: Association for Supervision and Curriculum Development, NEA, 1965).

Alice Miel, ed., *Creativity in Teaching: Invitations and Instances* (Belmont, Cal.: Wadsworth Publishing Company, Inc., 1961), pp. 4–6.

Figure 1 illustrates the relationships between curriculum, schooling, teaching, and instruction. It should be noted that teaching and instruction can be overlapping processes. If a person teaches in a highly structured way, he may be primarily instructing. On the other hand, the person who constantly is taking into account the many classroom variables as he interacts with pupils is probably doing more teaching than instructing.

FIGURE 1

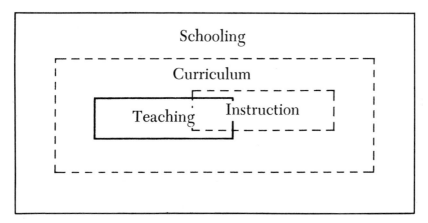

Actors in the Curriculum

The curriculum is a setting within which increasingly larger numbers of persons will be acting with the principal actor, the child. Insofar as these persons contribute to a planned segment of the curriculum, they are actors in the curriculum setting and therefore should be specially prepared to play their unique roles. Head teachers, regular teachers, auxiliary personnel, consultants in a special area, and others who work directly with children and youth should be groomed in their unique and overlapping responsibilities within the curriculum.

The curriculum thus becomes the major part of schooling in a setting which has many new elements which have not yet been adequately incorporated into the old structure of the school. Teaching and instruction become part of the curriculum. Persons, with their special competencies, play their parts in a curriculum designed to help children and youth develop into process-oriented persons.

The pages which follow present some ideas which need to receive high priority in today's school programs. Our intent is to invite the reader to contemplate these priorities and their place in the schools for which the reader has some reponsibility.

PART 2

New Priorities

3

A fool can look at the universe and see nothing, but the right man can look at a pinpoint, at a moth, at a cell and guess out the universe. That is the measure of the perceiving mind.

JOHN CIARDI

Perceiving:

THE STIMULUS FOR MAN'S BEHAVIOR

3

At the base of all man's peculiarly human functions, such as creating, knowing, valuing, and caring, is a mode of observing the world about him. What man notices influences the decisions he makes, the persons he prizes, the values he formulates, the ideas he communicates, and the knowledge he considers of most worth. No truly human person can hide from the panorama of ideas, values, forms, colors, persons, objects that continuously confront him during his waking hours. The truly imaginative and creative individual will use the mass of data which he is daily privileged to take in to make something beautiful of

---

Quote on opening page of chapter is from John Ciardi, "The Curriculum of Perception," in *Strength Through Reappraisal*, Sixteenth Yearbook of the American Association of Colleges for Teacher Education (Washington, D. C.: National Education Assn., 1963) pp. 115–116.

his own life and the activities in which he engages in the course of a day.

THE CENTRALITY OF PERCEIVING IN BEHAVING: THE NEED FOR CONSIDERATION

Because of the significance of perceiving in all of man's peculiarly human functions, it is critical that the school take a new and focused look at this process and school experiences that help develop it.

Although many educators acknowledge the importance of perceiving in learning, the curriculum often does not adequately provide for similarities or differences in perceiving that children bring to the classroom setting. One has only to consider how children from economically deprived homes fare in many classrooms to realize that their backgrounds and modes of seeing the world are not given sufficient attention in planning learning opportunities for them. Ascertaining the perceptions of students is one way to help determine what the school program ought to be. Curriculum planners can then determine what students know about a given topic or field, which learnings need clarification or revision, and what the new learnings ought to be in view of the backgrounds of the learners and the demands of the society.

If the school perceives its curriculum to be relatively static and appropriate to all students whatever their backgrounds and motivations, perhaps we do not need to be overly concerned about the phenomenon of perceiving. If in philosophy, however, we are concerned about the uniqueness of each individual, his welfare and potential contribution, then ideas relative to the worth of each child—his ideas, feelings, even his total self—need to go beyond statements of educational objectives and be evident in classroom procedures and practices. As consideration is given to the value of the individual student, we soon learn that the curriculum of perception is important, not only for groups of children receiving special attention, but for all children regardless of socio-economic backgrounds.

A major assumption of this chapter, therefore, is that how persons perceive, what they perceive, and why they perceive as they do are factors that should receive major attention if the school is to help develop persons who see the world with its richness, variety, and charm, and who are able to perceive with a minimum of distortion. Such persons have a wealth of material to use as they engage in the experiences of living.

THE MEANING OF PERCEIVING

Like many terms which are commonly and freely used, perceiving has several diverse meanings although common elements can be found in various definitions and descriptions of the term.

Definitions of Perceiving

The word is derived from the Latin *per-ápera* meaning "to take possession of" or "to obtain." In commenting upon the derivation Schachtel says that in perception there is an element of wanting "to take hold of the object, to wrest it from the infinite process of world and life, and to fix it at a definite point where we can take hold of it again, recall it, refind it."[1] Perception differs from sensation in that sensation is more fleeting and lacks the attempt to grasp.

Matson defines the term simply as "the act of noticing."[2] He goes on to elaborate that this "preliminary feature of human behavior ... has come to be regarded as central to the concerns of other departments and divisions of the field"[3] [psychology].

Russell says, " a percept may be defined as what is known of an object, a quality, or a relationship as a result of sensory experience."[4] A percept does not exist in isolation but tends to be reenforced by other related sensations and perceptions. According to Russell, a percept "shows three stages of development: (1) an indefinite, vague response to the whole situation; (2) analysis of the whole with some elaboration of separate sensory elements; (3) synthesis of the sensory elements into a new pattern, or 'percept': although some integration of sensations takes place, at any one instant only one, or a small group, can stand at the center of the sensory field."[5] Perception is an extremely important process, for it is the means by which raw materials of thinking become available for use. "Perception is the process of organizing and interpreting the sensations the organism receives from external and internal stimuli."[6]

The literature often relates perceiving to other human functions.

---

[1] Ernest Schachtel, *Metamorphosis* (New York: Basic Books, Inc., Publishers, 1959), p. 200.
[2] Floyd Matson, *The Broken Image: Man, Science, and Society* (New York: George Braziller, Inc., 1964), p. 181.
[3] *Ibid.*
[4] David H. Russell, *Children's Thinking* (Waltham, Mass.: Blaisdell Publishing Company, a Division of Ginn and Company, 1956), p. 66.
[5] *Ibid.*
[6] *Ibid.*, p. 70.

Thinking, communicating, valuing, relating to reality: all are integral to this phenomenon although writers point out that the level at which one perceives may influence the quality of his participation in other activities of life. Church says,

> We can recognize two major kinds of perception, each of which has a mature and immature version, and each of which represents a way of being mobilized toward reality. The first kind is what we have called *participation*, where we respond organismically in an unmediated reflex-like way to the dynamic, affective, physiognomic properties of the environment. The second is *contemplative perception*, where action is suspended in favor of inspection, judgment, and analysis. It is this kind of perception which the psychologist studies although it is the first kind which predominates in real life, even among adults.[7]

Selection and Perceiving

The concept of selection is found in many definitions of perception. The selective process involved in perception is closely allied to the degree of openness in thinking or creativity in production and behavior. Many writers, including Foshay,[8] Schachtel,[9] Combs,[10] and Thomas and Znaniecki,[11] equate openness in perceiving as prerequisite to creating and to living dynamic healthy existences.

Perhaps one of the most insightful descriptions of the relationship of selection to openness is Thomas and Znaniecki's "Three Types of Personality." In describing the "Philistine," the "Bohemian," and the "creative man," these authors differentiate them through the ways

---

[7] From *Language and the Discovery of Reality: A Developmental Psychology of Cognition*, by Joseph Church, p. 49. © Copyright 1961 by Joseph Church. Reprinted by permission of Random House, Inc.

[8] Arthur Foshay, "The Creative Process Described," in *Creativity in Teaching*, ed. Alice Miel (Belmont, California: Wadsworth Publishing Co., Inc., 1961), p. 24.

[9] Schachtel, *Metamorphosis*, p. 237.

[10] Arthur W. Combs, "A Perceptual View of the Adequate Personality," in *Perceiving, Behaving, Becoming: A New Focus for Education*, 1962 Yearbook (Washington, D. C.: Association for Supervision and Curriculum Development, NEA, 1962), pp. 56–59.

[11] William I. Thomas and Florian Znaniecki, "Three Types of Personality," in *Images of Man*, ed. C. Wright Mills (New York: George Braziller, Inc., 1960), p. 407. From "The Introduction" in *The Polish Peasant in Europe and America*, Vol. II, part IV: "Life Record of an Immigrant" (New York: Dover Publications, Inc., 1958 edition), pp. 1831, 1837–1838, 1850–1903.

they develop "general schemes of situations."[12] The schemes of the three types are characterized by different degrees of openness and degrees of tenaciousness to guiding principles which aid in the selection and rejection of percepts. According to these authors the creative, productive person is neither the one most open to experience nor the one who critically limits the numbers of perceptions he allows to enter his cognitive processes. Rather, the creative man possesses a "tendency to change, regulated by plans of productive activity, and the individual remains open to such influences as will be in line of his preconceived development."[13]

Perceiving as Transaction

The process of perceiving has many elements which make it illusive and difficult to describe. Perceiving is dynamic and ongoing. It involves the transaction of the organism with stimuli which can be either internal or external. Perceiving is a relationship of the self to another object, person, or idea even though the relationship may be only momentary because of the pace of the lives of most persons. The transaction is accompanied by categorization of the stimulus. This categorizing is dependent upon the modes of economizing that the individual has developed. Some persons have developed rather fixed categories that are few in number. Perceptions therefore are limited, for only a few can be held in the foreground simultaneously. Other persons have developed modes of categorizing which are more fluid, change being dependent upon some broader principles which help determine when old categories are obsolete and when new ones need to be formulated.

The process of perceiving demands the attention of the individual. Many persons lead rich and full lives even though their surroundings may appear limited. Such persons have learned to capture and subsequently categorize the many stimuli that come their way and have consequently become persons full of experience and wisdom upon which to draw. Other persons, even though their environment may be plush and full of potential stimuli to perceiving have developed inadequate criteria for seeing. They possess too few and rigid categories to have at their command the quantity, quality, and depth of experience characteristic of rigorous, sensitive persons. Attention has

---

12 *Ibid.*
13 *Ibid.*, p. 408.

been drawn off by too firm a commitment to very few categories. Bruner states, "Failure to perceive is most often not a lack of perceiving but a matter of interference with perceiving. Whence this interference? ... interference comes from categorizations in highly accessible categories that serve to block alternative categorizations in less accessible categories."[14]

Transaction involves the mobilization of resources. Since perceiving, as we indicated earlier, can operate at different levels, for we can *see* something tangentially, we can work at it, or we can *study* the object until it is known, it is important that the concept of action as related to perceiving be understood. Church says, "Both perception and action entail, initially, a total organismic *mobilization* ... in early experience perceptual mobilization is identical with response mobilization—that is, to perceive is to unify oneself with the object."[15] Unifying implies action, alertness, and astuteness in perceiving.

Perceiving, thus, is a human function in which a transaction is made between the perceiver and the person, object, situation, or idea being perceived. Perceiving may come about as a result of internal or external stimuli and is the process of categorizing those impressions which impinge upon the person. An individual can perceive with varying degrees of intensity. The more penetrating the perception, the more the individual becomes one with the object. Perceiving is noticing, but noticing is influenced by a variety of stimuli.

PERCEIVING, HUMAN FUNCTIONS, AND SCHOOL PRACTICES

The intent of this section is to consider briefly perceiving as it relates to certain aspects of communicating, loving, valuing, decision making, organizing, knowing, and creating. Our concern is primarily with perceiving in seemingly healthy, "normal" persons. Although researchers in the field of physical and mental abnormalities have long dealt with the phenomenon of perception, our intent is not to discuss distortions of the process but rather to consider perceiving in the person not needing special physical or mental attention. It is our

---

[14] Bruner, Jerome, "On Perceptual Readiness," in *The Cognitive Processes: Readings,* eds. Robert J. C. Harper and Others (Englewood Cliffs, N. J.: Prentice-Hall, Inc., 1964), pp. 223–256, p. 248.

[15] From *Language and the Discovery of Reality,* by Joseph Church, p. 28. © Copyright 1961 by Joseph Church. Reprinted by permission of Random House, Inc.

hypothesis that all persons could use their perceptual apparatus more effectively.

Perceiving and Communicating

The person who would communicate with freshness, vividness, and accuracy must learn to perceive fully. Perception of life and the world is prerequisite to communication, whatever form the message might take. Sartre, in discussing his childhood experiences, reports,

> I observed. It was a dismal and disappointing game: I had to stand in front of the stamped velvet chair and inspect it. What was there to say about it? Well, that it was covered with fuzzy green material, that it had two arms, four legs, a back surmounted by two little wooden pine-cones. That was all for the moment, but I would come back to it, I would do better next time, I would end by reading it inside out. Later, I would describe it; my readers would say: "How well observed it is, how accurately!! It's exactly right! That's the kind of thing one doesn't invent!" Depicting real objects with real words that were penned with a real pen, I'd be hanged if I didn't become real myself![16]

Perceiving, because it takes place in the brief instant of now, is fraught with problems. Church asks these questions:

> Do we really see an object move, or do we, as in viewing a motion picture, "piece together" a series of snapshots? How, indeed, can we speak of perceiving an event, when, at any given moment part of the event lies in the past, dissolved and gone forever, whereas the rest has yet to happen, and all we have to work with is memory, anticipation, and a tissue-thin instant of present time?[17]

Realizing that our perceptions move and change so rapidly, how can we ever hope to communicate that which has probably been viewed so swiftly that oftentimes only a blurred image is left? Is it ever possible to make life stand still long enough so that we can fully comprehend—soak in—that which we are seeing? In most instances the present rolls on so rapidly that ordinarily we are left with past

---

[16] George Braziller, Inc.—from *The Words* by Jean-Paul Sartre, p. 160; translated from the French by Bernard Frechtman. Copyright © 1964 by George Braziller, Inc., and Librairie Gallimard.

[17] From *Language and the Discovery of Reality*, by Joseph Church, p. 19. © Copyright 1961 by Joseph Church. Reprinted by permission of Random House, Inc.

impressions and future hopes. Thus what we communicate may become distorted through a lack of attention to the peculiar attributes of the character of the present moment. Yet, even the most sophisticated observers and reporters of the human scene cannot usually differentiate the three points in time and their effect upon perceiving because the past and the future so strongly influence the present.

Because of the rapidity of human perception and the tendency to interweave the past and the future with the present, care needs to be taken in assuring that the process of communicating takes into account these factors. As a perception is communicated, help should be given to students to enable them to differentiate reality from wishful thinking.

School practices can provide opportunity for students to report as accurately as possible present perceptions through a variety of experiences. Persons may wish to test or try these:

A student may be asked to report an event. He then analyzes the report in terms of incidents and other experiences in his background that have caused him to see the event as he did.

The teacher records something he has heard the child say. Teacher and child then examine the statement to see how much the teacher's own perceptual framework is influencing what he hears. The child is invited to restate what he has said if the teacher's words do not match what the child thought he has said.

The child is encouraged to express through some art form his present perceptions. He then uses words to describe the same event. A comparison is then made of the two modes of expression.

The individual communicates wishful thinking through some medium —words, paints, clay—then the child describes what elements of the message are not true to life.

Different children are asked to describe the same object or person. Comparisons are made of the descriptions. A discussion may follow of what is real.

Perceiving and Caring

Perhaps no one aspect of human experience causes more misunderstanding at the personal, national, and international levels than the misinterpretation of caring. Misinterpretation causes good motives to be wrongly perceived. Perception of affection is affected by the perceiver's past experiences, his future hopes, and what he feels is transpiring in the present moment. To perceive the intentions of another in the way that the other person desires demands open channels of communication and honesty in relations on the parts of persons involved. If blandness or insincerity characterizes the real world of either the perceiver or the perceived, there is room for distortion in the translation of the message.

Thus, the perception of a sense of care necessitates the ability to explain why an individual sees another's good intentions as he does. For example, a father may buy his child a bicycle, yet because the child desired a bigger and more elaborate vehicle than the father felt he could afford, the child's response may not be the gratitude the father had anticipated.

The perceiving of caring within the school setting is one that is easily distorted. The teacher who does a careful job of correcting a child's paper may be seen as rejecting the child when in actuality the teacher is attempting to communicate a sense of caring through a meticulous consideration of the student's written work.

Our concern in this chapter is not with an analysis of affection, for this topic is considered later in the book. What we are concerned about, though, is how a legitimate sense of caring is perceived by the one for whom the care is intended. The proper perception of caring is necessary if good intentions are to be reciprocated rather than challenged.

If persons are to learn to perceive and understand affection and caring both in their broader and more personal dimensions, then school practices might reflect these kinds of experiences:

The child is encouraged to write about or to discuss how something he did for another child was seen by the other child.

A selection from literature is discussed in terms of how an act of kindness is perceived by the person for whom it was done.

Children share experiences of how a well-intended act was misunderstood by another person.

Some teachers may wish to test these examples. For instance, one might reword the second item from the above list and test it:

If children have the opportunity to describe how an act of kindness, included in a selection from literature, was perceived by the person for

whom it was intended, they will be better able to describe mistaken
perceptions of affection than if they have not had such an opportunity.

Perceiving and Knowing

A fuzzy distinction exists between seeing and knowing. According
to the scholars in various fields of knowledge, each of the academic
disciplines or the school subjects has modes of perceiving and describing common to it. Must we teach multitudinous ways of looking,
seeing, and understanding if one is to perceive and come to know well
enough to function in this world? Bruner comments,

> There is perhaps, one universal truth about all forms of human
> cognition: the ability to deal with knowledge is hugely exceeded by the
> potential knowledge contained in man's environment. To cope with this
> diversity, man's perception, his memory and his thought processes early
> become governed by strategies for protecting his limited capacities
> from the confusion of overloading. We tend to perceive things schemat-
> ically, for example, rather than in detail, or we represent a class of
> diverse things by some sort of average "typical instance."[18]

As the individual comes to know, those objects and instances which
have real meaning to him are learned. Church says, "Here we are
saying two things: that the child perceives only personally meaningful
objects, and that what he perceives is not so much the objects as their
meanings."[19]

In dealing with perceiving and knowing, the school needs to realize
that each object, person, or idea with which the student has contact
has the potential for opening up to the student a wealth of new
meanings. On this point, Polanyi says,

> The sight of a solid object indicates that it has both another side and a
> hidden interior, which we could explore; the sight of another person
> points at unlimited hidden workings of his mind and body. Perception
> has this inexhaustible profundity, because what we perceive is an
> aspect of reality, and aspects of reality are clues to boundless undis-
> closed, and perhaps yet unthinkable, experiences. This is what the
> existing body of scientific thought means to the productive scientist; he

---

[18] Jerome S. Bruner, "Art as a Form of Knowing," in *On Knowing: Essays for
the Left Hand* (Cambridge: Harvard University Press, 1962), p. 65.
[19] From *Language and the Discovery of Reality,* by Joseph Church, p. 5. ©
Copyright 1961 by Joseph Church. Reprinted by permission of Random House, Inc.

sees in it an aspect of reality which, as such, promises to be an inexhaustible source of new, promising problems.[20]

As the world takes on personal meaning for the individual, he comes to learn that he categorizes stimuli in different ways. Some would claim that each discipline has its own unique way of dealing with percepts; therefore the individual needs to have at his command a great many tools for classifying knowledge. Others have attempted to group ways of knowing into larger wholes. For example, Russell suggests that percepts can be classified into the following nine categories:

1. Percepts of form	6. Percepts of numbers
2. Percepts of space	7. Social percepts
3. Percepts of time	8. Aesthetic percepts
4. Percepts of movement	9. Humor percepts[21, 22]
5. Percepts of weight	

Whatever view a school holds about knowledge, the likelihood is that the organizational constructs for knowing developed by curriculum planners and the constructs which students hold may be quite far apart. The case for utilizing the perceptions of children and youth in their pursuit of knowledge cannot be made too strongly.

Schooling that makes provision for continuously checking the perceptions of learners as they engage in the process of knowing might involve children in experiences such as these:

Ask children to describe something such as a tree, a view from a window, or a person in the language of an artist. Then describe the same scene, object, or person, in the language of a scientist. Ask children to compare the languages of these fields.

Give a student an opportunity to work with a scholar in a discipline for a period of time. Ask the student to describe why the scholar sees phenomena as he does.

---

[20] From *The Tacit Dimension*, by Michael Polanyi, p. 68. Copyright © 1966 by the author. Reprinted by permission of Doubleday & Company, Inc.

[21] Russell, *Children's Thinking*, p. 77.

[22] For another way of categorizing knowledge see Philip Phenix, *Realms of Meaning* (New York: McGraw-Hill Book Company, 1964), pp. 6–7.

Invite youth to compare a novel and an historical account of the same incident. Then determine in what ways the historian and the novelist see alike and differently.

Perceiving and Decision Making

The adequacy of a decision is partially dependent upon the number and quality of perceptions considered in making a decision. An individual can understand his own and the decisions of others more easily if he has some insight into how perceiving influences decisions.

In the classroom setting teachers can help children and youth study their own ways of perceiving and how their perceptions influence decision making. The setting can be structured so that students can see the points at which they tend to distort in their perceiving and thus make poor decisions. Teachers can also help students see patterns of decision making in school related activities and analyze why the decisions were made as they were.

Other activities which might be designed for children and youth to enable them better to see the relationship between decision making and perceiving could include the following:

Ask students to analyze an election for a school office. What perceptions of students seemed to influence the decision to vote for the winning candidate?

Ask students to indicate whom they think makes the decisions in the classroom relative to ongoing procedures. Then compare the students' and teacher's perceptions of who is making the decisions.[23]

Ask children or youth to compare why two persons made different decisions about the same issue. What differences in perceiving caused differences in the decision?

Perceiving and Organizing

How one perceives influences to a large degree how he organizes his own impressions and memories. The arranging of sense data of various kinds may take two forms. A person may arrange the data in terms of frameworks which have been predetermined. For example, each of

---

[23] For a study of decision making in one classroom, see Shirlyn Nash, "Young Children's Perceptions of Decision Making in the Classroom" (Milwaukee: School of Education, University of Wisconsin—Milwaukee, 1964, mimeographed). Summary statement of study in Bernice J. Wolfson and Shirlyn Nash, "Who Decides What in the Classroom?" *The Elementary School Journal*, LXV (May, 1965), 436–438.

the separate disciplines has broad boundaries, basic questions, and a language integral to the subject. The framework or organizational components have been imparted to some degree to the student so that the organization of the subject to a large extent has been determined apart from the student.

His perceptions, therefore, as he studies the subject will to a degree be capable of immediate organization in terms of the structure of the discipline. Thus, perceiving may involve the simultaneous identification of the framework and the substance which fits within the framework. Even if the fitting of content into the framework does not take place immediately, the teacher and the student usually can fairly easily categorize content.

Other predetermined frameworks include teacher-made outlines, or materials developed by commercial publishers in which the student is given rather precise instructions concerning the structure of the information. In other words, students are given not only content, but also the framework for organizing the content.

In cases such as those mentioned above, it is important that the student learn to perceive within the structure that has been shared with him. Distortion occurs when the materials are restructured so that they do not fit the author's intent.

On the other hand, much of life comes to persons in experiences which do not fit a readily discernible framework. Perceiving then must be accompanied by the development of an internalized framework which makes sense to the person.

Educators, therefore, concerned about helping students perceive accurately must give attention to externalized systems of ordering developed outside the individual learner and internalized systems which are unique to each person.

Schooling which attempts to help individuals relate their perceptions and ways of perceiving to organizing should provide opportunities like these:

Ask students to describe their perceptions of such fields of study as mathematics, biology, English, or history. Compare their perceptions with those of a scholar in the field.

Ask students to describe how they develop an outline for a writing project in which material is gathered from a variety of disciplines and sources.

Encourage students to record perceptions which do not fit into a pattern but seem to have merit for future thought and exploration.

Provide opportunities for students to examine distorted data in propaganda or other forms. Ask them to identify the points where information seems to have been misperceived.

Perceiving and Creating

Central to the act of creating is a mode of perceiving that allows for the intake of a variety of stimuli and possesses the mechanism to change and develop new categories rather easily. Creating is linked to perceiving in that economical, efficient ways of retaining perceptions in the form of memories and impressions have been developed. This enables the blending of ideas for rich syntheses when creation is taking place. To develop the kinds of categories which lend themselves to quick retrieval or necessary change is important to the creative process.

In addition, the perception of many other factors essential to creation is important. For example, the perception of the discipline of hard work, of insight, of the place of the irrational, of values, and of the achievement of focus are extremely critical to creating.

Children and youth can obtain better understanding of the relationship of perceiving to creating through experiences such as these:

Ask children or youth to record in a diary their perceptions of what they do, how they feel, what initiated the activity following a period when they feel they have been productive in some way.

Encourage students to compare perceptions of how they see themselves and how others see them during periods of creative production. Such items might be compared as friendliness, tendency toward withdrawal, concentration, what seemed to interest the person, etc.

Ask students to record impressions of live persons who have made a creative contribution of some note. Then make arrangements to interview the person to see how students' impressions coincide with the contributor's stated perception of himself.

Perceiving and Valuing

If valuing is defined as establishing priorities, then attention should be given to the perceptions that· influence the shaping of priorities. Accuracy in perceiving intangibles such as values is often more important than accuracy in perceiving objects. Unless criteria are developed by individuals to help them select among competing goods, then excessive energies will be drained off in engaging in good but mediocre kinds of activities rather than in ones which can make a significant difference to themselves and others. Thus, perceiving worth becomes extremely important, and valuing and perceiving become inextricably linked.

To help students learn to perceive priorities which they and others have established, assignments such as these might be given:

Ask students to read a current news item and to identify the values underlying decisions involved. Then let students compare their lists of values.

After students have read a selected novel, ask them to identify the values which led to certain actions. Encourage children to compare lists.

Ask students to identify values which seem to underlie some international event. How are the values different from those commonly held by persons in this country?

THE WONDER OF PERCEIVING AND THE SCHOOL OF THE FUTURE

How and why persons perceive as they do is not fully understood, yet enough knowledge is available to cause us to realize that school should give planned attention to this phenomenon. Ciardi has facetiously recommended three courses: "Visual Acuity I," "Visual Acuity II," and "Visual Acuity III." He suggests that more appropriate names for the courses might be: "Elementary Looking," "Intermediate Looking," and "Advanced Looking."[24] Perhaps Ciardi's suggestion should be taken seriously, for seeing is a sophisticated art affecting all other aspects of human behavior. Moreover, perceptions are inextricably interwoven with what we have seen before and our hopes for the future. There is no such phenomenon as "immaculate perception."[25]

Ability to perceive accurately and fully improves as persons practice the art of perceiving. "A work of art is determined always not by the thing looked at, but by the size of the mind that is doing the

---

[24] John Ciardi, "The Curriculum of Perception," in *Strength Through Reappraisal*, Sixteenth Yearbook of the American Association of Colleges for Teacher Education (Washington, D. C.: National Education Assn., 1963), p. 118.

[25] Lawrence S. Kubie, "Research in Protecting Preconscious Functions in Education," in *Nurturing Individual Potential* (Washington, D. C.: Association for Supervision and Curriculum Development, NEA, 1964), p. 39.

looking, that containment of anything within a mind."[26] Hopefully the containment becomes greater as persons engage in the art.

The school can play a major role in helping persons perfect their ways of perceiving. For some, teachers may need only to give encouragement, for students through various means have learned to perceive in healthy, adequate ways. Others may need help in perceiving so that what is seen matches the events in the world. This can be done in two ways: "either by the relearning of categories and expectancies, or by constant close inspection of events and objects,"[27] Whatever the task involved, young people will grow up to handle their lives more effectively if they have learned the wonder of perception, for perceiving is indeed the basis and stimulus for other human functions.

---

[26] Ciardi, "The Curriculum of Perception," in *Strength Through Reappraisal*, p. 115.

[27] Jerome Bruner, "On Perceptual Readiness," in *The Cognitive Processes: Readings*, p. 252.

4

How ridiculous, this need of yours to communicate! Why should it mean so much to you that at least one *person has seen the inside of your life?*

DAG HAMMARSKJÖLD

Communicating:

THE SHARING OF
PERSONAL MEANING

4

One of the strongest needs of man is to be understood—to present himself in such a way that he believes he has communicated clearly to others. Man also wants to understand others. Speaking, listening, writing, and utilizing silence appropriately are skills in which common symbols enable man to share his personal meanings.

Communicating through sight and sound is so essential to living that much compensating help is provided for the person deficient in one or both of these areas. Education often fails, however, to help the healthy person who has the use of these senses to utilize them in maximum ways. The school, therefore, at all levels, needs to rethink its communication programs in order to insure that children and youth are gaining necessary skills in communicating meaning.

Quote on opening page of chapter is from *Markings*, by Dag Hammarskjöld, p. 87. © Copyright 1964 by Alfred A. Knopf, Inc., and Faber and Faber Ltd. Reprinted by permission of the publishers.

COMMUNICATING: THE NEED FOR
AN EMPHASIS UPON INTERPERSONAL SKILLS

In keeping with our interest in process as ongoing, the discussion of communication is limited to the dynamism of the process. Because communication is not a static process, to delimit the topic is difficult. We are *not* treating communication, however, as reading, writing, speaking, listening, linguistics, or grammar. These separate facets have been given much attention in school programs. Our intent rather is to focus upon communicating as an interpersonal process which takes into account the traditional elements of programs of communication but may call for reshuffling them.

A need exists for an emphasis upon communicating as personal meaning for three broad reasons. First, we live in a highly complex world. Persons, ideologies, and cultures are becoming increasingly perplexing, necessitating great sophistication in communicating. Distortion of ideas is oftentimes apt to occur through inadequate facility in communication rather than through intent. To wrestle with the problems of complexity can bring rich rewards as skills in communicating are applied.

Second, communicating as the revealing of personal meaning is important because of the need to increase understanding among various groups of persons. Consider the family, professional and social groups, and the international audience.

Current writing about family life and the problems and satisfactions associated with it often calls attention to the fact that lack of effective communication deters mutually significant relationships. Family life can degenerate into a state of tolerance rather than be exalted into a network of relationships which provide sources of strength. Greater attention to those peculiar aspects of communication within the home that can make interpersonal relationships grotesque or beautiful is necessary if the backbone of our society is to be maintained.

In a nation characterized by fragmentation because individuals of various groups do not know how to communicate, we need to seek means for communicating between social, professional, and other types of groups formed for specific purposes. Despite the fact that a common language is spoken, we find, for example, academicians unable to exchange messages with those in related disciplines, and persons from related but dissimilar professions having difficulty in discussing overlapping concepts. Likewise, those interested in applied knowledge often cannot deal with theoreticians in the same field. Communication goes beyond knowledge of the language. We must find ways of bridging gaps between the conceptual frameworks of persons in different, but related, fields. Building the desire to understand the norms of the inner world and expectations from persons within various fields of human endeavor may help bring closer unity between persons who are working separately but should be working side by side.[1]

In dealing with the international audience, problems of communication are tremendous. In addition to language barriers, insensitivity to messages communicated nonverbally causes major problems. Distances and stances during conversation, the meaning of various tones of voice, and the relationship of business to social conversation are among the subtleties of communication viewed differently in various parts of the world.[2] Awareness of such differences is important to those wishing to communicate effectively in any culture.

Third, an understanding of communicating as sharing meaning is important in order that the individual select from a repertoire of skills those most important for the situation. *In short, we communicate to influence—to affect with intent.*[3] Influence involves many factors depending upon the audience and the purpose and substance of the message. At times influence may involve a highly analytical approach. At other times synthesis of ideas is evident in the message. Some persons send colorful messages; others tend to send drab ones. Techniques of propaganda may be employed in order to move the listener to a preconceived position regardless of validity. Thus, since communication skills can be used to produce certain effects, it is crucial that persons learn the appropriate technique and language to give the desired effect.

---

[1] For further reading on problems of interprofessional communication see Howard Baumgartel, "Some Human Problems in Interprofessional Communication," *Journal of Communication,* XIV (September, 1964), 172–182.

[2] For a fuller description of intercultural communication problems see:
Dominick A. Barbara, "Nonverbal Communication," *Journal of Communication,* XIII (September, 1963), 166–173.
Edward T. Hall and William F. Whyte, "Intercultural Communication," *Practical Anthropology,* X, No. 5 (1963), 216–232.
Edward T. Hall, *The Silent Language* (New York: Premier Books, Fawcett Publications, Inc., 1959).

[3] From *The Process of Communication,* by David K. Berlo, p. 12. Copyright © 1960 by Holt, Rinehart and Winston, Inc.

COMMUNICATING AS SHARING OF PERSONAL MEANING: MAJOR CONCEPTS

Traditionally much of what has been taught in the schools relative to communication has focused upon symbols and language. Less attention has been given to individuals in the process of communicating. Unless the person is seen as being central to the communication process, the school subjects of writing, reading, and speech have little meaning.

Assuming that the sharing of personal meanings is seen as the crux of the communication program, certain concepts should be developed. Three will be considered next: characteristics of the communication process; symbols, language, and meaning; and persons in the process of communicating.

Characteristics of the Communication Process

"Communicate" is derived from the Latin word *communicare* meaning "to enjoy," "share," "partake of," "use or enjoy in common." Webster has defined the word as "the ability to make one idea the property of two or more persons." The concept of sharing two worlds is often inherent in definitions of communication. On this point, MacLeod says,

> To understand another person is to reconstruct the world of the other person in such a way that it can be related to one's own. We can have complete communication only where there is full understanding, and this is never really achieved. Language presents so many obstacles that one sometimes wonders how it is that we understand one another at all.[4]

Weaver acknowledges that communication exceeds language and includes music, the pictorial arts, ballet, theater, in fact anything which involves human behavior. The important concept is that one mind affects another.[5]

Benda says, "Conversing postulates the attitude of turning to each

---

[4] Robert B. MacLeod, "Preface," in *Language and the Discovery of Reality,* by Joseph Church (New York: Random House, Inc., 1961), p. viii.

[5] Paraphrased from statement in Jurgen Ruesch, *Therapeutic Communication* (New York: W. W. Norton & Company, Inc., 1961), p. 452.

other in willingness to speak and listen. It is not 'dis-course' but 'dia-logue,' the fusion of two separate voices in one."[6]

Again, on the matter of the personal nature of communication, Kloman says, "The word *communication* has two separate, yet closely related meanings. It can mean the transmission or imparting of information (or a perceived sense of reality) from one to another person, or it can imply a joining together of one person with another."[7]

In addition, if communicating is sharing of personal meaning, the process is circular rather than linear. Its complexity is due to the nature of human personality in interaction. Since sharing of one meaning may induce feedback which somewhat changes the intent of the sender, communication is irreversible and unrepeatable. The rate of movement in the circular pattern is partially dependent upon the openness and integrity of the persons communicating. For example, an individual who tends to be indirect or veiled in his discourse may cause the understanding of meaning to be less rapid than the individual who sends direct and straightforward messages.

Another characteristic of communication is that it involves impression and expression. Impressions result from the intake of the present moment coupled with prior experiences which the individual unconsciously brings to bear upon what he is seeing or hearing. Expression is the speaking to one's self or others about reshaped or modified impressions. A rich intake of impressions should enable a rich sharing during expression.

Symbols, Language, and Meaning

In the interchange between either self and self or self and others, symbols and language are necessary tools to arrive at meaning. Symbols should "produce similar responses in more than one person."[8] Symbols are ideas, memories, purposes, or intentions organized,

6 Clemens E. Benda, *The Image of Love: Modern Trends in Psychiatric Thinking.* Copyright © 1961 by The Free Press of Glencoe, Inc. New York: The Free Press of Glencoe, Inc., a Division of the Crowell-Collier Publishing Company, p. 108. Reprinted by permission.

7 William Kloman, "Aspects of Existential Communication," *Journal of Existentialism,* VI (Fall, 1965), pp. 59–68, p. 59.

8 From *The Process of Communication,* by David K. Berlo, p. 172. Copyright © 1960 by Holt, Rinehart and Winston, Inc. Reprinted by permission of Holt, Rinehart and Winston, Inc.

adapted, or translated into some type of systematic system. "A symbol is an extraorganismic device which has been agreed upon to refer in a condensed way to a series of actions or events; it is used for coding purposes in order to transmit messages."[9] Symbols alone, however, are not the totality of the communication process. For economy of thinking and behaving, they must be sequenced in some way. A form of organization or a structure is imposed upon them.

As symbols are clarified and structured, a language is evolved. "Language is a purely human and non-instinctive method of communicating ideas, emotions, and desires by means of a system of voluntarily produced symbols. These symbols are in the first instance auditory and they are produced by the so-called 'organs of speech.'"[10] Although language has been defined in multitudinous ways, perhaps for our purposes the notion of "*verbal* systematic symbolism" is adequate.[11] How symbols are combined through meaningful methods is called *syntax*. "A *grammar* is the description of the structural characteristics of the language."[12]

Since language is one of the most objective, systematic, and common modes of communication, attention is given here to defining this term. The origin of language as a process can be described in the following way:

1. Language consists of a set of significant symbols (vocabulary).

2. The symbols of a language were chosen by chance. They are not fixed or God-given.

3. Man constructed his own language under the same principles of interpretation, response, and reward that govern all learning.

4. Man gradually created language in order to express his meanings to himself and others, to get other people to have the same meanings, and to make responses that increased his ability to affect.[13]

---

[9] Reusch, *Therapeutic Communication*, p. 453. Paraphrased from C. W. Morris, *Signs, Language and Behavior* (New York: Prentice-Hall, Inc., 1946).
[10] Edward Sapir, *Language: An Introduction to the Study of Speech* (New York: A Harvest Book, Harcourt, Brace & World, Inc., 1921, 1949), p. 8.
[11] Joshua Whatmough, *Language: A Modern Synthesis* (New York: Mentor Books, The New American Library, Inc., 1956), p. 20.
[12] From *The Process of Communication*, by David K. Berlo, p. 12. Copyright © 1960 by Holt, Rinehart and Winston, Inc. Reprinted by permission of Holt, Rinehart and Winston, Inc.
[13] *Ibid.*, p. 173.

The ability to be affected and to affect is central to the process of communication as we conceive it. For example, language, as language or linguistics, might be an appropriate stance from which to view the communication process. The study of language, linguistics, and other ways of viewing communication comes in as each area relates to the development of meaning.

Barnlund says the aim of communication "is to increase the number and consistency of our meanings within the limits set by patterns of evaluation that have proven successful in the past, our emerging needs and drives, and the demands of the physical and social setting of the moment."[14] He goes on to say, "A theory that leaves out man's communication with himself, his communication with the world about him, and a large proportion of his interactions with his fellowman, is not a theory at all, but a theory of speechmaking."[15]

In considering the significance of meaning of communication, it should be remembered that meaning is internal and not external to the individual. We indeed need increased understanding of what Vygotsky calls "inner speech" and how it differs from "external speech."[16] "Inner speech" as Vygotsky uses the term is not conveyed, for we do not convey meanings. We convey messages. However for effective communication, the message must mean essentially the same to the persons involved.

Berlo suggests the following about meanings and persons:

1. Meanings are in people. They are the internal responses that people make to stimuli, and the internal stimulations that these responses elicit.

2. Meanings result from (a) factors in the individual, as related to (b) factors in the physical world around him.

3. People can have similar meanings only to the extent that they have had similar experiences, or can anticipate similar experiences.

---

14 D. C. Barnlund, "Toward a Meaning Centered Philosophy of Communication," *ETC*, XX (December, 1963), pp. 454–469, p. 458.

15 *Ibid.*, p. 459.

16 For a full discussion of these terms see Lev Semenovich Vygotsky, *Thought and Language*, ed. and trans. Eugenia Hanfmann and Gertrude Vakar (Cambridge: The MIT Press, 1962), p. 131. See especially Chapter 7, "Thought and Word," pp. 119–151.

4. Meanings are never fixed. As experience changes, meanings change.

5. No two people can ever have exactly the same meaning for anything. Many times two people do not have even similar meanings.

6. People will always respond to a stimulus in light of their own experiences.

7. To give people a meaning or to change their meanings for a stimulus, you must pair the stimulus with other stimuli for which they already have meanings.

8. In learning meanings, people operate on the principles of (a) least effort, (b) noninterference, and (c) discriminative capacity.[17]

Persons in the Process of Communicating

If the sharing of meaning is considered to be the prime function of communicating, then persons should evidence or be helped to develop certain qualities.

A prerequisite to good communication is the ability to share openly and with integrity one's self—what one is organizing, creating, valuing, deciding. Without such honesty on the part of the sender, distortion occurs even before the message reaches the receiver.

A concomitant ability necessary to good communication is being able to listen to another with purpose, responding in terms that will help the other person sharpen, prize, and find deeper meaning in his own thoughts. "The behavior of young children suggests that when they are mobilized to speak, their hearing apparatus is turned off."[18] In light of this, most children need help in listening and coresponding.

Another facet that should be studied as persons communicate is change within their personalities. Persons engaged in real and vital communication often change not only one aspect of their thinking, but often their total outlook.[19] Other persons may see communication as "manipulation, a one-way conveying of meanings from the strong to

---

[17] From *The Process of Communication,* by David K. Berlo, p. 184. Copyright © 1960 by Holt, Rinehart and Winston, Inc. Reprinted by permission of Holt, Rinehart and Winston, Inc.

[18] From *Language and the Discovery of Reality,* by Joseph Church, p. 74. © Copyright 1961 by Joseph Church. Reprinted by permission of Random House, Inc.

[19] Adapted from Barnlund, *ETC,* XX, 460–461.

the weak, from the superior to the inferior. The communicator wants to change the other fellow's views, not his own."[20]

Although the term "communion" may be imprecise, another characteristic of a person in the process of communicating is the ability to unite his personality with that of the other person.

> The healthy mind is alert to the bonds that unite his personality with those of his associates. For communication depends upon communion, and communion is achieved through development of the social personality. It is this fact which is the primary guide for the development of healthfully purposive speech. Integrity demands that we say what we wish, but the most basic wish of our human lives is the desire to establish and maintain a sound relationship with our fellows.[21]

In brief, communication involves a union with one's fellows in which personal integrity and a caring for the other unite to make possible transactions in which one's own meanings become clearer because of mutual concern each for the other.

TEACHING COMMUNICATING AS THE SHARING OF MEANING

The teacher or curriculum worker interested in teaching communicating as the sharing of meaning can start at several points. The few suggestions that follow can be adapted, elaborated upon, or combined as a teacher sees fit.

Helping Another Clarify Meaning

Earlier, it was mentioned that meaning resides only in the person receiving the message, not in the sender of the message or in the message itself. What significant implications this concept has for schooling! Do not teachers often feel that if they have presented a clear, well-ordered lesson the students ought to have learned it? And

---

[20] Edgar Dale, "Instructional Resources," *The Changing American School*, ed. John Goodlad, the Sixty-fifth Yearbook of the National Society for the Study of Education, Part II (Chicago: University of Chicago Press, 1966), pp. 84–109, p. 90.

[21] Robert T. Oliver, "Purposive Speaking," in *The Healthy Mind in Communion and Communication*, eds. Robert T. Oliver and Dominick A. Barbara (Springfield, Illinois: Charles C. Thomas, Publisher, 1962), pp. 119–141, pp. 139–140.

is not the evaluation of teaching often based upon the results of tests whose purpose is to see how well students can recall what the teacher has said? The student who dares to interpret the lesson in terms of his own experience oftentimes risks school-created punishments. Teachers often use words which have meaning for them expecting students to know the teacher's inner world. Lewis Carroll illustrates this point in an insightful conversation between Alice and Humpty Dumpty:

"I don't know what you mean by 'glory'," Alice said.

Humpty Dumpty smiled contemptuously. "Of course you don't—till I tell you. I meant 'There's a nice knockdown argument for you!' "

"But 'glory' doesn't mean 'a nice knockdown argument,' " Alice objected.

"When I use a word," Humpty Dumpty said, in rather a scornful tone, "it means just what I choose it to mean—neither more nor less."

"The question is," said Alice, "whether you *can* make words mean so many different things."

"The question is," said Humpty Dumpty, "which is to be master— that's all."[22]

Obviously the implications of the dialogue between Humpty Dumpty and Alice are clear for the purposes of schooling. If the aim of the teacher is to help students develop stable, coherent self-images in which their personal meanings enable them to live rich, full lives, then the teacher's task is to check continuously the perceptions of students. Likewise, the teacher would encourage students to interact with each other in such a manner that they freely share areas of confusion or lack of clarity in personal discourse. Such teaching would encourage interaction between teachers and students, and students and students instead of an overemphasis upon discourse planned primarily by the teacher.

Clarification of meaning is particularly important in areas where children bring a different conception of the English spoken by teachers or taught in the school. Symbols possessing one meaning for the teacher may connote to the students something quite different. Opportunities for continuous comparison of ideas may help to bring

---

[22] Lewis Carroll (Charles Dodgson)', *Alice's Adventures in Wonderland, Through the Looking Glass, and the Hunting of the Snark* (New York: The Modern Library, Random House, Inc., 1925), pp. 246–247. Reprinted in Berlo, *The Process of Communication*, pp. 190–191.

reported meanings closer together and to increase communication than if such opportunities did not exist.

Development of Attentiveness

The teacher who wants to insure the clarifying and sharing of personal meaning will stress attentiveness in his own listening and that of his students. Attentiveness is listening in which one attempts to let preconceived biases and prejudices recede into the background in order to hear what is really being said. Such listening is not easy, for most persons mobilize to speak again as soon as the other person opens his mouth. Absolute attentiveness may require periods of sustained, unembarrassed silence so that the listener can frame his thoughts to respond within the meaning of the speaker. Children and youth may need practice in learning to cope with the quietness that periods of thought necessitate.

If the listening has been attentive, the response might be a question inviting clarification of intent. Or it might be an invitation to illustrate a point. Sometimes the respondent may admit he does not have the background to understand what the speaker has said. Practice in repeating what he thinks he has heard may help the student decide whether he has made a point of contact.[23]

Attentiveness in communication cannot be stressed too strongly, for since individuals are constantly undergoing change, meaning at one time may be different from that at another because of some new insight. The person truly skilled in the communication process is sensitive to signs of new meanings for old symbols or new arrangements of old ideas.

Questioning and Meaning

If meaning is seen as the critical element within the communication process, much attention should be devoted to the art of questioning. Benda says,

> Man is not only a speaking animal but, on a higher level, a questing and, thus, a questioning being; indeed, since the Socratic dialogues, it

---

[23] For further elaboration of helping children enhance their listening skills see: Helen F. Mackintosh, ed., *Children and Oral Language* (Association for Childhood Education, International; Association for Supervision and Curriculum Development; International Reading Association; and National Council of Teachers of English, 1964).

Robert T. Oliver and Dominick A. Barbara, *The Healthy Mind in Communion and Communication* (Springfield, Illinois: Charles C. Thomas, Publisher, 1962).

has been claimed that questioning is the true commencement of wisdom. Talking is taking oneself for granted and pouring one's own views into the other channels; but questioning reveals a consciousness of isolation, of one's own limitations. Alone in the face of such a great world, the questioning person starts out to seek the help of others; he is a true person in communication, open to others and no longer self-sufficient. He has transcended his own lonely position in entering the community of speaking people.[24]

Attention has been given to questions that help children think. For example, Sanders has focused upon questions related to such thinking skills as interpretation, analysis, synthesis, and evaluation.[25] Raths has developed techniques for helping children clarify their values and develop their thinking skills.[26] Berman has developed a construct of the thoughtful person and has sought to give examples of assignments that might foster such a person.[27]

Despite the fact, however, that questioning has been a favorite mode of instruction for centuries, our educational literature is lacking in advice for teachers who wish to help youth ask the kinds of questions that enable more precise understandings among persons.[28]

Meaning and Motivation

Because we cannot see the inner self, the school needs to provide opportunities for children to indicate their motivation. Vygotsky says,

> To understand another's speech, it is not sufficient to understand his words—we must understand his thought. But even that is not enough—we must also know its motivation. No psychological analysis of an utterance is complete until that plane is reached.[29]

---

[24] Benda, *The Image of Love*, p. 108. Reprinted by permission.

[25] Norris M. Sanders, *Classroom Questions: What Kinds?* (New York: Harper & Row, Publishers, 1966).

[26] Louis E. Raths, "Clarifying Values," in *Curriculum for Today's Boys and Girls*, ed. Robert Fleming (Columbus: Charles E. Merrill Publishing Company, 1963), pp. 315–342.

Louis E. Raths, Merrill Harmin, and Sidney B. Simon *Values and Teaching* (Columbus: Charles E. Merrill Publishing Company, 1966).

Louis E. Raths and Others, *Teaching for Thinking: Theory and Application* (Columbus: Charles E. Merrill Publishing Company, 1967).

[27] Louise M. Berman, *From Thinking to Behaving: Assignments Reconsidered*, Practical Suggestions for Teaching, ed. Alice Miel (New York: Teachers College Press, Columbia University, 1967).

[28] Literature from related fields of psychology and communication theory may give some help. For example,

Oliver and Barbara, *The Healthy Mind in Communion and Communication*, pp. 69–72.

[29] Vygotsky, *Thought and Language*, p. 151.

As motivations become somewhat clear to teacher and youth, assignments can be planned which enable the individual to do that which is of significance to him. In this way, integrity of action and communication are encouraged. Children are not merely carrying out tasks to please an adult without seeing a need for undertaking them. Superficiality of thought and action is encouraged when integrity of thinking and communicating is not prized.

Reporting on a study of suburban children, Miel indicates that to the query "What do you do when you're good?" primary graders replied, "Do things I'm asked to do."[30] If we are concerned about communicating meaning, the child needs more opportunities to be good by doing what he, rather than some adult, sees to be good, necessary, and interesting.

The Idiom of the Day versus the Idiom of the Self

Man is a social being whose transactions with others change both him and the groups of which he is a part. Very often the same symbols have essentially the same meaning for the group and for the individual; however, in many instances, the individual may have derived meanings for common symbols which do not coincide with the ideas of the group. In such cases it is essential for the individual to realize if his concepts differ from those held by his friends or peers; otherwise, serious problems of communication are likely. An individual should be able to say, "This is the meaning I hold for this word, but this is what I think the group ascribes to the word." The problem of being able to maintain individual identity within a group can be lessened if persons learn to develop their own meanings for common terms, share them, and become aware of the multiplicity of meanings the same term may have for others.

Symbols, therefore, have a meaning of the day but also of the self. To the degree that the two mesh is conversation apt to be fruitful and satisfying. The implications for schooling are twofold: (1) That students learn that the meaning they commonly ascribe to a word may not be a common meaning, and (2) that individuals have the opportunity within the school setting to know the joy and satisfaction that can come from sharing personal meaning. To help children see the many meanings each word can have, it is important that time be

---

[30] Alice Miel with Edwin Kiester, Jr., *The Shortchanged Children of Suburbia,* Institute of Human Relations Press Pamphlet Series No. 8 (New York: The American Jewish Committee, 1967), p. 47.

allotted to the study of words—their roots, ascribed meanings by various groups, and individual meanings of the child.

As individuals seek to understand verbal encounters, they should also learn to be sensitive to and aware of signals other than words. Tone of voice, inflection, facial expressions, gestures, posture, manner of dress, individual surroundings—all tell something about personal meaning. In a constantly shrinking world, it is becoming impossible to handle adequately the problem of language. Increased understanding seems to reside in a fuller conception of nonverbal symbols. Many who work abroad know the language of another country but are not sensitive to nonverbal symbols and, therefore, are less successful than those who are less sophisticated in the language but who are attuned to other kinds of messages. Teachers could provide more opportunities for analyzing nonverbal symbols such as facial expression, tone of voice, manner of dress, inflection, and treasured possessions.

For example, Dimitrovsky discovered that children become increasingly sensitive to facial expression and tone of voice as they mature.[31] It would appear, therefore, that with practice children might develop heightened sensitivity beyond that left to mere chance or random teaching.

Through an analysis of pictures, such as those in Ruesch and Kees' *Nonverbal Communication,* students can become familiar with the variety of symbols which are helpful in truly understanding people.[32] Stick figures depicting various emotional states, dramatizations, and role-playing are other ways of helping children and youth become aware of the importance of the nonverbal in the communication process.

Musicians and artists have long felt that our culture has not adequately taken into account the impact of things which are unspeakable and can only be expressed through media other than words.[33] While learning to be exacting and accurate in the use of words, students should search for ways to understand what is not easily thought or said.

---

[31] Lilly Dimitrovsky, "The Ability to Identify the Emotional Meaning of Vocal Expressions at Successive Age Levels," in *The Communication of Emotional Meaning,* eds. Joel R. Davitz and Others (New York: McGraw-Hill Book Company, 1964), pp. 69-86.

[32] Jurgen Ruesch and Weldon Kees, *Nonverbal Communication* (Berkeley: University of California Press, 1959).

[33] For a fuller treatment of the place of the arts in the process of communications see Susanne K. Langer, *Philosophy in a New Key* (New York: Mentor Books, The New American Library, Inc., 1942 and 1951).

Levy found that sensitivity, expressiveness, and self-understanding are positively interrelated. That is, people who are accurate in identifying the emotional expressions *of* others are more effective in expressing emotional meanings *to* others. They are also more accurate in identifying the meanings of their own expressions. These interrelations were investigated only in the vocal mode of communication, but for this mode at least, the positive relation between transmitting and receiving emotional messages is unequivocal.[34]

From the above statement we can hypothesize that if the school helps the student understand the nonverbal emotional behavior of others, he will learn to understand and deal with his own behavior with greater precision.

Analyzing the Communication Process

Within the school setting, the teacher plays various roles. At times he is a clarifier, a stimulator, an introducer of new concepts, a learner, or merely another individual acting spontaneously within a teaching-learning situation. There are occasions when to establish maximal learning conditions the teacher might engage in therapeutic communication. During therapeutic communication, the teacher will not be so much concerned about the dictionary meaning of his words as the emotional impact of the vocabulary.

Therapeutic communication thus presupposes the presence of several people, one of whom must be wiser, more mature, and more skilled in communication than the others; and if this more able person uses his skills to develop the communicative functions of the immature, young, or seriously disturbed individual, then he is engaging in therapeutic communication. At times, this process is referred to as therapy; at other times as education; some call it counselling; others simply friendship. But regardless of the label given, the criterion of whether an exchange becomes therapeutic or not is tied to the perception that the other person has a certain readiness to understand, to acknowledge, and to reply.[35]

In therapeutic communication, the therapist must be adaptive in his behavior. He is skilled in spacing, timing, and appropriately selecting his responses so that they are in reply to the patient.[36]

---

[34] Joel R. Davitz, *The Communication of Emotional Meaning* (New York: McGraw-Hill Book Company, 1964), p. 180.
[35] Ruesch, *Therapeutic Communication*, p. 31.
[36] *Ibid.*, p. 35.

Teachers need to understand when they are playing the healing role of the therapist. Obviously, this role is not used frequently since ordinarily teachers are not taught the necessary skills. Older children, through study of selected literature, might become aware of some of the dynamics of communication as therapy but again should be advised of the pitfalls.

Another body of literature which is helpful in the understanding of communication is the work being done on teaching as verbal interaction. Although many of the categories developed by the researchers of this school of thought are gross and inappropriate to the essence of what we are saying, nonetheless the procedures of getting feedback through coding, tape recordings, movies, and videotapes might be adapted for use among child and child, and teacher and child.[37]

The analysis of the communication process within the classroom can provide insights for helping individuals and the teacher improve their performance in the sharing of personal meanings. At the same time, because the sharing of meaning is a delicate, sensitive process, to catch it entirely through existing procedures may mean more loss than gain. Analysis of any communication should therefore be used with awareness of the inability to capture the total setting.

COMMUNICATING AND THE SCHOOL OF THE FUTURE

If we accept the assumption that the aim of communication is the sharing of personal meaning, the teaching of communication will change rather sharply. The development of skills to which much time is now devoted will be taught much more rapidly. Means will be available to diagnose the stage of development at which a child is. We will also know the most appropriate way to reach a given child. Hence skills of reading, writing, and listening will be taught in multiple and individualized ways. Some children will work primarily with the teacher on these skills. Others will learn more efficiently through forms of automated instruction.

Children will begin to use their senses differently. For example, children will not always use commonly taught eye patterns and will grasp the image of a page of print even as they grasp the image of a

---

[37] For further information, see Arno A. Bellack, ed., *Theory and Research in Teaching* (New York: Bureau of Publications, Teachers College, Columbia University, 1963).

picture.[38] They will have learned to use their hearing equipment more efficiently and will assimilate the message from a tape recorder played at triple speed as though it were played at the normal speed. They will be able to use two or more senses simultaneously and thus work with two or more media at the same time.[39] For example, they will be able, efficiently, to study a graph and to listen to a commentary on a tape recorder. Most persons at the present time would attend primarily to one of the two media at a time.

Speed reading, scanning, and reading to spur thinking will be the order of the day. Reading problems should be greatly minimized.

The major emphasis of the schools, however, will not be upon the skills as cited. It will be upon those aspects of communication which enable the psychological freedom to deal with one's inner life—ideas, feelings, constructs. It will be upon developing modes of expression which indicate integrity and concern.

We may have such areas of study in the elementary and secondary school as communication and conflict, communication and integrity, nonverbal communication, cross-cultural patterns of communication, communication and the inner life.

Whatever titles are given to areas of study, we will be concerned that communication help us shed the formalities that cause us to cloak ourselves so the true self cannot be seen. Children and youth will be learning the strength and vitality that can come from real sharing of personal meaning.

Hypotheses for Testing

If children and youth are given the opportunity to learn some of the components of nonverbal behavior, then they will describe more nonverbal components of communication in a non-structured setting than if they were not helped to become aware.

If children are given practice in repeating what they hear another say before responding, they will respond more in line with the other person's intent more frequently than if they do not repeat before responding.

---

[38]Informal conversation with Leslee J. Bishop, Executive Secretary, Association for Supervision and Curriculum Development, NEA, 1967.
[39] *Ibid.*

If teachers analyze their own teaching through the use of an objective device which gives feedback on what they have said, their speech in the classroom over a period of time will be more congruent with intent.

5

*If I speak in the tongues of men
and of angels, but have not love, I am
a noisy gong or a clanging cymbal.
And if I have prophetic powers, and
understand all mysteries and all knowledge, and if I have all faith, so as to
remove mountains, but have not love,
I am nothing. If I give away all I have,
and if I deliver my body to be burned,
but have not love, I gain nothing.*

I CORINTHIANS 13:1–3 RSV

Loving:

HUMAN EXPERIENCE AS CO-RESPONDING

5

When basic human functions or processes are discussed, it is natural that attention should turn to man's relationship to man. Men turn to others with varying degrees of feeling and interest; hence, we can describe in a number of ways how persons relate to each other. They can be aloof, kind, angry, loving, or hateful. In this chapter our purpose is to strike directly at one of the most central areas of human feeling and relating—loving.

First, consideration is given to the *need* for a critical examination of the concept of love. Then attention is focused upon the nature of love and its relationship to certain other facets of human existence. Finally attention is given to a few suggestions concerning the school's role in helping children and youth develop as persons who are able to give and receive love—to co-respond.

LOVING AS CO-RESPONDING:
THE NEED FOR EMPHASIS

The concept of loving has been characterized in such tawdry terms that the reader may well wonder about the inclusion of this area of human experience in curriculum planning. From the many synonyms the word has, however, educators can derive ideas which should be included in the theoretical construct of the process-oriented person.

At the present time, possibly because of the distorted emphasis created by mass media, some elements of the concept of love have been excluded, others overplayed. Consequently, the immediate image of love that comes to the minds of many adults and children is associated with sex, materialism, and the satisfaction of immediate desires.

It is indeed unfortunate that twentieth century man has allowed himself to be swayed by the superficial and inadequate concepts of this powerful and vital human process. Basically, the study of human love leads to a fuller understanding of man and his nature. Benda says,

> Man's nature reveals itself more in human love than in any other contact with the world. Being at one and the same time a beast (whose primordial needs and instincts have not changed over thousands of years) and the image of God—of *his* god—man reveals in his love the whole range of his existence. As the image of the gods whom he serves, man's love in its immediacy unveils his values and the framework of his thinking, the structure of his conscious world. In no other domain is man's nature state and the imagery of his spiritual world better reflected.[1]

Although love is a predominating factor in human nature, many persons have less understanding of its components than of other emotional states, such as joy or sadness. For example, Davitz points out that in a series of research studies involving hundreds of subjects, none asked what anger, joy, or sadness meant. However, a few questioned the meaning of love.[2] The presence or absence of love is often

---

[1] Clemens E. Benda, *The Image of Love: Modern Trends in Psychiatric Thinking.* Copyright © 1961 by The Free Press of Glencoe, Inc. (New York: The Free Press of Glencoe, Inc., a Division of the Crowell-Collier Publishing Company), p. 3. Reprinted by permission.

[2] Joel R. Davitz and Others, *The Communication of Emotional Meaning* (New York: McGraw-Hill Book Company, 1964), p. 194.

noticed, but to verbalize what is present or absent is often difficult. Because love involves subtle qualities, its study involves rigorous, yet sensitive examination.

An understanding of loving in its broadest sense is essential to effective relations with those near and far. Often an act designed to show love and concern for another may be perceived as an expression of aggressiveness, possession, or other qualities incompatible with the intent of the bestower. Problems of perceptions of love, concern, and caring often are evident in relations between husband and wife, child and parent, teacher and student, supervisor and supervised, and nation and nation.

Clarification of the term is important so that intent not be misperceived. At a time of increased international tensions, it is also crucial that overtones of kindness be enmeshed in concepts of caring rather than self-getting or self-protection if nations are to operate upon principles of mutual respect and admiration. If the term were defined more adequately, overtures to friendship on the part of one nation would not be so easily misinterpreted by others.

At the personal level, as the individual gains increased understanding about love he can better place his various commitments and attachments in perspective. The vision which a person creates for himself helps determine the persons, projects, and ideas to which the individual will devote his time, resources, and energy. Love is related to vision, for vision provides a basis for selection of persons with whom the individual will not only relate, but also co-respond—a term denoting a more honest, mutual, and pervasive kind of relating.

The need is indeed great for understanding the process of loving. Love goes beyond mere acceptance. It helps provide intensity in a mutually rewarding experience. Such is necessary for man to attain his true humanness.

LOVING AS CO-RESPONDING: MAJOR CONCEPTS

Through the ages love has been viewed from many stances. Each stance has accentuated certain aspects of love and deemphasized others. For example, poets, dramatists, and artists have used love as a common theme. Their stance is one in which love is very particularized and is usually epitomized as human expression resulting in close relationship between a man and a woman.

Theologians take a different stance. Although love is particularized, it is also generalized in that most religions advocate, in addition to individual relationships, a reaching out to and caring for the multitudes.

Behavioral scientists, such as psychologists, psychiatrists, and sociologists, give us another body of knowledge concerning man's relationship to man. Unfortunately, the data which psychologists and psychiatrists gather often are from persons who have problems in relating to others; hence love may be seen in a distorted form. We have little knowledge about love in "normally" functioning persons. Our information has left us with little from which to derive guidelines for parents or teachers who wish to provide the setting where children and youth can develop normal, healthy, caring relationships with others.

Lewis has developed a construct which describes love in four overlapping categories: affection, friendship, eros, and charity.[3] Briefly, affection is best seen in the love of a parent for his child; friendship in love emanating from common concerns and interest; eros involves the love of man for woman and woman for man; charity, the love of God which enriches and nourishes all other forms of love. Much of his analysis, particularly of the first two forms, is helpful in understanding the nature of love and its meaning for schooling.

We shall now consider some qualities of loving, the term being defined in such a way that the school is seen as an institution that can provide a setting where children have the opportunity to grasp the essential meaning of co-responding.

Qualities of Loving

Unlike many things which wear out with use, love increases with use. The person who loves finds he is able to include within the boundaries of his caring increasingly larger numbers of persons. The intensity of his affections do not decrease.[4]

Love involves selectivity as well as universality. Although children are often encouraged to care for others in a broad universal sense, such caring may actually only be a dim awareness rather than tenderness or intensity of feeling.

Love is often a serendipity. It is not sought. For example, when two or more individuals have the opportunity to work together on a

---

[3] C. S. Lewis, *The Four Loves* (New York: Harcourt, Brace & World, Inc., 1960).

[4] For an elaboration of the point that love breeds more love see Abraham H. Maslow, *Eupsychian Management: A Journal* (Homewood, Ill.: Richard D. Irwin, Inc., and the Dorsey Press, 1965), p. 92.

common task, or to play together at something which both enjoy, or to view a scene new and vibrant in its appeal, the end might be deeper meanings between persons.

Love involves the kind of caring which asks nothing in return. Hammarskjöld says, "Our love becomes impoverished if we lack the courage to sacrifice its object."[5] Love is simultaneously self-fulfilling and other-fulfilling. Individual integrity and freedom are respected by both parties.

Love is marked by tenderness. If boundaries for loving are established by principles of morality, rationality, and feeling, then evidence of consideration and concern may follow. To withhold an indication of one's affection when another inspires it is to cut off mutually satisfying relationships for both parties.[6] A heavy emphasis upon objectivity and a denial of the feeling components of man can cause tenderness to be seen as an unworthy aspect of human experience.

Love is both empathic and detached.[7] It can enable the person to become one with the other. It can also, on occasion, cause the person to stand back and analyze his relationship to the person for whom he cares. To stand back occasionally and analyze is necessary if one is to know whether love is co-responding or a selfish type of relationship.

Love is concerned primarily with inner qualities. Visible symbols, such as material resources, status, accomplishments, and roles are not central to the process of caring. Rather, such inner qualities as modes of cognition and ways of perceiving and valuing are integral to the relationship between persons. At a superficial level persons might look at external qualities in relating to others. At a fundamental level, however, the quality of the inner life as evidenced by outward behavior is of great significance. Chart 1 (see p. 68) explains this point.

Loving as an All-Encompassing Process

If love is seen as related to man's peculiarly human qualities, it can be described as an all-encompassing phenomenon. Perhaps it is in the process of truly caring for others that man's finest qualities are seen.

Among the elements involved in love is the rational. It seeks to hear in open-ended ways—to understand. Hora says,

---

[5] From *Markings*, by Dag Hammarskjöld, p. 56. © Copyright 1964 by Alfred A. Knopf, Inc., and Faber and Faber Ltd. Reprinted by permission of the publishers.

[6] For an expansion of this idea see Søren Kierkegaard, *Works of Love* (New York: Harper Torchbooks, Harper & Row, Publishers, 1962), p. 29.

[7] For further discussion of empathy see Robert L. Katz, *Empathy: Its Nature and Uses* (New York: The Free Press of Glencoe, 1963).

Love is essentially a mode of cognition. Love is concerned neither with feeling good nor feeling bad. Love is concerned with understanding. Love listens to hear. Love is a state of complete attention, without intruding thoughts and motivations. Contrary to general belief, love is not just a feeling or emotion. The opposite of love is not hate, as is generally assumed. *The opposite of love is calculative thinking.*[8]

Although Hora says that love is not concerned with feeling good or feeling bad, the affective does enter into the act of loving. One has only to read the poets. The problem is that attention generally is given only to the affective with inadequate attention to other dimensions.

Another component of the process of loving is morality. True love is a moral process in which all concerned are enhanced. The morality of love is not enforced; rather it is a natural concomitant of concern for the other. "Enforced morality which is not integrated into the individual unity and uniqueness will never inspire the creativeness of love."[9]

CHART 1

Differences Between Caring
at a Fundamental and a Superficial Level

Item	Evidence of Caring at Superficial Level	Evidence of Caring at Fundamental Level
1. Attention to group norms	1. Person relates to others in terms of what he perceives to be the norms of the group.	1. Person seeks to become aware of what may be group norms but behaves in terms of what seems to be best within the situation whether or not group norms are violated.
2. Attention to status and roles	2. Person evidences great awareness of the status and role of another and behaves in a way which he deems appropriate	2. Although awareness of status and role may be evident upon occasion, major attention is upon displaying integrity and

---

[8] Thomas Hora, "The Epistemology of Love," *Journal of Existential Psychiatry,* now *Journal of Existentialism,* II (Winter, 1962), pp. 303–312, p. 304.

[9] Edith Weigert, "The Role of Sympathy in the Psychotherapeutic Process," *The American Journal of Psychoanalysis,* XXII, No. 1 (1962), pp. 3–14, p. 8.

depending upon whether the other is seen as subservient or superior to himself.

transparency in relationships.

3. Attention to social and economic symbols

3. Person evidences interest in finding out about social and economic factors through attention to clothes, schooling, financial status, organizational memberships, etc.

3. Person evidences interest in outward symbols of socio-economic status only as they are contributing factors to inner qualities such as stability, caring, dynamism, etc.

4. Attention to visible accomplishments

4. Person evidences interest in visible accomplishments in order to know what the person *does.*

4. Person looks at outer accomplishments in order to understand what the person *is.*

5. Attention to inner qualities

5. Person evidences interest in qualities such as thinking, perceiving, caring, etc., only mildly.

5. Person vitally interested in ways of thinking, perceiving, caring of the other.

6. Goal of relationships with others

6. Person sees relationships with others primarily as self-enhancing.

6. Person sees relationships with others as enhancing other prior to self. In most relationship both stand to benefit.

7. Basis for selection of others

7. Person selects others to whom he relates closely on basis of external symbols.

7. Person selects others to whom he relates closely on basis of inner qualities as evidenced in outward behavior.

8. Beginning of relationship

8. Person views one aspect of the other—his sex, kinds of resources he can provide—as basis for relating.

8. Person views other in totality first and later particularizes.

9. Desire for power

9. Person desires power to excel, dominate, compete, use the other for personal advantage.

9. Person desires power in order to show increased sympathy, empathy, understanding, potential in co-responding.

In addition to rationality, feeling, and morality, love involves the undivided attention of the one who loves. As long as persons, events, ideals, or ideas come between the one who cares and the one cared for, complete love cannot ensue. Undivided attention is no easy price to pay for love. Assumptions and preconceived notions must give way to the understanding of the inner life of the other.

Time, Space, and Love

Time and space are important to caring. Educators face the challenge of helping children relate to those who are near and distant in time and space. How time and space can contribute to man's relation to man is another factor needing attention.

In planning homes, architects have played with space, sometimes constructing dwellings so that togetherness is fostered, at other times building so that privacy is provided for each member of the family. Schools are increasingly giving attention to planning space so that children can alternately work in solitude and be with others in various kinds of relationships. Opportunities for co-responding are somewhat determined by the setting. Parents and teachers should realize that needs for shared time and space ordinarily decrease as the child gets older. Rebelliousness and stubbornness on the part of adolescents might be somewhat alleviated if children were given more freedom in making decisions about the use of time and space.

Time, too, affects growth in love. Instead of "falling" in love, one grows into love. This growth pattern starts not in adolescence or maturity, but in infancy. During the first days of existence the infant begins to express love. Through the years he attaches himself to a series of love objects.[10] Time usually changes the worth he attaches to certain objects. In adult life persons often have problems resolving conflict between a variety of persons, ideas, and objects that demand attachment.[11] Further understanding is needed of how children, adolescents, and adults shift their love objects from age to age. We need to know more about the awareness and discriminations that characterize the shifts.

---

[10] Karl Menninger, *Love Against Hate* (New York: Harcourt, Brace & World, Inc., 1942), p. 261.

[11] For further discussion of love as attachment, see Allan Fromme, *The Ability to Love* (New York: Farrar, Straus & Giroux, Inc., 1965). Also available in Pocket Cardinal Editions.

In addition to the growth element, love also savors the present moment. One cannot truly love who sees others only as they were or as he hopes they will be. True love accepts others and responds to them in terms of the moment.

> Love requires man to let go of the past. The loving mode of cognition can only come into being when consciousness is emptied of memory traces, assumptions, and strivings. Truth cannot be organized purely on the basis of past experiences. What is required is an unequivocal commitment to understanding of what takes place from moment to moment. When light enters darkness vanishes. Light dissipates darkness. The truth of what really is dissolves the preconceptions.[12]

Loneliness and Its Relationship to Loving

Any relationship which has the potential for strength, positive feelings, and productivity also possesses the potential for dissatisfaction, unproductivity, and unhappiness. Because of fear of unsatisfying consequences many persons hesitate to care for others in a mutually beneficial way. Hence loneliness may result.

Loneliness may also ensue when satisfying relationships have been established but severed because of separation, death, or illness. On this point Moustakas says,

> To love is to be lonely. Every love eventually is broken by illness, separation, or death. The exquisite nature of love, the unique quality of dimension in its highest peak, is threatened by change and termination, and by the fact that the loved one does not always feel or know or understand. In the absence of the loved one, in solitude and loneliness, a new self emerges, in solitary thought. The loneliness quickens love and brings to it new perceptions and sensitivities, and new experiences of mutual depth and beauty.
>
> All love leads to suffering. If we did not care for others in a deep and fundamental way, we would not experience grief when they are troubled or disturbed, when they face tragedy or misfortune, when they are ill and dying.[13]

---

[12] Hora, *Journal of Existential Psychiatry*, now *Journal of Existentialism*, II, p. 309.
[13] Clark E. Moustakas, *Loneliness*, © 1961. Reprinted by permission of Prentice-Hall, Inc., Englewood Cliffs, New Jersey, p. 101.

In considering loneliness one must distinguish between loneliness and aloneness. "Loneliness is here defined as the feeling of no relationship and is distinguished from aloneness. Aloneness is often constructive, whereas loneliness is destructive. Apparently, loneliness is related to the unfulfillment of a need for intimacy instinctual in nature . . ."[14]

The ability to love and to care is particularly difficult as these processes relate to persons who are unique in their ideas or in the position which they have attained. A vicious cycle is in motion since resentment is apt to accompany the person who is "different." In turn, the unusual individual may not know how to cope with situations caused by the extraordinary circumstances in which he finds himself. Oliver Wendell Holmes said, "Man must face the loneliness of original work." Commenting upon this statement, Wood says,

> It is apparent that the man who thinks beyond a point to which his associates can accompany him must be alone in that respect at least. As a thinker ahead of his time, he has no way to escape his loneliness. Men cannot give him an understanding beyond their powers even if their will toward him is the best in the world—and often it is not. Men tend to look upon new ideas with skepticism and hostility, particularly if these ideas contain a threat to the established theories upon which the security of their own positions rests.[15]

In brief, the capacity for loneliness is related to the degree of intensity of other basically human functions. The person who can love intensely can also feel sharp pangs of loneliness. One cannot know loneliness, however, if he has not experienced the wonder of satisfying relationships.

TEACHING FOR CO-RESPONDING

Perhaps of all the processes discussed in this book, none is learned so well through direct experience as the process of loving. The child who enters school with experience in rich, spontaneous interactions with others is ready for activities which will help him bring to the

---

[14] Antonio Ferreira, "Loneliness and Psychopathology," *The American Journal of Psychoanalysis*, XXII, No. 2 (1962), pp. 201–207, p. 206.

[15] Margaret Mary Wood, *Paths of Loneliness* (New York: Bureau of Publications, Teachers College, Columbia University, 1953), p. 90.

level of awareness the meaning of dynamic, purposeful relationships with others. Although some children, because of positive past experiences, may be ready to establish warm relationships with teachers and peers, others may come with an impoverished background in giving and receiving affection and will need all the help the school can give.

The school needs to assume leadership in providing opportunities for co-responding. In addition, the home and outside agencies need to see their responsibility in creating conditions in which caring can flourish. What are some things that can be done if teachers are to provide a setting conducive to co-responding?

The Wise Use of Solitude

If children are to co-respond, an important learning is the wise use of solitude. Since much of the school day is oftentimes spent in working alone, teachers can help students use their solitary moments in ways which will help them relate more easily to others. Activities that are usually carried on alone in the school need to be reconsidered in order to insure that children and youth are having time to synthesize their learnings and to wrestle with new ideas. Only as new impressions are sharpened, shaped, and interwoven with memories and purpose can unique and meaningful freshness of thought occur.

One major deterrent to satisfactory co-responding is the individual's apathy about his own experiences. The individual who is boring to himself is undoubtedly boring to others, thus cutting off mutually satisfying relations. Hence, one of the tasks which the school must set for itself is establishing a climate where children can sift through their intake of knowledge in order to find what makes sense to them. Otto says, "... one needs to develop in childhood the psychological strength to define his own tasks, to create his own vision and not be deflected from it."[16]

Uniqueness of person and vision are necessary for co-responding that goes beyond the superficial. The person who truly cares for another seeks to bring constant freshness. The habit of finding that newness can be cultivated in school.

Human Difference and Co-responding

One of the tasks of a school in a democracy is to help children and youth learn to relate to a variety of kinds of persons. In addition

---

[16] Herbert A. Otto, ed., *Explorations in Human Potentialities* (Springfield, Illinois: Charles C. Thomas, Publisher, 1966), p. 215.

to learning to relate to those with whom an affinity is rather easily established, children and youth need to examine their perceptions of those unlike themselves if they wish to include a range of differences among those for whom they care. As children learn to look in a penetrating way at why they like some persons and don't like others they may find ways of caring for persons who appear different. Youth might identify behaviors in others which indicate modes of decision making, of thinking, or of creating that are more significant than may appear on the surface.

Grouping for Co-Responding

One's associates can do much to encourage or cut off feelings of concern for other persons. The individual within a group who feels rejection, loneliness, humiliation, or scorn is apt to develop different feelings toward his peers from the one who feels pride, happiness, and acceptance. For this reason, schools should provide opportunities for many kinds of groupings. Social-emotional as well as intellectual aspects of children should be taken into account in planning for classes within the school or groups within the class.[17] For optimum development, fluidity of grouping should characterize a school. Children, then, have the opportunity to establish mutually satisfying relationships with a variety of different kinds of persons.

Teachers need to plan, also, for interpreting to children and allowing for children to clarify for themselves what is transpiring within the group. Without such clarification and interpretation, experiences may not accomplish the planned intent.

This is particularly appropriate to schools which are being integrated. Poor experiences without the chance to verbalize what is affecting persons negatively may be worse than no experience at all with children of another race.

The child also needs the opportunity to work with one or two persons of *his* choice. What can be accomplished by persons compatible in their viewpoints has not been exploited by the school. We talk about the importance of the one-to-one relationship, but oftentimes it is not given enough consideration.

---

[17] For discussion of ways of grouping see John L. Tewksbury, *Nongrading in the Elementary School* (Columbus, Ohio: Charles E. Merrill Publishing Company, 1967).

The Moment of Now and Co-Responding

One way in which the school differs from other institutions, such as the family, is that tentative relationships are often developed. Children usually work with a teacher for only a specific number of months. Scheduling plans may cause friends to be separated shortly after they have established close ties. The mobility of society necessitates forming new relationships rather frequently during the period of formal schooling.

If many relationships during the school years are brief, steps should be taken to insure quality relations—relations which are dynamic, inspiring, warm—relations which evoke a positive co-response. Teachers, therefore, need to possess a liveliness of mind and feeling which cause students to be better students for having shared mutual moments of insight. The program needs flexibility so that children can weave in and out in their relationships and can also select persons with whom they can form close mutually satisfying relations.

The moment of *now* is important in schooling. Moments can be dull and uninteresting, or they can be stimulating and exciting depending upon how transitory relationships within the school setting are viewed. Teachers need to communicate, "While I work with you, I care, and I will try to provide situations where you learn to care for each other, but you will move on . . ."

Love and School Subjects

Teachers concerned that children and youth learn to give and receive affection should reconsider school subjects to see how they might best enhance the student's personal effectiveness. The student learns in order to contribute and is not seen as an empty vessel into which a subject is poured. Dynamic rather than rote experiences are important to learning. Individual perceptions are more crucial than scholars' treatises. The unproved insights of the humanities are perhaps more important than the proved facts (which may prove false tomorrow) of the sciences. In brief, school content should be selected for its potential impact upon the central core of the person rather than for its logical organization by the scholars.

Love should be treated as a topic for consideration within existing school courses. The social sciences provide a setting where person-to-person, group-to-group, and nation-to-nation relationships can be analyzed in terms of factors that facilitate or deter co-responding.

Literature is an obvious subject to deal with person-to-person co-responding. Sex education has traditionally been assigned to physical education or the biological sciences. Many educators are currently feeling that the way sex is taught needs to be reexamined in order to link it more intimately with man's emotional and spiritual make-up and view about the family.

Our concern is that children early learn to form relationships from which mutual satisfaction can be derived. In this way they can become the kind of persons who are capable of relating to a variety of persons in time and space.

CO-RESPONDING AND THE SCHOOL OF THE FUTURE

If we accept the assumptions that loving is co-responding and that the schools can teach for co-response, then the school of the future will provide a setting in which human interaction is stimulated. Opportunities will be provided for children and youth to come to know themselves better. Through the use of videotapes, movies, systems of interaction analysis, and other types of feedback mechanisms, individuals will learn about their relationships with others.

In addition to getting feedback, children will study problems of co-response as it relates to different types and groups of people. Age, prior knowledge, and maturity will partially determine how children go through units of work based upon the theme of caring. Children will study problems of mutuality with persons like themselves, persons different from themselves, and persons with whom there is a legal relationship. Problems of co-responding in the child's increasingly larger world will be another aspect of the curriculum.

Concepts of intimacy versus aloofness, the need for privacy versus the need to be with others, and aloneness versus "loneliness" will be treated. Students will be given the opportunity to do much with simulated materials dealing with problems of co-responding. The curriculum will also provide for much informal activity followed by periods when a student's behavior in relation to others is brought to a level of awareness.

Love will be taught as a highly sophisticated concept. If love is co-responding, it takes the utmost sensitivity on the part of the parties involved to find the most appropriate way to reach the other person at a level that has meaning for him. We can move toward increased mutuality, but a completely satisfying relationship is probably impossible. We can, however, help the school child catch glimpses of what loving as co-responding is.

Hypotheses for Testing

If children and youth study in a systematic way such concepts as affection, love, caring, and relating, then students will exhibit more of an awareness of the factors influencing their choice of friends and those persons to whom they relate than if they did not have planned study.

If two friends work together on a task they will accomplish it more efficiently and creatively than if two strangers are assigned the same task.

6

*There is only knowledge from a point
of view—*

JEAN-PAUL SARTRE

Knowing:

THE METAMORPHOSIS OF IDEAS

6

One of the purposes of schooling is to provide a setting where a person can learn to be a productive, thinking, creative being, both in his own eyes and in the eyes of others. Such an individual must have at his disposal tools which enable him to satisfy his curiosity about the world about him and to engage in the metamorphosis of ideas so that they have meaning for him.

KNOWING: THE NEED FOR AN EXAMINED EMPHASIS

Curriculum workers have long sought to understand how to deal with knowledge in order to make it real and relevant in the life of the learner. Questions are often rasied as to the most fruitful ways of helping the child develop an awareness of his world. Should the focus of the curriculum be upon facts, skills, principles, generalizations, or modes of inquiry? Should the concern of the school be primarily with public or personal knowing? Should the major emphasis be upon helping children learn knowledge of the past or upon helping them develop new knowledge? We must define how experiences for knowing can best be designed for children and youth.

The need for a new emphasis upon knowing arises out of new conceptions of knowledge in the curriculum that have been generated since about 1960. Academic scholars have assumed leadership in studying and prescribing what the schools should be teaching. As scholars with curriculum planners have entered the arena of determining appropriate content and methodology, fundamental questions concerning the nature of knowledge have come to the fore.

A complicating factor in the problem of knowing is the increasing fragmentation of knowledge. What were formerly well-established fields of study are now being divided and subdivided so that interrelationships are difficult to ascertain. Furthermore, discourse among scholars in related fields is often extremely limited. The lack of communication among scholars from related disciplines makes school planning for knowing difficult, since much that children need to know is interdisciplinary in nature.

Another reason for increasing emphasis upon the nature of knowing is that the myth of knowledge explosion bears examination. Because of new techniques of communication, knowledge that previously was primarily private has now become public. In addition, whereas prior knowledge was often derived from practical experience and judgments, today more quantified and systematized knowledge is available.

It is not critical to argue whether knowledge is increasing or whether it is the type that is increasing. Rather, it is critical to find ways to help children and youth learn, utilize, and create knowledge. If the schools are concerned about the addition of new to old knowledge, the task is indeed hopeless. If the schools, however, concern themselves with helping children see knowing as the metamorphosis of ideas, the task can be exciting. Metamorphosis is a creative process rather than an additive one. It involves an approach to curriculum development quite different from the additive approach.

KNOWING: ITS MEANING AND CHALLENGES

The concept of knowing has baffled learned men for thousands of years, hence to attempt to define the term within a few pages is an impossible task. What can be done, however, is to consider some ingredients which characterize the process and appear to be vital for school programs.

Definitions of Knowing and Knowledge

The verb *to know* is action-oriented. Whether the base is used in a verb form (knowing) or noun form (knowledge), the word denotes such transactional concepts as apprehending "immediately with the mind or senses" (Webster). Webster also ascribes meanings such as having cognizance, consciousness, or awareness of to the term knowing.

Broudy describes knowing or knowledge as the grasping of "essential characteristics." He says,

> For Plato, Aristotle, and their counterparts down through the Middle Ages, to know something was to grasp its essential characteristics. The essential characteristics of a chair or a horse are precisely those qualities that make one object a chair and the other a horse. By careful use of the senses and intellect, these essential characters of objects could be determined and formulated into real definitions. Every real thing, it was held, belonged to a genus and had characteristics which differentiated it from the other species that made up the genus, and this was shown in the definition. If one can conceive of the world as a vast but thoroughly organized set of pigeon-holes within pigeon-holes that supplied every real entity with one and only one proper place, then it is not unreasonable to conclude that to know means to classify correctly. The test for this kind of knowing is the ability to define the object, *i.e.*, to state its genus and differential. One can learn these definitions by observation, inquiry, and reasoning, but one can also memorize them from a book.[1]

In addition to the view of knowing as the grasping of essential characteristics, Broudy goes on to describe three other views. His second view is epitomized in the philosophy of John Dewey and the school of Experimentalism.

> ... to know is to find out what *in fact* has solved a problem; what in fact clarified a situation, what permitted interrupted action to resume its course. To know is not to grasp an essence but rather to restore

---

[1] Harry S. Broudy, "The Nature of Knowledge and the Uses of Schooling," Lecture I (Washington, D. C.: National Education Assn., 1964, mimeographed), p. 1.

continuity to action and thought. Truth is warranted assertion, Dewey liked to reiterate, and knowledge is the fund of such assertions which a fortunate culture accumulates.[2]

Dewey goes on to describe his own view of knowledge in the following words:

It [knowledge] signifies events understood, events so discriminately penetrated by thought that mind is literally at home in them. It means comprehension, or inclusive reasonable agreement. What is sometimes termed "applied" science, may then be more truly science than is what is conventionally called pure science. For it is directly concerned with not just instrumentalities, but instrumentalities at work in effecting modification of existence in behalf of conclusions that are reflectively preferred. Thus conceived the characteristic subject-matter of knowledge consists of fulfilling objects, which as fulfillment are connected with a history to which they give character.[3]

Knowledge as linked to problem solving and the rational processes, although deemed important by many, was not considered adequate by many to explain the values and understanding necessary to cope with the human predicament. Thus, the necessity for a third view of knowledge, one which stresses coherence.

Knowledge, therefore, it is urged, has to be a growth of coherence, a growing insight into what makes for a unity of feeling and action with thought. Truth, beauty, and goodness in the beginning were one. Only man's perversity has split them off from each other. Truth, on this view, is that judgment which takes into account the widest range of experience. A solution which solves a problem intellectually, morally, or aesthetically but not in all three modes is a false solution. The theoretical foundation for such a view is abstruse and controversial, and pedagogically the task of blending in the pupil what is separated out in the culture is difficult, but the need for such unification is not controversial. Philosophy, religion, art, psychiatry, and common sense agree that human health demands integration of the self as well as the cultivation of its diverse powers.[4]

---

2 *Ibid.*, p. 3.
3 John Dewey, *Nature and Experience*, p. 161, quoted in *Intelligence in the Modern World*, ed. Joseph Ratner (New York: Random House, Inc., 1939), p. 945.
4 Broudy, "The Nature of Knowledge," p. 5.

Broudy describes a fourth form of knowing as remaining human in the human predicament.

> Knowing takes on the dual dimensions of understanding and commitment. To know is to understand the human predicament, to accept it, and to assume the responsibility for remaining human in it. Only the knowledge which is a kind of being can make life coherent for only by this kind of knowing do facts become valuable and values actual. Coherence in education is not simply avoiding overemphasis on this or that subject. The solution is not simply to mix up as many ingredients as possible and to call it interrelatedness. To know and to live coherently, on the contrary, is to see with painful clarity the crises of relevance at every turn of life.[5]

The concept of coherence has been explored by other writers about knowing. It is central to a major work of Oakeshott.

> ... the process of knowledge is not a process of mere accretion. To speak of "adding to knowledge" is misleading. For a gain in knowledge is always the transformation and recreation of an entire world of ideas. It is the creation of a new world by transforming a given world. If knowledge consisted in a mere series of ideas, an addition to it could only touch the raw end. If it were a mere collection of ideas, increase could affect only the circumference. But, since it is a system, each advance affects retrospectively the entire whole, and is the creation of a new world. Knowledge, in the view I have suggested, is not the extension of a mere series, or the enlargement of a mere collection of ideas; it is the achievement of the coherence of a given world or system of ideas by the pursuit of the implications of that world.[6]

The concept of the coherence of knowledge is comforting in a world where much emphasis is upon the addition of knowledge. Coherence implies a system, a whole. Addition implies parts and fragmentation.

To achieve coherence, it is necessary that some ideas be changed—that a metamorphosis take place. It is in this continuous shifting that ideas take shape—a shape that grows out of the total experience of the person and not merely isolated pieces of information.

---

[5] *Ibid.*, p. 6.

[6] Michael Oakeshott, *Experience and Its Modes* (London: Cambridge University Press, 1933), p. 41.

Metamorphoses of ideas comes about as we play with what is seen. On this point Mackinnon says,

> ... *ledge,* the second element in the word knowledge means sport. Knowledge is the result of playing with what we know, that is, with our facts. A knowledgeable person in science is not, as we are often wont to think, merely one who has an accumulation of facts, but rather one who has the capacity to have sport with what he knows, giving creative rein to his fancy in changing his world of phenomenal appearances into a world of scientific constructs.[7]

To assure fresh and vital outlooks upon knowledge, it is important that we play with what we know about the subject. Whatever views of knowing are accepted, our view is that knowing is a vital, active process and should be treated in this way in curriculum planning. In planning for teaching, three knotty areas to which attention ought to be given are: (1) the categorization of knowledge, (2) the "structure of the disciplines," and (3) the dichotomy of personal versus established knowledge. Attention is now given to each of these topics.

Public Categorization of Knowledge

One of the most baffling problems of persons attempting to order knowledge is the development of handles. At times the categories include such a small body of knowledge that the interrelatedness and common dimensions of knowledge are not clearly seen. At other times, knowledge is so broadly categorized that to see the uniqueness of various facets of it is almost impossible. Hence, the necessity exists to develop categories which enable the viewing of knowledge both in its separateness and its interrelatedness.

One attempt to arrange knowledge in meaningful classes was made by Phenix. He categorizes knowledge into six different types of discourse which include:

1. symbolics: ordinary language, mathematics, nondiscursive symbolic forms.

2. empirics: physical sciences, life sciences, psychology, social sciences.

---

[7] D. W. Mackinnon, "The Nature of Creativity," in *Creativity and College Teaching* (Lexington: College of Education, University of Kentucky, 1963), p. 23.

3. esthetics: music, visual arts, arts of movement, literature.

4. synnoetics: philosophy, psychology, literature, religion, in their existential aspects.

5. ethics: the varied special areas of moral and ethical concern.

6. synoptics: history, religion, philosophy.[8]

Phenix proposes that the selection of school learnings should come from among the six realms of meanings. If attention were given each year to some aspect of each of the realms, students would obtain a comprehensive view of knowledge in the course of their schooling. Each realm of meaning would have its own set of tools, its ultimate ends, and its modes of inquiry. Phenix's proposal allows for the interrelatedness of knowledge while at the same time providing for certain types of discreteness within the academic fields.

Tykociner has helped identify the myriad of discourses of knowing that man has developed. "If our knowledge is to become a coherent unified system, it should be disseminated by treating it as a whole. And that is the function of education."[9]

Those who have attempted to categorize knowledge often are dealing with knowledge that has already been communicated to others—the realm of public knowledge. In this type of knowledge, an attempt is made to clarify meanings so that those dealing with the same phenomenon see it with as much commonness as possible.

Private knowledge, illustrated by the existentialist school of thought, is not easily categorized since each individual's internal world is seen to be of prime importance. That public knowledge exists is questionable, according to the bulk of existentialist writers. Those interested in scientific thought see little way of advancing knowledge if concepts are not shared and made precise.

Thus the categorizing of knowledge is a dilemma. Each curriculum worker must solve the dilemma to his satisfaction and work out school programs accordingly. To ignore the problem is to establish the base for a bland curriculum. The topic is explored further in a later section of this chapter.

---

[8] Philip Phenix, *Realms of Meaning* (New York: McGraw-Hill Book Company, 1964), p. 28.
[9] Joseph T. Tykociner, "Zetetics and Areas of Knowledge," in *Education and the Structure of Knowledge*, ed. Stanley Elam, Fifth Annual Phi Delta Kappa Symposium on Educational Research (Chicago: Rand McNally & Co., 1964), p. 147.

The Structure of the Disciplines

Related to the concept of categorizing knowledge is the emphasis since the early 1960's on "the structure of the disciplines."[10] According to Schwab, a spokesman for this point of view, "The structure of a discipline consists, in part, of the body of imposed conceptions which define the investigated subject matter of the discipline and control its inquiries."[11] The new look at the disciplines, as discussed by Schwab and others, involves a consideration of the nature of the discipline and the operations which enable truth finding and the language in which the truth will be couched.[12]

The consideration of the disciplines has invigorated educational practice by drawing closer together academicians with curriculum specialists. Together these persons have sought to answer two questions: (1) What is the essence of the discipline? (2) How should it be treated with school children and youth? Specialized vocabularies, the boundaries of the discipline, and basic questions inherent in the discipline have found their way into school programs as a result of the intensified look at the disciplines as a source of curriculum content.

In a provocative discussion of "The Disciplines as Communities of Discourse," King and Brownell summarize dimensions of a discipline as follows:

A discipline is a community of persons.

A discipline is an expression of human imagination.

A discipline is a domain.

A discipline is a tradition.

A discipline is a syntactical structure—a mode of inquiry.

A discipline is a conceptual structure—a substance.

A discipline is a specialized language or other system of symbols.

A discipline is a heritage of literature and artifacts and a network of communications.

---

[10] Arthur W. Foshay, "A Modest Proposal for the Improvement of Education," in *What Are the Sources of the Curriculum? A Symposium* (Washington, D. C.: Association for Supervision and Curriculum Development, NEA, 1962), pp. 1–13.

[11] Joseph J. Schwab, "The Concept of the Structure of a Discipline," *The Educational Record*, XLIII (July, 1962), pp. 197–205, p. 199. Reprinted in *Professional Reprints in Education*, No. 8001 (Columbus: Charles E. Merrill Publishing Company).

[12] *Ibid.*, p. 205.

A discipline is a valuative and affective stance.

A discipline is an instructive community.[13]

The emphasis upon the structure of the disciplines has been fruitful in that central rather than peripheral questions related to the various fields of knowledge have been asked. The answers have been important only as they contribute to further questioning at a more introspective level.

Emphasis upon the structure of the disciplines does not solve' all curricular problems, however. One challenge has been caused by the disagreement among scholars within a selected field of knowledge about the substance of the field and the tools by which new knowledge is derived. Since the disciplines do not usually come neatly ordered, curriculum planners must struggle with the challenges of the scholars. Oliver and Shaver point out the problem in the area of the social sciences.

> Four important modes which fall outside the social sciences, and which would appear to be important for the social studies, are the historian as poet and wise man (e.g., Morison); the broad-ranging socratic or prophetic philosopher (e.g., Tillich); the political activist or lawyer-statesman (e.g., Martin Luther King); and the journalist (e.g., Lippman).[14]

In the same vein Oliver and Shaver go on to state that social studies programs involve more than a dispassionate consideration of events. They say,

> It is clear that attitudinal and temperamental as well as intellectual dimensions run through the objectives of any social studies program— dimensions such as commitment, willingness to become engaged in society's political processes, detachment and perspective, and the inclination to use one's conceptual power and knowledge to modify old concepts. When one views a potential social studies program with such objectives in mind, focus on the academic scholar as the model of intelligent citizenry seems inadequate.[15]

---

[13] Arthur R. King, Jr., and John A. Brownell, *The Curriculum and the Disciplines of Knowledge: A Theory of Curriculum Practice* (New York: John Wiley & Sons, Inc., 1966), p. 95.

[14] Donald W. Oliver and James P. Shaver, *Teaching Public Issues in the High School* (Boston: Houghton Mifflin Company, 1966), p. 231.

[15] *Ibid.*, p. 232.

In addition to the potential neglect of certain areas of human functioning, the structure of the disciplines approach might be a contrivance fascinating to the adult but uninteresting to the child. Is the immature child and adolescent as enamored with the structure of a field of knowledge as the scholar in the field is? The assumption that the child is interested in the scholar's approach pervades much of the discourse concerning the new approach to the disciplines. The concept needs rigorous examination lest what is gained in logic be lost through lack of interest and motivation.

Despite the fact that the structure of the disciplines approach, if utilized solely, can lead to the fragmentation of knowledge and despite its heavy emphasis upon logic to the partial exclusion of other vital human functions, the movement has brought a new vitality to the area of knowing.

Personal versus Established Knowledge

Perhaps of all the problems of human knowledge none is so crucial as the relationship between knowledge that is commonly accepted within a culture and the knowledge an individual personally feels is of much worth.[16] In describing these two forms of knowledge, Thelen says,

> This (*established* knowledge) is what is in the book, the sacred text, the entombed wisdom of the ages, the funded capital of human experience. The second is *personal* knowledge. This is what a person knows in a situation—regardless of whether somebody else wrote it in a book. Personal knowledge may or may not be opinionated, warranted, valid, or true. But it is the knowledge with which one operates . . .[17]

The interplay between Personal and Established knowledge is one to which close attention should be given. If Established knowledge is of prime importance, we can more rapidly and easily codify, record, and disseminate material, for the assumption is that agreement can be

---

[16] Two sources of discussion of the relationship of Personal knowledge to Established knowledge are:

Michael Polanyi, *Personal Knowledge: Towards a Post-Critical Philosophy* (Chicago: University of Chicago Press, 1958).

Herbert A. Thelen, "Insights for Teaching from a Theory of Interaction," in *The Nature of Teaching: Implications for the Education of Teachers,* ed. Louise M. Berman (Milwaukee: School of Education, University of Wisconsin—Milwaukee, 1963), pp. 19–32.

[17] *Ibid.,* p. 27.

obtained among large numbers of persons. Such agreement indeed makes communication easier, for individual perceptions are not given as much credence.

On the other hand, if Personal knowledge is highly prized, great significance is given to an individual's perceptions of and reactions to a situation. The personal meaning that each individual derives from a situation is of utmost importance.

Either position carried to its extreme can create major problems within a society. If Established knowledge were not prized, modes of communication, of knowing with any degree of accuracy what has transpired in the past, of building upon the knowledge of another would not be very possible or likely. Each person would have his own communication system, his own system of values with little relationship to the larger scene. Hence, even though man's prizing his own thoughts, drives, aspirations, etc., is extremely important, his Personal knowledge is enhanced as he matches it against that which has been codified and recorded and changes both Established and Personal knowledge as these two constantly interact.

According to Thelen, such interaction cannot take place unless there is constant meditation.[18] Meditation involves a reorganization of experience as a result of the interplay between the two types of knowledge. The methodology employed in deriving knowledge which is Personal as opposed to that which is Established is rather succinctly described in a chart by Noll. His heading of "Scientific" somewhat parallels Established whereas "Humanistic" to a degree parallels Personal knowledge.

Scientific Method	*Humanistic Method*
Responds to objective problems	Responds to subjective problems
Uses externals	Uses internals
Is universally verifiable	Is individually verifiable
Analyzes particulars in an exclusive, prescriptive manner	Analyzes particulars in a far less exclusive or prescriptive manner
Emphasizes objective experience	Emphasizes personal experience
Attempts to build generalizations	Concentrates on single phenomenon rather than speculating on the universal

---

[18] *Ibid.*, p. 30.

Relies on accumulated and refined knowledge	Holds possibilities for cumulative effects, but not necessary to the fulfillment of the method
Attempts to control and limit valuational aspects in inquiry	Gives free rein to valuational aspects
Generally imposes conformity to fact	Promotes explorations beyond fact[19]

According to Noll, the scientific method is almost entirely a conscious process whereas the humanistic approach is partly conscious and partly subconscious.[20] Although in comparing Noll's and Thelen's viewpoints, we find many similarities, Thelen would probably accommodate to the notion that knowledge becomes established not only through verifiable, objective means but also through humanistic approaches. Established knowledge can be found in the arts and the humanities as well as in the sciences. Likewise, although much of the scientific is based upon logical analysis and interpretation, real breakthroughs in terms of new ideas and foundations may be initiated in personal knowledge—personal hunches which the individual feels warrant further investigation and study.

Before a school or a curriculum planner can develop learning experiences he needs to be very much aware of his views of knowledge. Our position is that knowledge is not primarily additive in nature. Rather, it is a result of the continuous transforming of experience. Such a view of knowing focuses upon the synthesis, wholeness, coherence, and interrelatedness of knowledge. If this conception of knowing is accepted, what are the implications for schooling?

KNOWING AND SCHOOL PRACTICES

Traditionally the imparting of knowledge has been ascribed to the school. Knowledge has usually been viewed as dealing with the known.

The rapid communication of knowledge caused curriculum de-

---

[19] James Noll, "Humanism as a Method," Educational Forum, XXIX (May, 1964), pp. 489–495, p. 494. Reprinted in Professional Reprints in Education, No. 8819 (Columbus: Charles E. Merrill Publishing Company). Reprinted here by permission of Kappa Delta Pi, An Honor Society in Education, owners of the copyright.
[20] Ibid.

velopers to reconsider the place knowledge has in school programs. Because an awareness existed that far more public knowledge was available than school children and youth could assimilate, the concept of helping children understand the structure of the disciplines captured the interest of many forward looking educators. Unless a way of getting at central and basic ideas were developed, it was feared that children would become swamped with a vast sea of facts—many of them unimportant or outworn.

The reconsidered academic disciplines promise much hope in school programs, especially since they enable the person to understand future as well as past and present knowledge. Therefore this movement should be explored further.

Development of New Curricula with a Special Emphasis on Knowing

Any knowledge which is confined to one discipline is incomplete. Complete knowledge involves the total experience of the person. Nonetheless the fragments of public knowledge which the disciplines represent are an aid in the individual's development of his own understandings. In dealing with the reconstructed disciplines, educators and academicians are exploring and identifying major concepts, questions, and frameworks within the disciplines.

Many school programs are now built around "packaged" curricula which have emerged as a result of the dialogue between educators and academicians. Some materials are very complete. Others are presented within a broader framework, the individual teacher or school being expected to develop the details.[21,22]

Neither a systematic nor a comprehensive view of current curriculum projects which focus heavily upon the process of knowing can be included in a volume of this nature. A few examples of projects are included, however.

Man, A Course of Study, by Jerome S. Bruner. In introducing the course, Bruner says, "The more 'elementary' a course and the younger

---

[21] For a review of some of the curricula emerging as a result of academicians and educators working together, see Association for Supervision and Curriculum Development, *New Curriculum Developments,* ed. Glenys G. Unruh (Washington, D. C.: The Association, NEA, 1965).

[22] For a discussion of the adaptation of many curricular projects for the educationally disadvantaged, see Joseph O. Loretan and Shelley Umans, *Teaching the Disadvantaged: New Curriculum Approaches* (New York: Teachers College Press, Columbia University, 1966).

its students, the more serious must be its pedagogical aim of forming the intellectual powers of those whom it serves."[23] The substance or the structure of the course is within the social studies and addresses itself to three recurring questions:

> What is human about human beings?
>
> How did they get that way?
>
> How can they be more so?[24]

Man is studied through five great humanizing forces: "tool-making, language, social organization, the management of man's prolonged childhood, and man's urge to explain."[25] Three types of techniques are used in helping the student grasp the substance of the five forces: contrast, "games," and the stimulation of "self-consciousness about assumptions."[26]

Bruner suggests five ideals inherent in the social studies program:

1. To give our pupils respect for and confidence in the powers of their own mind.

2. To give them respect, moreover, for the powers of thought concerning the human condition, man's plight and his social life.

3. To provide them with a set of workable models that make it simpler to analyze the nature of the social world in which they live and the condition in which man finds himself.

4. To impart a sense of respect for the capacities and plight of man as a species, for his origins, for his potential, for his humanity.

5. To leave the student with a sense of the unfinished business of man's evolution.[27]

Kits for teachers contain talks to teachers, queries and contrasts, devices, model exercises, documentaries, and supplementary materials.[28]

---

[23] Jerome S. Bruner, "Man: A Course of Study," *ESI Quarterly Report* (Watertown, Massachusetts: Education Development Center, Summer–Fall, 1965), pp. 85–95, p. 85.
[24] *Ibid.*
[25] *Ibid.*
[26] *Ibid.*, p. 92.
[27] *Ibid.*, p. 93.
[28] *Ibid.*, pp. 94–95.

Project English. Funded by the United States Office of Education, eleven centers for the study of English have been established in various parts of the United States. Although the relative emphases and the levels of the public school program may vary, certain commonalities do appear in the various studies. Ability being taken into account, attention is given to sequence of learning experiences often resulting in a spiral curriculum. Language study involves structural linguistics and transformational grammar. Stress is upon composition and rhetoric. Specific teaching materials are emerging; there is a strong emphasis on testing, and teacher training involves inductive teaching.[29]

An example of a program in Project English is that at Florida State University under the direction of Dwight L. Burton. At the junior high level, three experimental programs have been developed, each one taking a group of children through three years.

One program, the "tri-component," has separate units in linguistics, written composition, and literature planned for each year. The second curriculum is literature centered and is organized into thematic units concerned with four basic humanistic relationships: man's relation to deity, to other men, to nature, and to himself. In this program, rhetoric and linguistics are related to the literature program. The third program is based upon cognitive processes.[30]

High School Mathematics. Developed by Max Beberman and Herbert E. Vaughan, this course gives attention to the inherent structure of mathematics in the following ways:

(a) It builds in careful, logical steps upon prior knowledge of arithmetic, enabling him to discover properties of the real numbers.

(b) It gives the student opportunities to explore the logical relationships among these properties of the real numbers.

(c) It introduces elementary ideas of set-theory when needed and uses them thereafter to unify and simplify the development.

(d) It is consistent in terminology and symbolism.[31]

---

[29] Erwin R. Steinberg, ed., "Curriculum Development and Evaluation in English and Social Studies," A report on the Research and Development Conference for Personnel of USOE Curriculum Study Centers in English and Social Studies, USOE Cooperative Research Project No. F-041 (Pittsburgh: Carnegie Institute of Technology, 1964), pp. 6–10.

[30] *Ibid.*, pp. 19–23.

[31] Max Beberman and Herbert E. Vaughan, "Mathematics Text Makes News," Announcement of *High School Mathematics,* Course I (Boston: D. C. Heath & Company, 1964).

In an attempt to bring the knowledge of the mathematician and that of the educator together, the course claims to build upon principles of student discovery, "deferment of verbalization," "mathematical consistency," "precision of language," "student-interest," and "new teaching devices and techniques."[32] The Beberman text is not unlike other mathematical materials which appeared about the same time, designed for elementary and secondary pupils. A look at the inherent structure of mathematics was common to many of these texts and materials.

Physical Science Study Committee. In constructing courses for junior high school students, the writers of this science series indicate two purposes: "on the one hand to be a sound foundation for future physics, chemistry, and perhaps biology courses; and on the other hand to furnish sufficient nourishment in the essence, the spirit, and the substance of physical science to be a good terminal course for those who will not study physical science later on."[33]

In discussing skills and values of the course, Haber-Schaim says,

> . . . we want to give a feeling for the kind of human effort that is involved in the development of science. We want to put across that the root of all science is phenomena and that the names come later. We should like the student to get his information from the original source, from nature itself. This calls for real investigations in the laboratory. But science is not all laboratory work. We have to correlate and generalize our observations. We have to construct models or theories which can be manipulated logically and which will raise new questions. Later we do other experiments to seek answers to these questions.[34]

In developing curriculum patterns focusing upon the academic disciplines, a variety of persons need to be involved: scholars of the disciplines, curriculum workers understanding scope and sequence, psychologists with competence in motivation and evaluation, and sociologists skilled in helping to build the bridges between a child's past and his potential for the future. Instruction should be such that psychological, logical, and pedagogical aspects of teaching may be considered simultaneously. When these three aspects have been

---

[32] *Ibid.*

[33] Uri Haber-Schaim, "Objectives and Content of the Course," in *Introductory Physical Science: A Brief Description of a New Course,* Preliminary Edition (Watertown, Massachusetts: Education Development Center, 1964), p. 2.

[34] *Ibid.*

considered the teacher "translates a curriculum into a planned series of learning tasks. The task is not merely a section of a textbook to be studied, a concept to be understood, or a skill to be mastered. It is rather a sequence of operations in which teacher and pupil each has a part . . ."[35]

These operations, when the disciplines are used as a base for the content of the curriculum, are often related to the thought processes and modes of inquiry central to the development of new knowledge within each discipline.

Thinking and Knowing

Thinking is closely allied to the process of knowing since many of the components of knowing in the various academic fields involve the rational processes. Hence, if the process of knowing is to be well taught, the teacher needs to know how each student seems to think. Students may not have similar thought patterns; therefore the necessity for consideration to individualizing and personalizing of instruction. Individualizing here means more than pacing. It means the development and use of materials for each student which will enable him to develop thought processes currently needing refinement and to enhance those modes of thought already well developed.

The relationship of thinking to knowing is critical in a day of automated instruction. As materials are programed, careful attention should be given to the thought processes evoked if knowing and thinking are seen as being closely allied.

In addition to knowing the thought processes involved in various types of programed instruction, teachers need to know the thought processes characteristic of the children for whom they are responsible. Does the child tend to be analytical, synthesizing, or creative in his thinking? To try to fit a program to a child may be difficult unless the thought processes of the child are considered in the planning. Rather, emphasis should be placed upon having a range of materials and ideas available so that materials may be selected for learning which are in line with the thinking skills the child needs and wants to develop.

Furthermore, the child should begin to learn early the relationship between the tasks related to knowing which he performs and the thought processes. To assign work to students who have little notion

---

[35] Harry S. Broudy, "The Teacher as the Mediator of Knowledge," (Washington, D. C.: National Education Association, 1964, mimeographed), p. 4.

of the reason for the work may defeat the purpose of the task. Children need to know the why of learning a given body of content and the why of developing skill in using certain thought processes.

Knowing and Other Processes

Processes such as decision making, caring, creating, communicating, organizing, and perceiving are seen to be processes that overlap but in some ways are distinct from knowing. Each of these processes must find a place in the curriculum; hence, in order to provide time, the concept of knowing may need to be revamped in order to treat it courageously and vitally and still to allow for adequate treatment of the other processes. This means several things.

First, the relationship of each of the processes to knowing must be worked out. In this way knowing can be treated simultaneously with the development of the other processes. For example, attention to perceiving physical phenomena can be given in biology or to perceiving social phenomena in sociology.

Second, instead of the eclectic textbook, which usually fails to take a viewpoint and presents content in a watered down manner, students should be using materials in which the viewpoint is sharp, the underlying assumptions clearly stated, and the logic adequate.

Third, the irrational thought processes in the disciplines will be given attention even as the rational processes are. This means that persons will respect intuition, realizing that insights derived in this manner can be later studied and made more precise.

Knowing as the Metamorphosis of Ideas

The ultimate goal of knowing is harmony with one's self and one's intake of ideas. Current studies often use inquiry as a procedure.[36] Inquiry is synonymous with interrelating as well as analyzing. A balance has to be found between questioning and synthesizing if we are to help children become mature adults.

We are faced with a curricular challenge that the synthesis of knowledge within the individual can never be wholly dependent on how it is taught. King and Brownell state,

> Never assume that curricula or studies organized on sweeping themes, broad fields, surveys, symposia, and syntheses of many fields, pro-

---

[36] See the work of Richard Suchman, currently with Science Research Associates, Inc.

duce a unity of knowledge in the minds of students. Synthesis is personal.[37]

KNOWING AND THE SCHOOL OF THE FUTURE

In teacher preparation programs of the future, hopefully increased attention will be given to different concepts of knowing so that teachers can knowingly select the stance from which they will teach about knowledge. Currently, educators talk about the "knowledge explosion," but this term may be used because of an inability to synthesize knowledge, to formulate over-arching generalizations, and to transform ideas so that a coherent pattern emerges.

Within the framework of knowing about knowing we might imagine that knowledge could be viewed by teachers and curriculum planners in these rough categories: additive, systematized, and metamorphosed.

By *additive* is meant the adding of ideas and bits of information without any attempt to develop form. By *systematized* is meant the categorizing of knowledge so that principles and generalizations emerge. By *metamorphosed* knowledge is meant the emergence of a coherent framework which makes something fresh and vital of ideas or impressions.

Knowledge can be seen on the one hand as *public* or *established* and on the other hand as *private* or *personal*. Public knowledge is widely shared and communicated. Private knowledge is internalized. No one person can truly see the private knowledge or world of another. This may be seen in chart form on page 98.

The school of the future will, in the early grades, begin the study of knowing so that by the time the child is in the upper grades he knows the difference between private and public knowledge and between treating ideas in an additive, a systematized, or a metamorphosed way. He will see knowing as an action verb and therefore will assume responsibility for being a continuing learner. Youth will continue to have their curiosity whetted as they progress through the grades so that the thirst for knowing becomes unquenchable. If teaching focuses upon the active elements in knowing rather than upon the known, persons should have a desire to become continuing learners.

Curriculum planners will need to give much greater attention to the

---

[37] King and Brownell, *The Curriculum and the Discipline of Knowledge*, p. 144.

CHART 2
STATE OF KNOWLEDGE

	Public Established External	Private Personal Internal
Additive		
Systematized		
Metamorphosed		

USE OF IDEAS

philosophic dimensions of knowing if children are to leave school knowing knowingly how to know.

Hypotheses for Testing

If children and youth receive systematic instruction relative to the differences between personalized and public knowledge, then they will be able to differentiate examples of each.

If children have practice in describing new knowledge which occurs as a result of additional information, they will be able to describe how an old idea was changed.

If children and youth are made aware of the thought processes which are being developed as a result of learning a school subject, they can better discuss their own rational processes than if they had not had such instruction.

7

Decision . . . is choice in face of bounded uncertainty.

G.L.S. SHACKLE

Decision Making:

THE PRESENT AS TURNING POINT BETWEEN PAST AND FUTURE

7

"The greatest of all sciences is the science of decision."[1] Perhaps no human function calls as many of man's essentially human resources into play as decision making, particularly when the consequences are apt to be long in duration, the persons affected many, and the opportunity to turn back unlikely. Although most decisions which a person makes in his lifetime are not apt to have far-reaching consequences, others may be critical in terms of an individual's own satisfaction and his contribution to others. Yet, whether the decision is minor, such as what to wear or what to eat, or whether the decision is more consequential, such as whom to marry, many elements of the decision making process—though not all—are the same. Persons need

---

[1] D. Elton Trueblood, "Deciding for the Difficult," in *Education for Decision*, eds. Frank E. Gaebelein and Others (New York: The Seabury Press, Inc., 1963), pp. 31–42, p. 31.

to understand the decision making process in order to make minor decisions efficiently and effectively so energy can be conserved to make more major decisions in as creative a manner as possible.

Despite the ever-present need for choice making and despite the fact that many persons do not realize their full potential because of poorly made decisions, at the present time most schools do not deal in a systematic way with this important human function. Hence, our purpose is to present a case for making the teaching of decision making an integral part of the school program, to discuss some of the ingredients of decision making which should have a place in the curriculum, and to derive implications from some of the concepts considered for schooling.

DECISION MAKING AS TURNING POINT: THE NEED FOR EMPHASIS

Each reader can probably recall a decision, either well made or poorly made, that has affected the course of his life in a major way. Persons who prepare prospective executives or administrators are aware of the importance of wise decision making and plan programs of preparation which include study of the decision making process. Such programs, however, usually are more concerned with public rather than private decision making.

Our concern is primarily with individual rather than community decision making. Oliver and Shaver say, "Decisions which affect the community we shall call public decisions; those which affect only an individual or a small private group we shall call private decisions."[2]

Decisions vary in complexity. Fortunately, more mature persons are usually called upon to make the more difficult decisions, yet if children have not had opportunity to begin to make them and to analyze the process, they may reach adult life with inadequate resources to make wisely the vital decisions of life. A critical need exists, therefore, for the school to give planned attention to the decision making process for several reasons.

First, much decision making is highly complex. "Decision is hard because the answers are indeterminate and because it is the glory of

---

[2] Donald W. Oliver and James P. Shaver, *Teaching Public Issues in the High School* (Boston: Houghton Mifflin Company, 1966), p. 57.

man to be indeterminate."[3] Knowledge of the complexity of the decision making process may lead to increased tolerance for ambiguity and to increased ability to accept the consequences of an occasional poorly made decision.

Second, a need exists to become aware of the decision making process so that persons will develop an understanding of the use of data in making a decision. Seldom will one have readily available all the data necessary. The individual will need to know when to search for additional data and when the cost of the search in terms of time, money, and energy probably is not worthwhile.[4]

Third, a study of decision making enables one to see the relationship between goals, action, and decision. Goal attainment can be facilitated or deterred by the quality of decisions made. Griffiths says,

> Decisions are closely interrelated with action. A decision may alter the present course of such action to a noticeable degree. A decision may adjust a present course of action, merely correct it; or a decision may be made to permit the present course of action to continue.
>
> Decisions are totally pragmatic in nature—that is, the value of a decision is dependent upon the success of the action which follows it. Since all rational action is in terms of goals, the value of a decision is related to the degree to which the goals are attained.[5]

Fourth, decision making should be studied so that persons can learn to ascertain the quality of the decision. To differentiate between the merits of possible consequences of choices is a necessary learning. In the rush of accomplishing daily tasks, persons often fail to consider long term consequences of present actions, to see relationships among decisions, or to develop a framework for priorities. Ideally, however, each decision is not seen as a separate entity, but separate decisions are seen in relationships to a larger pattern, a comprehensive plan. Decisions are therefore made upon a broader base than present dissatisfactions. They are made on what seems to be best in terms of long range commitments. Dill says, "we make decisions for the present, with the idea that we can remake them in the future. We tend to accept alternatives that at most can be described as 'satisfacto-

---

[3] Trueblood, "Deciding for the Difficult," in *Education for Decision*, p. 32.

[4] For further development of this idea see David Braybrooke and Charles E. Lindblom, *A Strategy of Decision: Policy Evaluation as a Social Process* (Glencoe: The Free Press of Glencoe, 1963), p. 47.

[5] Daniel Griffiths, *Administrative Theory* (New York: Appleton-Century-Crofts, 1959), pp. 75–76.

ry for the time being' because we are better judges of what is 'better' than of what is 'best.' "[6]

A fifth need to study decision making stems from our relationships with others. The acceptance of the principle of individual freedom of choice helps the person realize that he himself does not enter into the decision of another except as the other person chooses to let others enter into the decision. In the last analysis each person selects those individuals, facts, or situations which he is going to allow to influence his decision making. The person sees "he does not *cause* pleasure or pain. He understands the free relationship between himself and the other person, where each offers something which the other may freely accept or reject. He knows now that 'you hurt me 'means 'I choose to hurt myself about you,' and 'you make me love you' means 'I choose to care about you.' "[7]

Sixth, persons need to understand decision making since it is so critical to other human processes and functions such as showing gratitude, aspiring, and caring.

Decision making is affected by how one perceives, the values one holds, the knowledge one prizes, the persons one admires, the modes of communication one utilizes. The process does not stand alone.

Consider the results of Child and Whiting's study of aspiration. Each of the five statements could be analyzed in terms of decision.

1. Success generally leads to a rising of the level of aspiration, and failure to lowering.

2. The stronger the success, the greater is the probability of a rise in level of aspiration; the stronger the failure, the greater is the probability of a lowering.

3. Shifts in level of aspiration are in part a function of changes in the subject's confidence in his ability to attain goals.

4. Failure is more likely than success to lead to withdrawal in the form of avoiding of setting a level of aspiration.

---

[6] William K. Dill, "Decision Making," in *Behavorial Science and Educational Administration*, ed. Daniel Griffiths, The Sixty-third Yearbook of the National Society for the Study of Education, Part II (Chicago: University of Chicago Press, 1964), pp. 199–222, pp. 209–210.

[7] Richard L. Sutherland, "Choosing—as Therapeutic Aim, Method and Philosophy," *Journal of Existential Psychiatry*, now *Journal of Existentialism*, II (Spring, 1962), pp. 371–392, p. 383.

5. Effects of failure on level of aspiration are more varied than those of success.[8]

Seventh, a fuller understanding of the decision making process enables better determination of which kinds of decisions can be made by machines and which necessitate human thought. Much current study is being undertaken on the technology of decision. We need to give much thought to the kinds of decisions that demand peculiarly human thought. Technology can help in implementation once a major decision has been made, but technology cannot do the creative decision making characteristic of frontier thinking.

In brief, we need to teach decision making so the individual can live a more vital life. The individual who fails to see the range of choices available to him may live a routinized life within narrowly defined boundaries. The person who sees that the present may be a turning point between the past and the future may learn the beauty, symmetry, delight, novelty, and potential good for one's self and others that can emerge from well designed decisions.

DECISION MAKING AS TURNING POINT: MAJOR CONCEPTS

"Two persons given the same alternatives, the same values, the same knowledge, can rationally reach only the same decision."[9] This statement would certainly facilitate the decision making process if two elements were always present: (1) Any two persons could be found who possessed the three stated variables in common, and (2) the decision making process were governed only or even primarily by rational variables.

When decision making is taught, it is often treated as a series of overlapping steps. Ordinarily the element of rationality is important in the process. Litchfield says,

Decision making may be rational, deliberative, discretionary, purposive, or it may be irrational, habitual, obligatory, random, or any

---

[8] I. L. Child and J. W. M. Whiting, "Determinants of Level of Aspiration: Evidence from Everyday Life," in *The Study of Personality*, ed. H. Brand (New York: John Wiley & Sons, Inc., 1954), pp. 495–508, p. 508.

[9] Herbert Simon, *Administrative Behavior* (New York: The Macmillan Company, 1950), p. 241.

combination thereof. In its rational, deliberative, discretionary and purposive form, it is performed by means of the following subactivities: (italics removed)

a. Definition of the issue
b. Analysis of the existing situation
c. Deliberation
d. Choice.[10]

Although the five steps proposed by Litchfield are logical, nonetheless study of each of the steps would indicate that nonrational elements as well as rational are critical. For example, in the "analysis of the existing situation," one's perceptions of the situation will color the analysis. Perception is an emotional as well as a cognitive process that is influenced by preconceptions.

A similar series of overlapping steps is proposed by Griffiths. He states them as follows:

1. Recognize, define, and limit the problem.
2. Analyze and evaluate the problem.
3. Establish criteria or standards by which solution will be evaluated or judged as acceptable and adequate to the need.
4. Collect data.
5. Formulate and select the preferred solution or solutions. Test them in advance.
6. Put into effect the preferred solution.
   a. Program the solution.
   b. Control the activities in the program.
   c. Evaluate the results and process.[11]

Attention is now directed to certain concepts which, in addition to those mentioned earlier, should be taught in school programs if skill in decision making is an anticipated outcome of school learning.

Awareness of the Availability of Choice

One of the prerequisites to creative, successful decision making is the knowledge that one has freedom of choice. Availability of choice means that the world is seen as nondeterministic and non-

---

[10] Edward H. Litchfield, "Notes on a General Theory of Administration," in *Education Administration: Selected Readings,* eds. Walter G. Hack and Others (Boston: Allyn & Bacon, Inc., 1965), pp. 312–337, p. 322. Originally published in *Administrative Science Quarterly,* I (June, 1956), 3–29.

[11] Griffiths, *Administrative Theory,* p. 94.

mechanistic. To the degree that an individual feels that he lives in a world of compulsion or fate, to the same degree will he be a decision-less being, feeling that outside forces rather than inner resources determine his course of action. "Decisionlessness makes man divided and unfree, conditioned and acted upon. It is failure to direct one's inner power. Decision, in contrast, means transforming one's passion so that it enters with its whole power into the single deed."[12]

The realization of freedom is critical to choice making. The awareness of possibility rather than probability is also necessary, for probability has an element of doubt.[13] If doubt, uncertainty, and determinism are key factors influencing a person's thinking, decisions cannot be as creative as when openness, possibility, and a degree of confidence influence a person's choice making.

Decision as a "Cut"

"Decision . . . is a cut between past and future, an introduction of an essentially new strand into the emerging pattern of history."[14] Decision occurs in the "solitary moment"[15] which must be considered exclusive of calendar or clock time. The incisive time cannot be reckoned in terms of seconds or instants. Yet, when it has occurred, the past is seen in new perspective, and the future has an essence of newness though total knowledge of the future may be unclear.

If decision is seen as a cut, it is possible to help persons begin to identify when the cut, or the turning point, has occurred. As persons reach this level of awareness, the cuts can be made more precisely and with an effective utilization of knowledge.

Decision and Knowledge

Decision making seldom occurs with complete knowledge available. "Decision . . . is choice, but not choice in face of perfect foreknowledge, not choice in face of complete ignorance. Decision, therefore, is choice in face of bounded uncertainty."[16] Utilization of knowledge is critical to decision making, but equally critical is the

---

[12] Maurice Friedman, "Will, Decision, and Responsibility in the Thought of Martin Buber," *Review of Existential Psychiatry and Psychology,* I (November, 1961), pp. 217–227, p. 219.

[13] G. L. S. Shackle, *Decision, Order, and Time in Human Affairs* (London: Cambridge University Press, 1961), p. 12.

[14] *Ibid.,* p. 3.

[15] *Ibid.,* p. 4.

[16] *Ibid.,* p. 5.

facility of being able to identify and locate the most pressing gaps in information and being able to make an adequate decision when the location of additional information is too costly or impossible. Knowing when to delay a decision is another concept relative to the utilization of information that children and youth should be considering in school programs.

The Effect of Time and Place upon Decision

Fletcher discusses "situation-sensitive decision making."[17] Although it has been indicated that decision making can be a very imaginative process, on the other hand it is bounded by the limitations of the time and setting. What may be an appropriate decision at one time or place may not be so within a different setting or at another period in time.

Ascertaining how the present situation can be utilized is a skill of the imaginative decision maker. Time and space limitations are part of the fabric of the decision rather than limiting factors. If boundaries of time and place did not exist, decision would become a different kind of process, lacking the challenge which currently abounds in the process.

Inspiration and Decision

Most decisions which individuals make daily are minor in their consequences. Patterns should be established for the making of such decisions so that energy and resources can be conserved for decisions where the impact of one well made will be rewarding. The consequences of critical decisions usually cannot be reversed. Important decisions demand a bringing to bear upon the problem all the resources the individual can muster coupled with such elements as novelty and intuition.

The individual who seeks inspiration in his personal decison making prizes and utilizes his inward impressions, feelings, thoughts, longings, and personal knowledge as he views external circumstances. The subjective is of prime importance in the creative decision.

The role of imagination and inspiration in decision making is somewhat different from their role in creative thinking, where the immedi-

---

[17] Joseph Fletcher, *Situation Ethics: The New Morality* (Philadelphia: The Westminster Press, 1966), p. 14.

ate outcome may be unimportant in terms of implementation. In important decisions, the result is usually crucial; therefore imagination is constantly linked to the possible, to the congruous, and to the present situation. Heightened inspiration for decision making is linked to continuous examination of the consequences of a given course of action. The mind is not free to wander at will, for the expectation of new insights which will cause a creative person to cut between past and future demands attention to the existing situation. Yet, "The discipline of paying attention to each mental state as it arises with the intention of choosing its course, leads to a clearer awareness of living here and now."[18]

Decision making involves many logical processes, but inspired decision making also involves awe, wonder, and mystery.

Decision and Acceptance of Consequences

Decision making is a risk-taking venture. Risk taking, like decision making, is learned. The individual who has risked much with success in his decision making will probably anticipate future key decisions. The individual who has been unhappy about past decisions may be hesitant and move toward decisionlessness or little creativity in decisions.

It is important, therefore, that individuals learn to analyze the results of decisions, to see how the decision might have been made in more satisfying ways, and to accept the consequences of the decision, whether well or poorly made. To maintain a positive outlook on the process is crucial if decision making is to be seen as something exciting and dramatically human.

For the individual who has risked himself too far and is suffering the consequences of a poorly made decision, help can be provided. The individual can be encouraged to accept the frustrations and unhappiness of the decision and to make far-reaching decisions again when *he* is ready to do so.

Attitudes toward mistakes will greatly influence the types of decisions made. The person who cannot tolerate error will be much more circumscribed in his decision making than the one who can. In brief, the emotional concomitants of decision making are as important as the logical processes.

---

[18] Sutherland, *Journal of Existential Psychiatry*, now *Journal of Existentialism*, II, p. 383.

DECISION MAKING AND SCHOOL PRACTICES

Decision making is such an awesome topic that its dimensions overlap many of the other concerns of this book. Nonetheless, certain of the broader aspects of the topic are discussed as they relate to the several aspects of schooling, such as teaching, curriculum development, and counselling.

Decision Making and the Teaching of School Subjects

In the chapter on knowing, reference is made to teaching school children the tools of the scholars in the various academic fields. Such an emphasis would involve teaching skills of analysis. To be able to analyze is extremely important to decision making, for however decision making is described, data gathering is part of the process. Knowing which information is central and which is tangential to a problem is critical if adequate decisions are to be made.

In addition to learning skills of analysis, school subjects should teach thinking skills related to synthesizing information. How to make sense out of facts from many disciplines is often part of the decision making process.

Attention to how content is taught—whether from a problems approach, a discipline centered approach, or some other way of organizing—will enable curriculum planners to see that decision making is receiving adequate consideration within the overall curriculum.[19]

Decision and Language

As teachers study opportunities to learn decision making skills in their classrooms, one place they might want to look is at the language of the classroom. Appropriate questions for study might be the following:

---

[19] The reader is referred to two sources. The first deals with a way of organizing the curriculum so that both the academic disciplines and a problems approach are given attention in the curriculum. The second source is a discussion of how decision making can act as a structure for instruction within the social studies program.

Alice Miel, "Knowledge and the Curriculum," in *New Insights and the Curriculum*, ed. Alex Frazier, 1963 Yearbook (Washington: Association for Supervision and Curriculum Development, NEA, 1963), pp. 71–107.

Shirley H. Engle, "Decision Making: The Heart of Social Studies Instruction," in *Readings for Social Studies in Elementary Education*, eds. John Jarolimek and Huber M. Walsh (New York: The Macmillan Company, 1965), pp. 195–202. Reprinted from *Social Education*, XXIV (November, 1960), 301–304.

Who is making the decisions within the classroom?

Do teachers and children have the same perception of who is making decisions within the classroom?[20]

What opportunities are provided to clarify or explain the decision making process?

Are children aware of the factors they take into account in making various kinds of decisions?

Data concerning classroom language can be gathered in many ways. With portable videotape machines, pictures and sound can be captured of situations which merit later study because of relevance to some aspect of decision making. Tape recorders and eight millimeter sound cameras are other means of recording what is transpiring. Verbatim accounts can be scrutinized in terms of decision. Categories of behaviors related to decision making can be developed and observations recorded within the predetermined categories. Through the gathering of material relative to what is being said, teachers and students not only come to understand the process better but also can see whether behavior is congruent with intent.

The Direct Teaching of Decision Making

An examination of most curriculum materials at almost any level indicates that scant, if any, attention is given to the direct teaching of the decision making process or any of its components. For example, seldom does one see a unit of work titled "Decision Making" or "Choice Making." It seems to be taken for granted that persons will automatically become good decision makers, yet observation and experience indicate that such is often not the case.

If decision making is seen to be an area that merits increased attention, three types of activities should be included in the school program. First, experiences should be designed which give direct experience in making decisions. Decisions might be concerned with questions of priorities among competing assignments. They might be of a more personal nature, such as the selection of another child with whom to play after school.

---

[20] See Shirlyn Nash, "Young Children's Perceptions of Decision-Making in the Classroom" (Wisconsin: University of Wisconsin—Milwaukee, 1964, mimeographed), a study of the insights of young children concerning decision making.

After children have had opportunities to make many decisions on their own, they should have help in bringing to the level of awareness some of the factors that enter into the decision making process. Concepts of choice, responsibility, and freedom should be discussed with the child as they relate to his own experiences.

At a third level, children and youth should be exposed to material which is directly relative to components of decision making. For example, responsibility should be taught as one of the central foci of education.[21] Children need to learn the meaning of responsibility through appropriate assignments, geared to age, maturity, and other circumstances.

Choice making is another aspect of decision which should be available to children through direct experience and through teaching about the process. Children should have the opportunity to "feel" what it is like to have to select betweeen two important alternatives and to have later the opportunity to discuss the basis for their choice making. They need to come to an understanding of how availability, attitudes, the situation, other persons, and values affect their choice making.

The Setting for Teaching Decision Making

The setting in which decision making is taught has certain characteristics. Consider a few.

Risk taking is invited. The setting has an atmosphere of excitement and of anticipation. Doing the unusual is often rewarded above doing the expected or anticipated.

Teachers appear to be risk takers, too, especially when the goal is worthwhile and the chances of attaining it likely. In addition to being risk takers themselves, teachers display a combination of buoyancy and sympathy so that they can apply healing ointment to a child's hurt feelings and frustration when the risk has resulted in unfavorable consequences for the child.

The risk taking atmosphere is dealt with openly, and children and youth have learning activities designed to help them cope with failure as well as success. The setting is such that the message of newness rather than staticism rings out.

Group process is utilized with sophistication. With the exception of

---

[21] For further development of the meaning of responsibility for choice making see Bruce L. Hood, "Human Nature, Existentialism, and Education," *The University of Kansas Bulletin of Education*, XX (Spring, 1966), 99–109.

decisions having to do with more mundane matters, most decisions are better made alone than in groups. If the assumption is accepted that inspiration and insight enter into more creative decisions, one can see that many decisions cannot be well made by a group unless credence is given only to the logical, rational elements of decision making. Insight, creativity, and newness often arrive to the person working in solitude rather than in a group.

Three conditions, therefore, should be established for students. First, students need to be given time, stimulus, and help in making creative decisions. Second, students need the opportunity to work with others at points in the decision making process when others can be particularly helpful, for example, at the beginning of the decision making process, when brainstorming is a useful technique to produce quantity of ideas. Third, students should learn to work with appropriate others in implementing a decision so that good ideas are not lost.

The balance between individual and group work is critical in the classroom in which attention is given to decision making. How to provide for individual creativity and freshness in a setting which also prizes democratic principles is an area demanding much consideration and study.

Decisions about classroom management are made by the group. Decisions can be grouped along a continuum from very creative ones with far-reaching implications to less creative but important ones. Decisions relative to classroom management ordinarily are in the latter category. They are highly significant, for management decisions well made and carried out can provide time for the individual to make more creative decisions. Encouraging children to make decisions relative to management helps them learn about choice, freedom, and responsibility. They also begin to get some feeling about the differences between public and private decision. Children, in cooperation with the teacher, can create a setting conducive to reflective decisions.

Decision Making and Counselling

Teachers and professional counsellors are regularly called upon to help children and youth make decisions which may be long lasting in their consequences. Such counselling can be patternless, the exigency of the moment being handled in as propitious a manner as possible, or the counsellor may use a framework which makes the decision making involved as productive as possible.

Teachers and counsellors in the secondary school are constantly being called upon to help students select appropriate courses. Gelatt suggests the following for this purpose:

The objective would be to select an appropriate program of courses. Information related to the objective would be organized and considered. Test results, previous course grades, interests, and the relation of this decision to future choices are examples of data to be used. In order to discuss the possible outcomes of alternative choices and their probabilities it is essential to know something about the degree of relevancy these data have for each alternative. What is the empirical basis for the relevance of a particular datum for a specific decision? Can success be predicted? Would other data be more suggestive? These and other questions are part of the strategy. Then the possible outcomes are evaluated in terms of some scale of desirability and the actual selection of a decision is made utilizing a criterion based on the purpose.[22]

Figure 2 shows in diagram form Gelatt's conception of decision making as it applies to counselling. The notion that the individual is as integrally involved as possible in decisions which affect him is central to the counselling process.

DECISION MAKING
AND THE SCHOOL OF THE FUTURE

Except in very unusual situations, teaching about decision has been left to chance. The school of the future will see decision as one of its central themes.

Young children will have many opportunities for choice even as they have in many schools today. However, instead of the range of choices being narrowed as children mature, increased numbers of opportunities to make decisions will be available.

In addition, from early grades through the secondary school and higher education, children will be given much opportunity to view themselves as decision makers. Feedback will be available to them on growth in decision making, and children will have information so they can change their patterns as they see fit. Children will also learn the concomitant emotional states that are apt to accompany both creative

---

[22] H. B. Gelatt, "Decison-Making: A Conceptual Frame of Reference for Counselling," *Journal of Counselling Psychology*, IX, No. 3 (1962), pp. 246–251, p. 249.

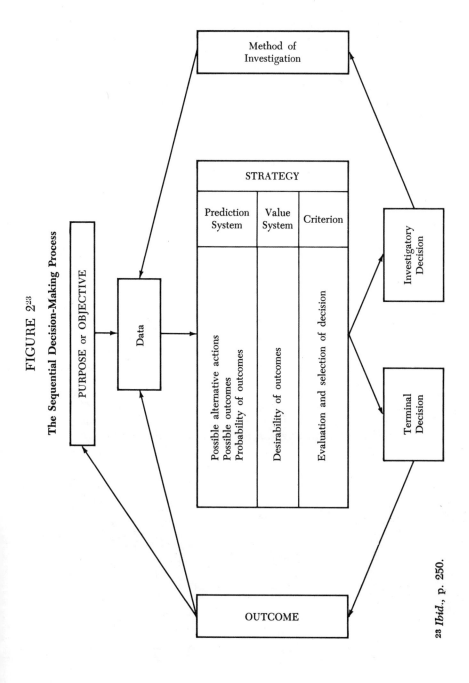

FIGURE 2[23]

The Sequential Decision-Making Process

Method of
Investigation

PURPOSE or OBJECTIVE

Data

STRATEGY

Prediction System	Value System	Criterion
Possible alternative actions Possible outcomes Probability of outcomes	Desirability of outcomes	Evaluation and selection of decision

Investigatory
Decision

Terminal
Decision

OUTCOME

[23] *Ibid.*, p. 250.

115

and noncreative decisions. As they gain this knowledge, they can decide whether they wish to make bold and daring decisions or decisions which have less far-reaching consequences. This decision will influence to some extent the kind of schooling a child gets. Potential leadership may be tapped rather early and special programs developed which are designed to focus heavily on the outcomes of radical decisions.

Children will learn to prize the moment of *now*, for they will learn that how it is used can mean the difference between a full, worthwhile life or a safe, but dull, existence.

Hypotheses for Testing

If children and youth learn the various components of the decision making process, they will feel greater satisfaction with their decisions than if they did not have such school-related help.

If children learn that frustration and dissatisfaction may accompany decisions in an area which is new to the individual, they will be better able to cope with their emotional states when dealing in a new area than if they did not have such knowledge.

If means are used to help children receive feedback relative to how they make decisions, they will make better ones in the future than if they did not have such information.

8

For the creative order, which is an extension of life, is not an elaboration of the established, but a movement beyond the established, or at the least a reorganization of it and often of elements not included in it.

BREWSTER GHISELIN

Patterning:

THE SYSTEMATIZING OF HUMAN EXPERIENCE

8

If life were to come to each of us neatly ordered and packaged, no need would exist for an examination of the process of patterning. For all persons, however, predictability of human experience is possible only to a degree. Many facets of life are constantly being modified and rearranged as a result of man's peculiarly human qualities and of certain forces outside man over which he has little control.

The need for constant rearrangement of concepts, percepts, experiences, memories, and plans for future action may be seen when a new element within a situation causes old ideas and plans to become obsolete. For example, a new job, a move to another city, the death of a friend or family member may necessitate a total reorganization and

---

Quote on the opening page of the chapter from Brewster Ghiselin, ed., *The Creative Process.* Copyright © by the Regents of the University of California. (New York: Mentor Books, 1952), p. 14.

reconstruction of one's life's activities. Such reconstruction may mean disaster in the lives of some persons. For others, it may be the gateway to a total reconsideration and new patterning of experience.

When the consequences of rearrangement of concepts, memories, and impressions are not far-reaching, persons can learn to organize and systematize so that they will be better able to do so when the consequences have more meaning. For example, new ideas which the person gathers through the printed page might spark a train of thought which causes an old framework to become obsolete. The individual can learn to accommodate to or ignore the stimulant. Accommodation might mean the development of a new organizing framework for ideas. Particularized help on the part of the school can help children and youth develop the tools for the patterning of experiences, whether the end product is of major or minor importance.

SYSTEMATIZING EXPERIENCE:
THE NEED FOR CONSIDERATION

Although a surface examination of human existence reveals that life itself is composed of a series of orderings and reorderings of experience, the curriculum oftentimes has not included the direct teaching of the process of patterning. Exercises in outlining, classifying, or engaging in some other form of patterning or systematizing may be a part of a larger unit within the school program, but if tasks focusing upon patterning exist, children may not be given deliberate instruction in the meaning of the tasks for the broader functions of life. Hence, one reason why a reexamination should be given to the process of patterning is that the teaching of the process may be buried under layers of "content" and therefore not receiving high priority in school programs.

School children and youth spend much time learning the outlines, organizational patterns, and schemes of others, yet as with other human functions discussed, the process by which schemes, outlines, and the like have been formulated is often more important than the product. We are proposing, therefore, that in addition to learning the formal patterns which others have developed, children learn *how to* pattern or systematize.

In the teaching of the process, a need exists to consider this function in a developmental way. A person cannot be expected to come up with a new and far-reaching synthesis of ideas if he has not had practice in combining ideas of less magnitude and consequence.

Intellectual survival in the days to come will depend more and more, as Jerome Bruner puts it, on growth in our students' abilities at grouping and encoding information so that what is known is grouped in simpler, more usable form, is categorized in ways that establish connectedness and in ways that maximize recombination and inventive regrouping of data.[1]

Since man can drown in a sea of disconnected perceptions, it is essential that he see large groupings of ideas and facts rather than bits and pieces of picayune detail.

A second reason for attention to the process of patterning is that certain research exists which indicates that more creative persons have a need and desire to formulate far-reaching and complex patterns.[2] Creative individuals prefer to deal with complexity as opposed to simplicity when new patterns or designs seem possible.

If creative individuals have the tendency to enjoy making new orders, perhaps one of the functions of the school should be to help all children examine their own preferences for order and disorder since all have some propensity toward creativity. Such knowledge might cause some to seek to examine causes for liking or disliking complexity and hence to come to a better knowledge of themselves. Self-understanding can lead to a more productive use of self. The individual needs to understand where he places himself on an order-disorder continuum when the potential for new order seems to be available.

A third reason for giving attention to the process of ordering is that existence itself is not always well-planned and ordered. Unforeseen circumstance can mar the best laid plans. Furthermore, tomorrow's children will be faced with a new set of challenges because of the impact of technology upon them. The order that work gives to life will be substituted by a state of flux which often is a concomitant of leisure.

---

[1] William G. Hollister, M. D., "Preparing the Minds of the Future: Enhancing Ego Processes Through Curriculum Development," in *Curriculum Change: Direction and Process,* ed. Robert Leeper (Washington, D. C.: Association for Supervision and Curriculum Development, NEA, 1966), pp. 27–42, p. 30. Reprinted with permission of the Association for Supervision and Curriculum Development and William G. Hollister. Copyright © 1966 by the Association for Supervision and Curriculum Development. Bruner paraphrase from J. S. Bruner and R. R. Oliver, "Development of Equivalence Transformations in Children," in *Basic Cognitive Processes in Children,* eds. J. C. Wright and J. Kagan, Monograph of the Society for Research in Child Development XXVIII, 1963 (n.p.), 125–141.

[2] Frank Barron, "The Psychology of Imagination," *Scientific American,* IX (September, 1958), 150–166. Reprinted in *A Source Book for Creative Thinking,* eds. Sidney J. Parnes and Harold F. Harding (New York: Charles Scribner's Sons, 1962), pp 227–237.

Henry B. Clark II, a member of the faculty of New York's Union Theological Seminary, says that one reason people fear the idea of not having to work is their "fear of a perpetual state of flux."

"Work," says Clark, "has been that ordering principle which told you what you had to do every morning when you got up; you didn't have to think about what you ought to do." Fear of flux, he adds, may lie back of some fear of sexual freedom. "There, too, the traditional ethic provides an orderly framework through which one finds security. One may not find happiness but at least one has order and meaning."[3]

Persons need help in handling the freedom that technology will be bringing since old patterns that brought security in past generations may no longer be available. Since life is and will continue to be composed of tangled skeins, the task of the school is to help persons weave something beautiful from the twisted threads. The learning is a developmental process.

A fourth reason for attention to the pattern of organizing is that one must learn how to develop new categories and to know when old categories are no longer appropriate. Categories should be such that they facilitate the storage and retrieval of vital knowledge. New categories may open the way for finding more up-to-date knowledge which is in accord with what we already know. Menninger says, "A new classification can be very fruitful, therefore, if it helps put old observations in a new light and generates new questions for research. But no classification can be any better than the classifier's knowledge and understanding of the observations he is classifying."[4]

Our classifications of persons, for example, as white, or Negro, or Protestant, or Jewish, or male, or female may cause us to see the person only in this category and thus close out our observation of other important aspects of his being. The less encompassing the category the less likelihood of seeing the person as a whole.

A fifth reason why educators should give attention to the teaching of patterning within school programs is that the person who can pattern efficiently and effectively can hang on to a wider range of concepts than the person who has not learned to order his thinking.

---

[3] "The Spectre of a Leisure-Ridden World," *The Futurist*, I (June, 1967), pp. 36–37, p. 36. Also see Charles De Carlo, "Educational Technology and Value Systems," *Motive*, XXVII (March/April, 1967), 19–25. The total issue of *Motive* is devoted to technology's impact upon man and is summarized in the article in *The Futurist*.

[4] Karl Menninger, *The Vital Balance* (New York: The Viking Press, Inc., 1963), p. 16.

Patterning is a way of economizing the mental energy required to hold onto a large number of ideas. Through the arrangement of concepts, handles are provided by which a myriad of concepts can be grasped at once.

A sixth reason why attention should be given to patterning is so that children can learn how incomplete but public patterns or systems related to human behavior have emerged. They can then learn the functions of these systems and how a person can maintain his internal individuality while simultaneously conforming to some external system. For example, there is the legal way of acting and behaving.

Law is thus seen as a special kind of ordering process, a special type of process of restoring, maintaining or creating social order—a type of ordering which is primarily neither the way of friendship nor the way of force but something in between.[5]

Then there is the social way of acting—the demonstrating of behaviors appropriate to a time and situation within a given culture. Social behavior is passed on from generation to generation through customs, manners, and the spoken and written word. It is found in the literature of sociology, anthropology, and related disciplines.

Another way of thinking is illustrated in religion. Symbolism which has common meaning holds groups of persons together in terms of common values and basic commitments.

The understanding of public ways of systematizing so that common elements of human experience can be shared is critical to life in an organized society. But of greater importance is the understanding of internalized order so that the individual truly utilizes wisely his interior freedom.

SYSTEMATIZING HUMAN EXPERIENCE: MAJOR CONCEPTS

Thus far, terms such as organizing, patterning, classifying, and systematizing have been used rather loosely. Our intent in this chapter is to take a brief look at definitions and then to move to the broader topics of facets that need to be considered when attention is given to the concept of systematizing human experience.

---

[5]Harold Berman and William R. Greiner, *The Nature and Functions of Law* (Brooklyn: The Foundation Press, Inc., 1966), pp. 6–7.

An Attempt at Definition

One of the terms that should be understood as the phenomenon of patterning is analyzed is the concept of *categorizing*. Yet, Webster gives little help here, for he says a category is "one of the most abstract and universal terms, concepts, or notions."

Fortunately, however, psychologists have studied the meaning of categorizing and have come up with more definitive analyses. In discussing the "achievements of categorizing," Bruner, Goodnow, and Austin make several points:

(a) By categorizing as equivalent discriminably different events, the organism *reduces the complexity* of its environment . . .

(b) Categorizing is the *means by which the objects of the world about us are identified* . . .

(c) The establishment of a category based on a set of defining attributes *reduces the necessity of constant learning* . . .

(d) A fourth achievement inherent in the act of categorizing is the *direction it provides for instrumental activity*. To know by virtue of discriminable defining attributes and without need for further direct test . . . is to know in *advance* about appropriate and inappropriate actions to be taken . . .

(e) A fifth achievement of categorizing is the opportunity it permits for *ordering* and *relating classes of events* . . . We map and give meaning to our world by relating classes of events rather than by relating individual events . . .[6]

Although categorizing is a universal but somewhat ambiguous phenomenon, we are not sure to what extent the process is innate and to what extent it is learned. Whatever the origin, categorizing can be improved through appropriate kinds of attention.

Classify is a term similar to categorize. According to Webster, to classify is "to group or segregate in classes that have systematic relations usually founded in common properties or characters." Classify is synonymous with sort.

Thus categorizing and classifying have in common the grouping of elements with common properties. A relationship is evident within the groupings, but relationships among groupings is not necessarily evident.

---

[6]Jerome S. Bruner, Jacqueline J. Goodnow, and George A. Austin, *A Study of Thinking* (New York: Science Editions, Inc., 1962. Also, New York: John Wiley & Sons, Inc., 1956), pp. 11–13.

Ordering is closely related to these terms. It means interrelating things in a reasonable way "so that system is achieved or confusion or friction is eliminated," according to Webster. The notion of confusion or friction is relative to discussion later in the chapter, for it is the tolerance of disorder that often causes new interrelations to come into being.

Organizing is another term integral to this discussion. It is the developing of an organic structure "into a coherent unity in which each part has a special function or relation," according to Webster. Smooth interrelations are an integral part of organizing.

Systematizing, according to Webster, means arranging methodically or reducing to order. It involves a "coherent unification." System is defined as "an organized or methodically arranged set of ideas, theories, or speculations," "an orderly scheme of thought." Systematizing therefore would involve the making of such orders and schemes.

Terms such as ordering, organizing, classifying, and categorizing are helpful in that they enable the grouping of phenomena into classes. These terms provide ways of economizing in dealing with learning and ideas. "According to Piaget, one of the characteristics of logical thought is the ability of the thinker to think in class terms, e.g., classes such as animals, vehicles, and natural phenomena."[7] Individuals learn to see the relevance of one thing to another but do not necessarily see the whole.

Terms like patterning, systematizing, or mapping denote a fully developed form or model. Hence, the categories and classifications of the earlier group of terms is seen in relation to a totality which may be a scheme, plan, or network, as well as in their singular states. The individual, therefore, who has worked out a pattern has arranged various categories, orders, and classifications so that they have interrelatedness and meaning for him. The pattern may be simple or complex. It may give more emphasis to some categories than to others. It is in the establishing of points of priority and importance that man brings his judging and creative skills together with his skills in sorting.

The Determination of Categories

One of the problems of classifying is the determination of the appropriateness of categories. In the emphasis upon "the structure of

---

[7] Irving Sigel, "Child Development and Social Science Education. Part IV: A Teaching Concept Derived from Some Piagetian Concepts," Publication No. 113 of the Social Science Education Consortium, USOE Cooperative Research Program (Lafayette, Indiana: Purdue University, 1966), p. 2.

the disciplines," the trend is toward more discreteness of categories. Broad areas, such as the social studies, give way to the consideration of the separate disciplines within the social studies. Although the trend is toward using the academic disciplines as sources for school learning, large overall concepts may be lost in the desire to see the relationship of each to each within the disciplines rather than to consider broad concepts within larger, more meaningful wholes.

Menninger cites an instance of a colleague who wrote a textbook of psychiatry. In the book were listed 2400 species of mental disease. Three years later when the book was republished the 2400 species were reduced to four main ones.[8]

As study in any field increases, the relationship between threads may become more obvious and a pattern rather than separate skeins may emerge. A task, therefore, is to help individuals insure that the categories and classifications which they are formulating fit into a whole which possesses a high degree of interrelatedness. If such is to take place persons must become involved in the continuous process of developing criteria for selecting and deleting categories. The more apt the categories the more beautiful the symmetry of the patterning.

The individual who has given attention to the concept of patterning within his own life can often be recognized by the consistency of his behavior, the wide range of possibilities for which he makes provision, and his ability to tolerate ambiguity when the development of new categories is causing change in the total pattern.

Piaget's Contribution to the Understanding of Classifying

Although Piaget does not focus upon the individual's development of the broader aspects of patterning, he is known for his extensive theories concerning classifying. He starts from the concept of adaptation and from there is concerned with two complementary processes—"assimilation" and "accommodation."

> Assimilation occurs when an organism uses something in its environment for some activity which is already part of its repertoire . . . Piaget sees assimilation at work, for example, whenever a situation evokes a particular pattern of behavior because it resembles situations that have evoked it in the past, whenever something new is perceived or conceived in terms of something familiar, whenever something is invested

---

[8] Menninger, *The Vital Balance*, p. 11. The psychiatrist mentioned was Phillippe Pinel.

with value or emotional importance. Accommodation, on the other hand, means the addition of new activities to an organism's repertoire or the modification of old activities in response to the impact of environmental events.[9]

Piaget believes the intellect develops in a sequential order. Each child must go through the steps in order to arrive at the logical thinking associated with adults.[10] Piaget has identified four stages of growth which the child goes through. During each of these stages, which start at birth and go through adolescence, the child learns increasingly refined skills of categorizing.[11]

According to Piaget, the child begins with classifying objects in terms of one characteristic. As he develops he can classify objects in terms of two or more characteristics. When he reaches the fourth stage, during adolescence, "the child can form groupings of values, as of other classifications and orderings. He can systematize his values according to their relative priorities and their mutual affinities, so that his evaluations and his motives may be consistent with one another."[12]

Piaget's work is important to the consideration of order because he invites consideration of the adequacy and validity of categories[13] and the means by which persons classify.

Patterning and Human Emotions

Because of the complexity of human life, patterning which goes beyond the readily observable or knowable is no easy task. Old ideas may need to give way as new ones replace them. Sometimes new ideas are not easily absorbed into previously constructed frameworks. As the new and old intermingle, frustration, tension, and dissatisfaction may ensue. Very often the introduction of a new idea means that a totally new framework must emerge.

---

[9] D. E. Berlyne, "Recent Developments in Piaget's Work," in *The Cognitive Processes: Readings,* eds. Robert J. C. Harper and Others (Englewood Cliffs, N.J.: Prentice-Hall, Inc., 1964), pp. 311–323, pp. 311–312. Reprinted from *British Journal of Educational Psychology,* XXVII (1957), 1–12.

[10] Sigel, "Child Development and Social Science Education," p. 4.

[11] For a brief description of Piaget's four stages see Frank G. Jennings, "Jean Piaget: Notes on Learning," *Saturday Review,* L (May 20, 1967), pp. 81–83, p. 82.

[12] Berlyne, "Recent Developments in Piaget's Work," in *The Cognitive Processes,* p. 321.

[13] See Bruner, Goodnow, and Austin, *A Study of Thinking,* p. 17, for a discussion of the validation of categories.

Thus the person who would be open to developing new patterns of ideas must also be open to handling the emotional states which might accompany the emergence of a new system. If the person can tolerate discomfort as newness emerges, he is more apt to be a creative rather than a conforming person.

Patterning and Significance

The key to significant living is the patterning of one's experiences in such a way that life is shaped and designed so that one sees life as productive and fruitful both for himself and others. To gain a sense of such living is not easy, for this necessitates a sharp awareness of how the patterning of experience is influencing movement. The individual who has command of his patterning knows when to bring closure and when to leave an idea, category, or pattern open. This sense of timing is crucial to significant living—living that is inwardly satisfying and outwardly contributing.

Thus, patterning is important because it helps one categorize and classify events, situations, and ideas. The categorizing then becomes part of a pattern. The pattern may possess a beauty and symmetry which interweaves the many experiences of life, or the pattern may be lacking in form because the individual does not have command of himself in such a way as to fit the many parts together into a well conceived design.

Because of the tremendous doses of information which the child confronts daily we must give planned attention to what assistance the school can give in helping children and youth deal with the mass.

> Schooling which utilizes the child's endeavors to structure his world contributes to competence. Schooling which either tries to impose an order when the child cannot grasp it, or presents masses of data expecting the child to order them as the adult does, may lead to mental indigestion and feelings of incompetence.[14]

What can the school do to build competence in ordering? Here are a few suggestions.

---

[14] Ira J. Gordon, "New Conceptions of Children's Learning and Development," in *Learning and Mental Health in the School*, eds. Walter B. Waetjen and Robert R. Leeper, 1966 Yearbook (Washington, D. C.: Association for Supervision and Curriculum Development, NEA, 1966), pp. 49–73, pp. 68–69.

PATTERNING AND SCHOOL PRACTICES

Patterning and Definitions

If children and youth are to understand the meaning of patterning, they should learn to define at an intellectual level and in terms of their own experience such concepts as: order, disorder, symmetry, regularity, disintegration, organization, classification, categorization, arrangement, pattern, irregularity, and complexity.

In addition to dictionary and experiential meanings, children and youth might search for the meaning of these words as essayists use them. Or, older children might search the lives of literary characters to see whether these words had any meaning for them and if so what the meanings were.

Newspapers might provide another source of definition as children study systematizing and organizing in the lives of their contemporaries.

Patterning and Daily Living

Students may be encouraged to observe relationships in their everyday living—in their walks to and from school, in the commonplace settings of the town or city, in the unusual effects nature creates at various seasons of the year. In discussing the choreographer, Humphrey says,

> . . . he is not interested in, but fascinated with, all manifestations of form and shape. He notes the designs in his everyday living, wherever he may be. In the city? He sees architectural variation, the skyline, the tangled grotesqueness of water tanks, television wires, ventilators, the "feel" of the congestion, the preponderance of rectilinear lines, and the comedy of small defiant brownstones, squashed between the mammoth chromium and glass monsters. In the country? Nature presents a never-ending panorama of wind and cloud, shapes of growing things, animal life, plain and mountain and water. All this has much to teach him about form and relationships.[15]

Children should learn to keep records of new relationships they see. Perhaps after a period of time they can begin to identify any insights

---

[15] Doris Humphrey, *The Art of Making Dances* (New York: Rinehart & Company, Inc., 1959), p. 22.

they gain about themselves as they attempt to make a design or systematize previously unrelated elements.

Patterning and Categorizing within School Subjects

The ability to conceptualize categories is a basic cognitive strength that we could foster while teaching grammar, vocabulary, biology, mathematics, and other subjects. Already we are teaching the classification of biological phenomena by homologous structure or by analogous function. Chemistry is loaded with opportunities to teach categorization by common elements, common derivation, qualities of relationship, and consequences of interaction. Mathematics is a royal road to the study of various types of relationships such as linear, reciprocal, parallel, geometric, and algebraic. I am sure we already present many of the principles of categorization at widely divergent points in our present courses of study. Nevertheless, I wonder whether we identify these tool processes, so vital in data analysis in research or the understanding of human behavior, and whether we demonstrate their transferability to other kinds of data and problem solving situations?

I shall never forget a high school literature class I visited in which the vicissitudes of Silas Marner and his life companions were being analyzed. First, the class had listed its own criteria of maturity on the board, and they were day-by-day matching the behaviors of the various characters in the book against these criteria. Obviously they were learning that the quality of people's performance changed in maturity level from episode to episode. They were beginning to experiment with classifying relationships and behaviors in books, plays, TV programs, and real life. At a simple level, Silas Marner was coming alive as an instrument of learning to differentiate and think about human behaviors.

I am sure there are many such opportunities to do more than we now do, to train more explicitly the capacities to cope with the current cognitive overload and the ongoing task of ordering information. We need to provide learning experiences that range over the analytic, inferential, relational, and functional methods of grouping in a concerted and planful way. We perhaps should provide learning settings that not only confront the student with concrete and symbolic data but also semantic and behavioral kinds of data. Now that tests are emerging that will allow us to assess a student's levels of conceptualization and abstractions, we should be able to create a more comprehensive coverage of the various information-encoding processes of the mind and be able to test the impact of our curricular innovations.[16]

---

[16] Hollister, "Preparing the Minds of the Future," in *Curriculum Change*, pp. 30–31. Reprinted with permission of the Association for Supervision and Curriculum Development and William G. Hollister, Copyright © 1966 by the Association for Supervision and Curriculum Development.

Hollister, in the preceding statement, indicates that within the present curriculum the astute teacher can use school subjects to teach vital processes related to patterning. An important consideration is that means be established so that children can bring to a level of awareness the relationship between categorizing within school subjects and other areas of life. The teacher who is interested in children's learning the real meaning of systematizing will help children try to see the relationships.

Patterning and the Experiences of Original People

One way of helping children better understand the inner lives of those who have made original or creative contributions is through the arrangement of interviews with such persons. Students might prepare reports on such topics as:

The factors which caused the individual to strive after something new.

The point at which he found what he was seeking.

An analysis of what happened if a new type of patterning came about unintentionally.

The feelings which accompanied the new arrangement of ideas.

Patterning and Rules

One of the ways to understand how children systematize their thinking is to observe how rules are evolved at different age levels. Jennings reports that Piaget learned how to play marbles with children. He learned how to make good rules, bad ones, and even to cheat. "Rules and standards for three-year-olds, he found, are almost nonexistent. . . . The five-year-old sees and sometimes respects rules . . . Ten-year-olds can get together and modify rules to meet new conditions, and with the onset of puberty, adjustments are freely made to fit unusual cases."[17] Teachers can begin to keep records of the data children use in their rule making. Through sharing and discussing the data with the children, they can engage more wisely in further rule making.

Evaluation of Movement Toward Complexity in Patterning

If an individual is to improve in the process of organizing, classifying, and patterning, then he needs to have a means of evaluating

---

[17] Jennings, *Saturday Review*, L, 81–82.

growth. One way of evaluating growth is through ascertaining the individual's preferences for complexity and his ability to handle disorder.[18] Curriculum planners need to design activities which can be used to determine how children are learning to pattern and their preferences for complexity.[19]

The Phases of Patterning

Patterning, as indicated, does not come to any of us already structured. Rather, patterning takes place in phases. The first phase is that of pre-patterning. Pre-patterning involves the intake of a host of impressions which do not lend themselves readily to a preconceived framework. Children have the opportunity for pre-patterning during periods of self-selection of learning activities in which the intent is the intake of ideas.

For example, children may take a field trip with instructions to see and note as much as they can, the patterning of such impressions not having been predetermined. Children may be encouraged to read with abandon, the selections having been chosen by the child from a rather wide range of printed materials. They may be asked to create dance steps, melodic lines, pictorial creations from their own preconceptions—a formal school of thought or previously developed schemes of the child not being included in the instructions.

After the pre-patterning stage children might be encouraged to pattern. At this point the new thoughts, impressions, and in some instances outward manifestations of the child's thinking will emerge into a whole which has symmetry, unity, and design for the child and occasionally for the outside world. Encouragement to move from pre-patterning to patterning is through assignments which invite the child to relate his new ideas and impressions to the old in broad, bold outlines. For example, themes with broad titles, the composition of musical pieces which possess unity and coherence, the forming of a human relationship which has a thread of newness are instances in

---

[18] For further discussion of order and disorder see Frank Barron, "The Needs for Order and for Disorder as Motives in Creative Activity," in *Scientific Creativity: Its Recognition and Development*, eds. Calvin W. Taylor and Frank Barron (New York: John Wiley & Sons, Inc., 1963), pp. 153–160.

[19] For some specific suggestions relative to determining an individual's propensity for dealing with complexity, see Appendix.

which children can learn the process of patterning. The key to the assignment is the invitation to link previous broad concepts with newer concepts so that a new design emerges.

Patterning cannot stop here, however. It being a process means that attention must be given to post-patterning. This step involves the evaluation, the raising of questions, the bringing to the fore new insights which will keep the cycle moving. Post-patterning can be encouraged by asking the child to assess his product, by asking him to record how he would have done a task differently, by providing the opportunity for him to accomplish the same task in a different way. The challenge to the educator is that the child is encouraged to see that patterning can come about in numerous ways, that alternative routes may be equally good to achieve a desired end, that the desired end invariably opens up new trails which need to be blazed.

Figure 3 illustrates the continuity of the patterning process. After children have had the opportunity for planned experiences in various aspects of patterning, perhaps teachers can provide experiences which will give opportunity for verbalizing the process.

FIGURE 3

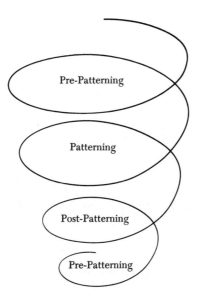

PATTERNING AND THE SCHOOL OF THE FUTURE

One process that helps to give consistency and order to life is patterning. Patterning is a developmental process which begins as the young child begins to classify and categorize those many impressions that he takes in. As the individual matures, he may seek a wholeness— a totality—of experience which causes life to have increased meaning. Our thesis has been that patterning can be taught, at least to a degree.

The teaching of patterning and related topics, such as categorizing and systematizing, will be carried out boldly and directly as the child goes through the school. Although the young child may need specific help in the categorizing of objects, he may also begin to learn to sort out experiences into those which he likes and those which he dislikes, those from which he has learned something new and those which were a repetition of a previous learning, those which demand primarily physical activity and those which demand primarily mental activity. In addition to learning to classify what is "out there," he will learn to classify what is internal—his perceptions and impressions of what he sees and feels rather than what he *thinks* he should feel and see.

Older children will study the classifying and synthesizing of concepts pertaining to valuing or relating to others. They will learn to look for and categorize subtle characteristics in others that make them easy or difficult to relate to. Through the use of videotape recorders or eight millimeter film, they will gather information about how they work and play with others so that they can see whether what they intend doing is actually congruent with observed behaviors. They will look for patterns of behaving in various kinds of situations and with different types of persons.

To help children gain feedback about themselves in relation to how they organize experience will take time and special preparation on the part of educators. We dare not do less, though, than provide the necessary aid, for the world of tomorrow has the potential for being even more confusing than today's. The person will need tools to create order—satisfying to himself at least.

Hypotheses for Testing

If the school provides children and youth opportunities to pattern series of seemingly unrelated items, they will de-

velop more fresh organizations of ideas when dealing with problems with which they have selected to work than if they have not had the opportunity to practice patterning.

If children are asked to describe the patterns they see in a situation, their drawings will show more attention to design than if they have not had such an experience.

If children have the opportunity to describe how they will organize the activities of a day and if they are helped to see various ways of organizing, they will describe more varied organizational patterns than if they did not have such practice and teaching.

9

Look for your own. Do not do what someone else could do as well as you. Do not say, do not write what someone else could say, could write as well as you. Care for nothing in yourself but what you feel exists nowhere else —and out of yourself create, impatiently or patiently . . . the most irreplaceable of beings.

ANDRÉ GIDE

Creating:

REACHING FOR THE UNPRECEDENTED

9

The possibilities inherent within each person to create a life satisfying to himself and worthwhile to others have scarcely been tapped. Many persons have established in various ways an uneasy truce between a bland, wearisome life and the human spirit's need for the refreshment of innovation. Few have been bold enough to pronounce as a way of life the creation of freshness and newness within themselves as persons and within the persons, ideas, and objects with whom they have contact. Lassitude and ennui pervade lives that could be rich and full while reaching for the unprecedented.

A glimpse of the occasional instant in which the primarily uncreative person has become involved in something new to him or the study of persons who have made the development of seemingly worthwhile newness a central part of their lives causes an awareness that man's true humanness is best seen in the acts of creating.

137

CREATING: THE NEED TO REACH
FOR THE UNPRECEDENTED

A society such as ours, which claims to value the individual, must examine itself to see whether the emphasis is truly upon what the individual is and can create or whether our utterances lack substance when it comes to day-by-day practices and beliefs.

Because of the diversity of cultures and subcultures represented within our society and because we claim to have "a system that provides for its own continuous renewal,"[1] it is imperative that attention be given to what is thought and known about creating. The self-renewing process which takes place as an individual creates is essential in a democracy, whose success depends upon the optimum development of each of its individuals. Persons must learn both individually and collectively to refine, change, and modify their ideas so that perpetual discovery and development are possible.

If man is given the opportunities to be a creating being, the need exists to push ahead rapidly in our study of and attention to what is required to reach new heights. Although the period from 1950 to the present has seen an increased interest in this phenomenon, much of the work has been replications of studies developed by a few individuals.[2] There have been few boundary breakers in the area.

As the creative process is rather generally discussed, the thoughtful person cannot help but be aware of the elusiveness of the meaning of the process. Although certain terms as irrational, open, and intuitive are used to describe the process, the description is not adequate to enable educators to develop programs and procedures to improve a person's creative potential. Hence, a need exists for increased proficiency in researching the process and developing practical suggestions and implications for the school setting.

Because of our inadequate knowledge about creating, persons who might be highly original and imaginative are allowed to slip into adaptive and adjustive ways. Such ways are easier to handle than patterns of behavior which innovate and create. We have not taught persons to cope with the realities of the creative process, partially because we do not know *in toto* what the process involves. Yet, we

---

[1] John Gardner, *Self-Renewal: The Individual and the Innovative Society* (New York: Harper & Row, Publishers, 1964), p. 7.

[2] E. Paul Torrance, "The Minnesota Studies of Creative Behavior: National and International Extensions," *The Journal of Creative Behavior*, I (Spring, 1967), pp. 137–154, p. 138.

have not shared the knowledge we have or helped individuals understand the meaning of the creative process for themselves. The need also exists for man to utilize his freedom of thought so that maximum good comes to himself and others. No machine can replace man in the thoughtful process of innovation. Machines can only implement once man has innovated.[3] The need exists for man to use his capacity for thinking freely in order to produce new ideas and approaches relevant to the situation and age in which he finds himself.

CREATING: ITS MEANING

The creative process has been described and applied, however inadequately, in a multitude of fields of human endeavor. Scientists, artists, theologians, writers, psychologists, businessmen, and educators all claim to have some understanding of the process. One only has to review the literature of recent years to see the increased interest in this phenomenon and to become aware of the variety of scholars interested in it. Whatever the application and outcome, whether the creative product be something tangible, such as a painting, an invention, or a piece of music; or whether it be something intangible, such as a new way of relating to people or a new mode of synthesizing ideas, the process seems to have similarities.

The process has been described in many ways, some literature analyzing only a portion of the process such as the ability to be original or to be fluent with ideas. Although studies of the components of the process are helpful, our interest is in the complete process. Creativity is the total process from the inception of an idea through to a completed product which is aesthetically pleasing or potentially useful, at least to the individual creator.[4]

In addition to involving a total process, creativity involves the total person. In an interrelated manner, the individual's cognitive skills, his emotions, his moral insights, and his physical being are brought to bear upon a significant creative act. It is from the perspective of the person that creating is briefly examined.

---

[3] "The Spectre of a Leisure-Ridden World," *The Futurist,* I (June, 1967), pp. 36–37, p. 36.

[4] For further development of the concept of creating as newness for the individual, see Alice Miel, ed., *Creativity in Teaching: Invitations and Instances* (Belmont, California: Wadsworth Publishing Co., Inc., 1961), pp. 6–7.

The Intellectual Skills and Creating

Although at various stages of the creative process, different kinds of intellectual skills are called into play, critical to creating are skills which precipitate wondering, being sensitive to problems, being able to build upon the idea of another, being able to express many ideas relevant to a topic in rapid succession, and being original. The intellectual skills which differentiate the creative individual from one less creative include those skills which enable the person to take a rapid turn of mind or to develop new and far-reaching syntheses.[5]

Also among the cognitive skills essential to creativity is a mode of perception. In a documentary at the Eastman Kodak Pavillion at the New York World's Fair, the following lines were found:

> The more we are able to see,
>   the more we look for . . .
>
> The more we question,
>   the more there is to question . . .
>
> The more we experience,
>   the more we want to experience . . .
>
> The more we contemplate,
>   the greater is our need for contemplation . . .[6]

The creative process is dependent upon richness of perception, for only through such perceiving does the individual acquire the images necessary to making new configurations of ideas. Richness of perception seems to be a natural phenomenon with many persons. Others, because experience has taught them to look for sameness in human and environmental surroundings, have developed what Combs and Snygg call "tunnel vision."[7] Such vision causes one to view in a narrow and restricted manner much of human experience.

---

[5] For a summary of thinking skills involved in creative thinking see Louise Berman, *From Thinking to Behaving: Assignments Reconsidered*, Practical Suggestions for Teaching, ed. Alice Miel (New York: Teachers College Press, Columbia University, 1967), pp. 7–10 and pp. 35–43. Also see work of E. Paul Torrance listed in Bibliography for more detailed discussion.

[6] From "The Searching Eye," produced and directed by Saul Bass, written by Paul David, a film for Eastman Kodak.

[7] See Arthur Combs and Donald Snygg, *Individual Behavior: A Perceptual Approach to Behavior* (New York: Harper & Brothers, Publishers, 1959) for a full discussion of how perception influences behavior.

The creative process functions within those persons who perceive and think in such richness and fullness that the obvious becomes the unusual, and the unusual becomes so real that it has meaning for the creator and oftentimes for the outside world.

To see in ways that are fresh and new is essential to creating. New data, new ways of organizing, and new wholes cannot emerge when persons continuously see in their same modes.[8] The fear of seeing something differently from the masses must be overcome if persons are to have the stuff out of which to create the new.

The Emotions and Creating

To our way of thinking, emotion and thought are so inextricably bound together that to discuss them separately seems like a false dichotomy. Nonetheless, much literature deals with man as though he could think without feeling and feel without thinking.[9]

Creating involves commitment which does not come by intellectual expertise alone. Newness and surprise often come through intense involvement in a task. The involvement is such that other interests are sublimated to internalized dedication to the product being shaped. Arthur Miller, in speaking of writing his work on D. H. Lawrence, says, "I was saturated with it, and I got obsessed and couldn't drop it. I didn't even sleep."[10]

Even though an occasional creative production may emerge without seeming involvement and commitment at the point of emergent newness, usually there has been intense work at some prior time. The study and deep involvement may have occurred much earlier, the creator therefore having time for the mental incubation and development of ideas. Serendipities do not usually come about in a vacuum. More frequently they are delayed reactions to previous immersion in a subject or problem.

If the principle is accepted that immersion in the topic is necessary for creative production, then the problem for which an answer is sought should be self-selected. An imposed problem is not as likely to arouse interest and curiosity. Williams says,

---

[8] For further discussion of this point see Ernest G. Schachtel, *Metamorphosis* (New York: Basic Books, Inc., Publishers, 1959).

[9] See Susanne Langer, *Mind: An Essay on Human Feeling*, Vol. 1 (Baltimore: The Johns Hopkins Press, 1967), pp. 3–32.

[10] Van Wyck Brooks, intro., *Writers at Work. The Paris Review Interviews*, Second Series (New York: The Viking Press, Inc., 1963), p. 171.

It has also been observed that highly creative school children become bored rather quickly with the discovery method—especially if they are expected to discover something that is not an immediate problem to them. Discovery for discovery's sake does not seem to encourage the creative process. Creative children usually know what they want and have an abundance of ideas for getting there.[11]

If an individual is to engage in creative activities, he must learn that varying emotional states may accompany the feeling of intense involvement. That it is common to experience frustration, dissatisfaction, and unhappiness during times of creation is a factor the person involved in creating must know. Otherwise he may quit before he has had the opportunity to give a potentially good or useful idea a try. The person in the act of creation should also know the positive feelings that may accompany the act—the release from tension and the joy of seeing unrelated items in a new pattern. The creator must be prepared to understand and cope with these emotions within himself and other creators.

The Morality of Creating

In the preceding paragraphs it was suggested that creating ordinarily requires intense emotional involvement. Our fragmented lives often do not allow for the kind of involvement that produces highly original products. The question might well be raised as to whether the allowing of fragmentation of time, energies, and reflective thought is not an immoral act. If the contributions of a person both to himself and others are always inconsequential, the likelihood is that the individual is spreading himself too thin. Obviously, each person has a host of day-by-day activities, relationships, and obligations of various types that must be fulfilled. Some are of more potential value than others. The person is wise who can determine priorities among the many things bidding for his time.

Competing good ideas and activities must be brought into some type of pattern so that the better among the good becomes increasingly significant. How one strives for or carries through the better becomes of utmost significance. If the better is treated only as the good, one is harming himself and those for whom he has some responsibility. Likewise, spending one's life accomplishing only the good can be

---

[11] Frank E. Williams, "Intellectual Creativity and the Teacher," *The Journal of Creative Behavior*, I (Spring, 1967), pp. 173–180, p. 178.

a waste of precious human life and resources. Only the individual can decide where his energy should be spent, but once that determination has been made, to be ethical the individual should carry through his commitments.

Our intent is not to say that creative genius must characterize the output of each individual in terms of masterpieces of art, literature, or music. An individual's modes of relating to others in his day-by-day contacts may be where he places his priorities. For him not to strive to perfect his relationships with others is seemingly an immoral act. To provide the setting for the creation of more significant others is a highly worthwhile act. Another individual may select to place her priorities upon child rearing. For her to let so many other good things crowd in that child rearing becomes secondary is an unethical act. Children should begin to see early that they will need to make choices as to how time should be spent.

No one can prescribe for another where his priorities ought to be. Each person must come to a full awareness of where his potential contributions might be and use his time, talents, and energies accordingly. Only then can each person satisfy his own needs and make the contribution which will enable him to be a producing rather than a parasitic member of society.

Our society is in the throes of program planning for upgrading the lives of persons bereft of certain material and social advantages. One way of helping these persons find meaning and purpose as opposed to idle wishes is to help them identify the points at which they can make creative contributions. Persons need more than to be seen as the objects of the giving of others. Provisions need to be made for them to give *to* others.

Thus, an important component of creativity is the morality which enables persons to select the better and the best from what appears good.

The Physical and Creating

If one has been truly creative, something of the individual departs. Not only do the intellectual and the emotional processes become involved in the act of creation; the bodily processes also quicken. Tension often ensues. The culmination of the creative product usually involves a relaxation of the physical processes which have stepped up during creation.

The acceleration of the physical processes as a result of engagement in the creative process must be carefully considered if the creative person is to continue to be productive. One cannot live at a perpetually accelerated physical pace without physical deterioration. Thus, the creative person learns to keep in check his physical being, alternating between times of intensity of output and more relaxed modes of input. Input may mean new experiences which can be derived from reading, contacts with new persons or places, or times of contemplation. Whatever the manner of input, it is essential for maximum creative production.

CREATING AND SCHOOL PRACTICES

If persons are to acquire tendencies and behaviors which lead to increased ingenuity in productivity, then certain experiences should be provided and conditions present for school-aged children and youth. It should again be noted that our emphasis is upon creativity which culminates in newness or freshness of product. Creativity is not merely one portion of the process such as openness in perceiving or a sense of commitment. It usually involves a range of qualities. Hence, the school that wishes to enhance the creativity of its students should provide experiences which do two things: (1) enhance some of the singular behaviors which combined provide for creative production and (2) encourage the totality of the creative process through experiences which may develop a variety of behaviors that are central to creativity.

Creating and Perceiving

In an earlier chapter modes of perception were discussed. Central to the creative process is a mode of perceiving, for unless one has learned to see in as open-ended ways as possible, one's vision stands in the way of maximal creativity. One must have the stuff out of which to create, and this does not come about from going through the world with blinders.

One way that students can be helped to perceive more fully is through asking them to describe a city block from the height of a hill or a tall building. The area they are asked to describe is then gradually made smaller until the individual is asked to tell what he sees within a square inch. The directions might be worded so that different types of reporting are evoked at different times. Occasionally one might aim for accuracy of expression, at other times for vividness of expression.

Myers and Torrance encourage perceiving as fully as possible with exercises such as the following:

> On the way home from school tonight see how many things you notice that you have never noticed before or that you haven't noticed for a long time. Be especially sensitive to changes in people, objects, plants, and animals. Use your nose, your hands, your ears, and your eyes. Make use of all your senses. See if there are differences in the atmosphere, in the movement of things, in your attitude toward the world, and in its attitude toward you. Write down as many of the things you have noticed as you can remember.[12]

It is extremely critical that the individual interested in creating learn the very basic skill of perceiving as fully and openly as possible.

Creating and Discovery

Since about 1960 much of the curriculum material written for use with children and youth has been based upon the principle of discovery. The assumption has been that through the discovery method children will understand better some of the basic assumptions, principles, and questions within the various domains of knowledge.

Since, as indicated earlier, creative children usually have problems of their own, Williams says they "prefer the teacher who gives them facts and information with freedom to set their own problems and find their own solutions, rather than having to discover an established answer to a set problem."[13] If one of the intended outcomes of the educational enterprise is that children be creative, we have yet to find the best ways to make available to them the knowledge of the culture, the knowledge that adults feel is important to the child but which may not be identified by the child as a problem area.

Creating and Error

The individual who treads into the unknown is bound to make more mistakes than the one who seldom tries something new. Freshness and newness may at times be synonymous with error. Hopefully,

---

[12] R. E. Myers and E. Paul Torrance, *Invitations to Thinking and Doing* (Boston: Ginn and Company, 1964), p. 5. See also the other books of activities for children developed by Myers and Torrance listed in the Bibliography in the back of the book for this chapter.

[13] Williams, *The Journal of Creative Behavior*, I, p. 178.

the creative individual has the judgment to evaluate an idea before it is executed. At times his enthusiasm may be greater than his judgment. If the critique of newness, however, becomes too severe, a potentially new and good idea may be lost. It is essential, therefore, that fear of error not stymie the development of a good idea. It is also important that children and youth know that what may appear to be an error at one point in time may be highly valuable when the climate is such that the new idea can be assimilated.

Since error is potentially useful to creative production, children need to be helped to see the possible contribution of mistakes to new knowledge. An analysis of why something did not materialize in the intended way may lead to something better than the original plan.

Perhaps at times children should have tasks in which they are to come up with anything but the "right" answer. Students are then asked to play with the unsatisfactory response until something meaningful emerges. Playing with inadequacies may lead to new answers far more satisfying than the old. In any event, children should learn early that if they are to reach for the unprecedented, the way will not be fully charted. Therefore, they need to develop the psychological stamina to handle mistakes and lack of acceptance of newness at a given point in time.

Creating and Psychological Support

Since, as we have discussed, the creative person is bound to make mistakes in his search for newness, it is important that the individual who is searching for the unknown have support. Without the sponsorship of persons who can help the individual when his newness has failed, many high powered persons may be lost from living full lives.

Teachers can act as sponsors to the highly creative student by exercising sound judgment in moving in and out of situations.[14] They can also provide opportunities for like-minded persons to come together to provide mutual support.

Creativity and an Internal Locus of Evaluation

It has been said that a new idea is always in a minority of one. Ideas do not just come into being. A person is behind them. To be

---

[14] For a discussion of this point see E. Paul Torrance, *Guiding Creative Talent* (Englewood Cliffs, N. J.: Prentice-Hall, Inc., 1962).

able to tolerate being in a minority of one is no easy task for most persons. Perhaps this is why many good ideas are never fully developed.

Related to the concept that the person with a new idea usually stands alone is the notion that we are a success-oriented culture. Nobody wants to fail, and to try out a new idea greatly increases the possibility of failure. To help the individual tolerate aloneness and failure is essential if creativity, which implies freshness and newness, is to flourish.

The development of new knowledge and ideas of meaningful personal knowledge calls for an internal locus of evaluation, for independence of judgment. Some of Torrance's work indicates that teachers value independent thinking but do not give as high priority to independence of judgment.[15] Although the creator seeks and should seek the judgment of others, it is ultimately his own feelings and knowledge that determine the worth of the creation for him.

Teachers are accustomed to evaluating the work of others. Yet, if creativity is prized, increased attention must be given to helping individuals develop their own loci of evaluation.

In a symposium on creativity held at Michigan State University, of the fourteen contributors, more than half discussed the need for an internal locus of evaluation as essential to creativity. Only one mentioned external evaluation as important to this phenomenon.[16] At this symposium, Carl Rogers said:

> Perhaps the most fundamental condition of creativity is that the source of locus of evaluative judgment is internal. The value of his product is, for the creative person, established not by the praise or criticism of others, but by himself. Have I created something satisfying to *me*? Does it express part of me—my feeling or my thought, my pain or my ecstasy? These are the only questions which really matter to the creative person, or to any person when he is being creative.
>
> This does not mean that he is oblivious to, or unwilling to be aware of, the judgments of others. It is simply that the basis of evaluation lies within himself, in his own organismic reaction to and appraisal of his product. If to the person it has the "feel" of being "me in action," of

---

15 Louise M. Berman, *Creativity in Education: A Guide to a Television Series* (Milwaukee: The Milwaukee Public Schools, 1963), pp. 17–19. Major portion of chapter on "Creative Individuals" written by E. Paul Torrance.

16 Harold H. Anderson, ed., *Creativity and Its Cultivation* (New York: Harper & Brothers, Publishers, 1959).

being an actualization of potentialities in himself which heretofore have not existed and are now emerging into existence, then it is satisfying and creative, and no outside evaluation can change that fundamental fact.[17]

Helping individuals establish a proper internal locus of evaluation is indeed a difficult task, for without needed restraints and controls, anarchy could develop. It is extremely important, therefore, that the teacher who is interested in establishing a setting where the student learns to value his own judgment also provide the opportunity for him to understand those areas of our culture where it is important that standards of the culture be given serious consideration and, for the most part, adopted. Consider, for example, the area of language. What would happen if each person were to develop his own symbol system without thought to the necessity of commonality of symbol forms? On the other hand, persons need to know the areas of life where, through exercising independence of thought and judgment, one can make a real and vital contribution.

That persons learn to value the opinions, advice, and criticism of others is also important in evaluation. Although in the last analysis, in many projects the judgments are the creator's to make, by soliciting suggestions, recommendations, and criticisms from peers and teachers, the creator can view his work with increased knowledge and precision prior to making definitive decisions about it. The teacher desiring to help the individual establish an internal locus of evaluation can provide a classroom climate where the student feels free to solicit suggestions, recommendations, and criticisms from peers and teachers. Children can learn to help their classmates through asking good questions, giving support, and helping another clarify his thinking. Essentially children can learn to behave in such a way that they seek the help of each other in their search for appropriate criteria for evaluation of their products.

Creating and Ideas

That teacher who would foster creativity in children and youth should study what he does with children's ideas. Is one type of idea usually accepted? What kinds of ideas are rejected? Are the same

---

[17] Carl R. Rogers, "Toward a Theory of Creativity," *Ibid.*, p. 76. Reprinted by permission from *ETC: A Review of General Semantics*, Vol. XI, No. 4; copyright 1954, by the International Society for General Semantics, pp. 254–255.

children continuously praised for their ideas while others have their ideas rejected, no matter what the quality? How the ideas of the maturing child are accepted and forwarded may partially determine how he prizes the new thinking of himself and others in later life.

Teachers may want to make tape recordings for later analysis in which the treatment of ideas is studied in some detail. Children might also be asked to consider how they treat the "strange" ideas of classmates. Ideas might also be studied for originality, for the degree to which they upset the *status quo*, for their potential for further development.

Only the human mind has the capacity to develop ideas of merit and quality. Only humans can innovate. As persons learn to respect their ideas they will find that the flow of ideas increases.

Capturing the Process of Creating

Synectics, or the study of process in motion, appears to be a fruitful way of understanding better what transpires during creative production. To halt something in motion for purposes of study is indeed difficult. Gordon says,

> The study of the creative process is encumbered by the fact that, being a process, it is in motion. Traditionally, the creative process has been considered after the fact—halted for observation. But when the process is stopped, what is there to observe? The synectics study has attempted to research creative process *in vivo* while it is going on.[18]

Through the use of tape recordings people can later go back and analyze their feelings and motivations during periods of group creative productivity. Since creativity involves the irrational as well as the rational, the analysis of these components of man's disposition and the part they play during the creative process is a fruitful mode of studying the process. Again Gordon says,

> We observed that certain people repeatedly selected ways of thinking about a problem which led to elegant solutions. These people confessed to a pleasurable feeling—a feeling of "being on the track"— long before their intuition was proved correct. They said they regarded the pleasurable feeling as a signal telling them they were headed in the right direction. Our technique used the tape recordings of sessions to

---

[18] William J. J. Gordon, *Synectics: The Development of Creative Capacity* (New York: Harper & Row, Publishers, 1961), p. 3.

teach people to look for this pleasurable feeling in themselves and act on it.[19]

Anything that enables the capturing of process should lead to a clearer perspective about how particular groups of persons create, the points at which they bog down, and the types of situations which allow increased productivity.

Individuals might be interested in getting motion pictures of themselves or others in the process of creating in order to get a clearer understanding of themselves or others. Later analysis may enable them to go about creating in the future with some awareness of what might "spark" the process.

Other persons might be interested in keeping anecdotal records of what causes them to feel like creating and what breaks the "mood" for creative activity. To capture the total creative process is difficult because so much of it is inward experience. Nonetheless, whatever can be done to help an individual understand himself in relation to the process should enable him to become a more creative individual, if he so desires.

CREATING AND THE SCHOOL OF THE FUTURE

Because life is becoming vastly more complex, the hope of man's retaining his humanness in terms of maintaining mastery of his universe depends upon how he uses his creative potential. With new media available to today's and tomorrow's schools, education has the opportunity to provide a setting in which children and youth can develop and test their own ideas. With more persons being prepared to work in the classroom in supplementary ways, children can have access to a wider range of persons to help them more fully clarify and identify the problems to which they wish to give attention. The crux of school programs must focus on what is of value and worth to children if creativity is to flourish.

Teachers' language will be much different from the language heard in many classrooms. Specific information to help solve a problem, the language of support and concern, and questions which stimulate thinking and reaching will be heard frequently.

---

[19] *Ibid.*, p. 29.

Children will be using materials for learning which have been produced to stimulate creative thinking. For example, here are some topics that might be developed on various kinds of media.

. . . creative individuals making a work of art out of their lives.

. . . utilization of principles of creative thinking and problem solving, *i.e.*, analogies, similes, paradoxes, metaphors, attribute-listing, deferring-judgment, check-listing, etc.

. . . present contemporary goals of society: learning how to learn, learning how to change, learning how to create, learning how to adapt rather than adjust.

. . . paradoxes of a field or subject.

. . . people in the process of toying with new information or ideas, *i.e.*, how to care for and nurture infant ideas.

. . . early life anxieties, conflicts, and uncertainties of highly creative people with an emphasis upon how such problems were overcome or contributed to their creating.

. . . the kinds of extended efforts which individuals need for invention, discovery, and creating.[20]

If a goal of the school is to help children live creatively, then specific experiences need to be designed which will enable students to gain competence in various components of the creative process. A body of knowledge about creativity is beginning to emerge which should help educators plan activities that develop elements which are usually associated with the creative process.

Hypotheses for Testing

If children are rewarded for new or fresh ideas, then they will describe more of their new or unusual ideas than if they do not receive such rewards.

---

[20] Frank E. Williams, "Chapter 13: Conference Overview with Models and Summary Lists of Tenable Ideas and Research Areas," in *Instructional Media and Creativity*, eds. Calvin W. Taylor and Frank E. Williams (New York: John Wiley & Sons, Inc., 1966), pp. 367–371.

If children are given the opportunity to rank creative ideas in terms of their worthwhileness, they will be more apt to consider the value of a creative idea before carrying it out than if they have not had such experience.

If children are encouraged to judge the worth of their own ideas, they will look to teachers less frequently to evaluate their ideas than if they have not had such encouragement.

10

If in our learning we are to aim not simply at knowing something important, we shall have to deal courageously and candidly with our commitments —both the teacher's and the student's: for importance implies the fashioning of our diverse experience into personal priorities. If we are to aim not simply at learning but at wisdom, we shall have to deal courageously with our standards—both the teacher's and the student's; for wisdom implies the fashioning of a descriptive knowledge into that discriminate weighing of experience which distinguishes between "higher" and "lower," between "is" and "ought."

LLOYD J. AVERILL

Valuing:

ENCHANTMENT WITH THE ETHICAL

10

Most persons responsible for inducting the young into the culture are concerned that they learn what the culture prizes. Through exhortation, but more frequently through example, the young become dimly aware of the more pervasive values peculiar to a given group of people. The level of awareness, however, it not usually such that what is important could be easily verbalized or arranged in any kind of hierarchical order.

Values are elements of human experience that are invested with great emotional meaning for people. For society, particularly society as we have described it, values represent the main source of "energy" in the operation of the component parts of that society. It is the energy

Quote on opening page of chapter is from Lloyd J. Averill, "The Climate of Valuing," *Current Issues in Higher Education,* 1963 Yearbook of the Association for Higher Education (Washington, D. C.: National Education Assn., 1963), p. 71.

which shapes the form of the main social institutions of the society. It is also the energy that provides the motivational bases for the behavior of individuals in a wide variety of social contexts.[1]

If man is viewed as a complex and intricate being, such as is the case within an open society or a democracy, then the valuing question becomes extremely difficult. In addition to answering the question, "What values shall I hold?" each individual must be concerned with the questions, "What priorities should be established in my ethical views?" and "What provision is made for changing my priorities?"

The fear of thoughtful persons within a democracy focuses upon the possibility of the society and its members becoming rigid or authoritarian. Hence, in describing the value dimension of a situation, such *laissez-faire* terms are used as "balance," "harmony," "equilibrium," "adjustment," "maladjustment," "organization," "accommodation," "function," "social process," and "cultural lag."[2]

Partially because of the difficulties inherent in the valuing process, we are prone to discuss values at an abstract level, oftentimes ignoring the meaning in terms of behaviors a person exhibits or operations which the school should perform. If children and youth are to gain skill in the process of valuing, then teachers must learn the "what" and "how" of dealing with this critical topic. The task is not easy, but the need is imperative.

VALUING: THE NEED FOR RENEWED ATTENTION TO THE ETHICAL

The place of the teaching of valuing in the curriculum needs reexamination for several reasons. First, man's intellectual and emotional qualities are so interwoven that the two must be studied simultaneously. Much of the curriculum, however, currently found in elementary and secondary schools places a heavy emphasis upon intellectual development to the exclusion of other kinds of growth. Averill says,

---

[1] Robert Perrucci, "Sociology," Publication No. 101 of the Social Science Education Consortium, USOE Cooperative Research Program (Lafayette, Indiana: Purdue University, 1966), p. 11.

[2] Gunnar Myrdal, *An American Dilemma* (New York: Harper & Row, Publishers, 1944 and 1962), p. 1055.

It is probably perpetuated, among college teachers especially, by one of the most durable of our academic myths, namely that a man's intellectual powers exist in isolation from his volitional, valuational, and affectional powers. So then, in order to be a good teacher on this view, it is only necessary to treat the student as an isolated intellect; and equally important, the teacher will feel obliged to expose nothing more of himself to the student than the content of his intellect. Volition, valuation, affection—these are the parts of the person which are assigned, not to the teacher but to the student personnel program and its administrative specialists.[3]

Through a new look at the concept of valuing, the schools may find additional resources for providing a setting which accommodates to the systematic teaching of the individual as a total person. Volition and affection will be planned for along with the intellect in dealing with value questions.

A second reason why schools should reconsider the question of values is that the term has multiple meanings. That everybody accepts the same definition of the term is not as critical as it is that the various attributes and components of the concepts be handled somewhere in the curriculum. Values are confused with "attitudes, motivations, objects, measurable quantities, substantive areas of behavior, affect-laden customs or traditions, and relationships such as those between individuals, groups, objects, events."[4] Although a wealth of material about values exists within the disciplines concerned with man, nonetheless the literature can be confusing to the reader unless he really digs, rearranges, and personalizes his findings so that valuing has meaning for him. If the school as a unit is to be concerned about values, then provision needs to be made for teachers to work in concert on this phenomenon. With the diverse and multiple demands made upon teachers, a study of the teaching of valuing and its meaning for a given locale is very apt to get lost.

Third, valuing needs to be reexamined so that educators clarify their own thinking and subsequent implications for the curriculum of

---

[3] Lloyd J. Averill, "The Climate of Valuing," *Current Issues in Higher Education,* 1963 Yearbook of the Association for Higher Education (Washington, D. C.: National Education Assn., 1963), p. 70.

[4] Clyde Kluckhohn and Others, "Value and Value Orientations in the Theory of Action: An Exploration in Definition and Classification," in *Toward a General Theory of Action,* eds. Talcott Parsons and Edward A. Shils (New York: Harper Torchbooks, Harper & Row, Publishers, 1962), pp. 388–433, p. 390. Originally published by Harvard University Press, 1951.

the relationship of cultural values and norms to internalized values. When values are discussed, teachers and students need to be clear whether one is referring to what is out there—the norms or standards of a group, be it country, classroom, or culture—or whether one is referring to something internalized which acts as a standard or norm for behavior. Kimball says,

> . . . that values and value formation are a consequence of the activities of individuals within a social setting. Such a position accounts for both the variability of value systems among peoples of diverse cultures and the changes which occur over time within a specific society. In other words, the meaning of things, of activities, and of relationships is a variable and arises out of participation and is affirmed in successive and repetitive events.
>
> The meaning and form of human behavior, however, must be understood within their context, one aspect of which is the cultural heritage. The cognitive tradition is found, in part, in the system of classification which gives order to experience—the categories of knowledge. But there is an additional psychic ordering which governs the responses of individuals to their experiences.[5]

A fourth reason why values and valuing need a relook in the schools is that although many teachers are interested in helping students formulate and clarify values, the process of valuing can be more effectively taught if teachers act in concert. Deep-seated change comes about slowly. Hence if teachers are to deal in the realm of values, opportunities for consistent teaching over a period of years must be planned. Evaluation of what has transpired can then take place over a longer period of time than if total school resources are not brought to bear within this important area.

A fifth reason why the teaching of values needs to be reconsidered is that the consequences of such teaching need to be spelled out and examined. Individual consideration of the underlying factors influencing spontaneous behavior may indicate a value orientation needing clarifying, changing, or creating of new values. Such a process may be painful. Yet, the person whose behavior exhibits a consistent, integrated value system possesses the potential for far greater personal impact than the one who is not the possessor of such a system. Only the

---

[5] Solon T. Kimball, "Individualism and the Formation of Values," *The Journal of Applied Behavorial Science,* II, No. 4 (October/November/December, 1966), pp. 465–480, p. 480.

sturdy are willing to assume the responsibility that may ensue from a set of values which may lead some to identify and carry out difficult tasks begging to be accomplished. Many of the elements of our society militate against persons becoming overly involved or committed. Gardner says,

> Instead of giving young people the impression that their task is to stand a dreary watch over the ancient values, we should be telling them the grim but bracing truth that it is their task to re-create those values continuously in their own behavior, facing the dilemmas and catastrophes of their own time. . . . a society is being continuously re-created, for good or ill, by its members. This will strike some as a burdensome responsibility, but it will summon others to greatness.[6]

A sixth reason is that increased attention needs to be given to the nature of value reasoning. Scriven suggests six principles underlying this type of reasoning:

1. If doing something will bring about a state of affairs that people value, that is a good prima facie reason for doing it.

2. If there are prima facie reasons for doing something and none against, we should do it. . . .

3. If there is a conflict of supportable prima facie reasons, due to an interpersonal conflict of interest, appeal must be made to a general moral principle. . . .

4. This egalitarian principle can be defended on the temporizing ground that we are already committed to it—politically in a democracy, and theologically in almost all systems of religious ethics. Or it may be defended directly, by a consideration of the advantages and disadvantages of this and alternative allocations of rights, as solutions to a strategy problem in game theory.

5. Prima facie equality of consideration means actual equality of consideration except where inequalities can be defended on the basis of equality. . . .

6. In particular, certain attitudes (values, wants, etc.) can be criticized as immoral if alternatives are humanly possible and would be more consistent with the equality axiom, *i.e.*, with morality. . . .[7]

---

[6] John Gardner, *Self Renewal: The Individual and the Innovative Society* (New York: Harper & Row, Publishers, 1964), pp. 126–127.

[7] Michael Scriven, "Student Values as Educational Objectives," Publication No. 124 of the Social Science Educational Consortium, USOE Cooperative Research Program (Lafayette, Indiana: Purdue University, 1966), pp. 8–9.

Perhaps educators can add to, change, or delete some of these principles as they move toward a way of thinking about values. Our attention is now directed to a fuller meaning of the term valuing.

VALUING AS ENCHANTMENT WITH THE ETHICAL: MAJOR CONCEPTS

To the playful in spirit, valuing offers untold opportunities. Because of its nebulous nature persons can toy with concepts, rearrange them, and formulate new dynamic responses to ethical questions. Perhaps no other basic human function offers as much chance to be open and flexible or to be rigid and closed.

The person who views values in a fixed, static form does not need the word valuing, for to him values are rules or laws which are to be obeyed under any and all circumstances. The shifting scene or new situations do not alter his values; therefore the -*ing* form of the word denoting process is unnecessary.

The individual, however, who enjoys playing with the ethical can find in the realm of valuing significant opportunities to formulate new combinations of ideas that can make life more meaningful, both for himself and for those in his world. Schools might strive to help their children and youth become enchanted with the ethical.

Contributions of Raths and Krathwohl to the Understanding of Valuing

Although much has been written about valuing, two contributions should be noted since their precision and specificity make these works particularly helpful for educators.

Raths, Harmin, and Simon have written a very practical volume for teachers. They indicate that valuing is based upon three processes: "Choosing, prizing and acting." In a summary statement the terms are briefly elaborated:

Choosing: (1)   freely
            (2)   from alternatives
            (3)   after thoughtful consideration of the consequences of each alternative

Prizing: (4)   cherishing, being happy with the choice
            (5)   willing to affirm the choice publicly

Acting: (6)   doing something with the choice
            (7)   repeatedly in some pattern of life

According to the authors, the "processes collectively define valuing. Results of the valuing process are called values."[8] According to Raths' explanation and definition of a value, most persons would hold very few.

Krathwohl, Bloom, and Masia have developed a taxonomy which allows for the description of a person's value scheme at various levels. A classification scheme in which categories are arranged in hierarchical order has been developed by these authors.

The categories and their subdivisions are:

1.0 Receiving (attending)
    1.1. Awareness
    1.2 Willingness to receive
    1.3 Controlled or selected attention

2.0 Responding
    2.1 Acquiescence in responding
    2.2 Willingness to respond
    2.3 Satisfaction in response

3.0 Valuing
    3.1 Acceptance of a value
    3.2 Preference for a value
    3.3 Commitment (conviction)

4.0 Organization
    4.1 Conceptualization of a value
    4.2 Organization of a value system

5.0 Characterization by a value or value complex
    5.1 Generalized set
    5.2 Characterization[9]

In their descriptions which amplify the hierarchy Krathwohl, Bloom, and Masia indicate that at a low level a person might accept a value, or what others might call a belief. At higher levels, commitment or conviction enters into the value structure. At the highest levels, integration and consistency of a value scheme are seen. Relationships and priorities among values have been established into a life view.[10]

---

[8] Louis E. Raths, Merrill Harmin, and Sidney B. Simon, *Values and Teaching: Working with Values in the Classroom* (Columbus: Charles E. Merrill Publishing Company, 1966), p. 30. The teaching of values is also discussed in an earlier work by Raths, "Clarifying Values," in *Curriculum for Today's Boys and Girls,* ed. Robert Fleming (Columbus: Charles E. Merrill Publishing Company, 1963), p. 320.

[9] David Krathwohl, Benjamin S. Bloom, and Bertram B. Masia, *Taxonomy of Educational Objectives, Handbook II: Affective Domain* (New York: David McKay Co., Inc., 1964), p. 95.

[10] *Ibid.,* p. 65.

Values can thus range from simple beliefs to carefully designed schemes which act as guides in the situations in which persons find themselves.

Attributes of Valuing

Valuing is a process in which the persons involved, other factors in the situation, and pervasive principles are critical factors. Most real life situations are such that priorities must be established among conflicting values or goods. Among the characteristics of values are the following:

First, *a value involves more than preference or desire.* Kluckhohn says, "A value is not just a preference but a preference which is felt and/or considered to be justified—morally or by reasoning or by aesthetic judgment, usually by two or all three of these."[11] Virtue says, "Value is not *merely* what satisfies desire; in a deeper sense, it *justifies* desire; *value is that quality of a process which makes it right aesthetically or morally* that it be desired."[12]

Second, *a value causes human behavior to move with a degree of consistency in certain directions.* Values cause predictability in human behavior. "Values are learned commands which, once internalized, coerce human behavior in specific directions."[13] Kluckhohn says, "*A value is a conception, explicit, or implicit, distinctive of an individual or characteristic of a group, of the desirable which influences the selection from available modes, means, and ends of action.*"[14] Kluckhohn later says that values do not arise out of "immediate tensions or immediate situation."[15] When a value is influencing a decision the individual does not stop to articulate the value either inwardly or verbally, yet his behavior indicates the presence of the value and at a higher level shows the integration of the value with related values. Over a period of time, persistence of the value may be noted whether it is articulated or not.

---

[11] Kluckhohn, "Values and Value Orientations," in *Toward a General Theory of Action,* p. 396.

[12] Charles F. Virtue, "Creativity and Symbolism," in *Creativity and Psychological Health,* ed. Michael F. Andrews (Syracuse: Syracuse University Press, 1961), p. 60.

[13] Chris Argyris, "T-Groups for Organizational Effectiveness," *Harvard Business Review,* XLII (March–April, 1964), pp. 60–74, p. 61.

[14] Kluckhohn, "Value and Value Orientations," in *Toward a General Theory of Action,* p. 395.

[15] *Ibid.,* p. 425.

Third, *a value possesses the quality of applying to a variety of situations.* The matter is very complex, however. Oliver and Shaver say,

1. It is important to distinguish between factual issues or beliefs, which are subject to the methods of objective verification, and values or valuations, which require a different kind of analysis and justification.

2. Values operate at different levels of generality. Some apply to specific groups; some apply to all men, some apply to specific situations. The more specific values often contradict the general values.

3. We attempt to "rationalize" values by finding facts or beliefs which are affectively loaded in the same direction as our values. Factual distortion and repression take place when the affective loading of our facts is inconsistent with our values.

4. There are two kinds of inconsistencies with which we have to deal: (a) inconsistencies between the loading of a fact and a social value and (b) inconsistencies between specific values and general values.

5. General values, those which apply to all men at all times, have a higher and more permanent status, at least as Americans see them.

6. When we stand on the threshold of a value conflict, we tend to deal with it by leaving one value in the shadow of our consciousness and making salient the value which supports our immediate behavior. In this way we try to avoid recognizing and coping with inconsistency.

7. Open discussion tends to force society to have before it the total range of beliefs and values, even those which conflict with one another.

8. Most Americans share the basic values of the culture. There is cultural unity at the general value level, but different individuals and groups share these general values with different degrees of intensity as they apply to different issues.

9. Since most Americans share the same general values, when public discussion lays bare our inconsistencies we feel compelled to deal with them.

10. As a "public" becomes increasingly sensitive to the fact that many of the specific beliefs supporting its values are erroneous,

it will be forced to alter the values. And as the public becomes aware of the inconsistency between the specific values and the more permanent and general values (e.g., liberty, equality, and Christian brotherhood), the specific values will gradually become modified and finally effect a change in behavior.[16]

Fourth, *a value is an internalized set of principles derived from past experience which has been analyzed in terms of its "morality."* These principles enable the individual, during a period of choice, to act with dispatch, predictability, orderliness, an awareness of consequences, and an internalized feeling of "rightness." To a degree the individual seeks to enforce the value and "sees to it that it is observed by others."[17]

Fifth, *values may be a compromise between the individual's prevailing predispositions and the imperatives of the situation in which he finds himself.* Without such compromise, the individual may lose close and vital contacts with persons within his environment. Social settings vary in the degree of compromise that is demanded of the individual in order to be an integral part of a group. For example, adolescents in the United States are notorious for their rather narrowly defined range of values as evidenced in outward behaviors that are necessary to be acceptable to the group. On the other hand, some groups very much prize individuality among persons composing the group.

Sixth, *values are restraining forces upon an individual.* Consciously or unconsciously, they cause self-imposed evaluation and kinds of self-inhibition and restraint. Values cause "internalized control." A value is "authentic" when behavior is sanctioned by it rather than by "external coercive sanctions."[18]

Seventh, *values are multi-dimensional.* Value "is not expressible as a simple, isolated noun but is shorthand for a three-sided relation, which includes (1) what is preferred, which involves, as well, what is rejected, (2) one who prefers and rejects (that is, discriminates), and (3) the context within which this activity takes place."[19]

---

[16] Donald W. Oliver and James P. Shaver, *Teaching Public Issues in the High School* (Boston: Houghton Mifflin Company, 1966), pp. 23–24.

[17] Otakar Machotka, *The Unconscious in Social Relations* (New York: Philosophical Library, Inc., 1964), p. 221.

[18] Philip E. Jacob and James J. Flink, "Values and Their Function in Decision Making," *American Behavorial Scientist Supplement*, V (May, 1962), pp. 5–34, p. 16.

[19] Evelyn Shirk, *The Ethical Dimension: An Approach to the Process of Values and Valuing* (New York: Appleton-Century-Crofts, 1965), p. 4.

Up to this point we have been concerned about definitions and attributes of valuing and values. Yet to talk about values within a vacuum is highly innocuous and lacking in practical value. Various writers have attempted to describe values and to ascribe characteristics to them.[20] Yet how the valuing dilemma is handled must be highly personalized. One view follows.

GUIDELINES FOR DEALING WITH VALUING: ONE VIEWPOINT

No man is a law unto himself. He must be concerned about bringing together the world of which he is a part and his ethical predispositions. Although staticism and inertness can slow down movement in the consideration of the value aspects of life, on the other hand lack of any basic moral underpinnings means that each new encounter necessitates a new set of guides to behavior. That the individual therefore formulate a broad base from which to view ethical or value-laden encounters is necessary. What are some guidelines for dealing with valuing?

Development of Personal Integrity

The ability to be one's self, to feel the freedom to give expression to one's thoughts and feelings is highly important if one is to be authentic both in his own eyes and in the eyes of others. Unfortunately, many factors militate against this type of forthrightness. "Good manners," "breeding," and fear of reprisal often cause persons to deny to themselves and others the opportunity to see themselves as they really are. Anything that causes one to hide behind a mask is not conducive to growth in the ethical.

That persons do not always communicate the true self is understandable, for directness and honesty may cause others discomfort or hurt. No sensitive person wishes to harm another. Thus a second guideline is necessary for the individual who would be honest in his relationship with himself and others.

Recognition of the Ongoingness of Human Nature

Each new insight a person has alters him as a person. While some changes may be only slight and rarely perceived by the outsider,

---

[20] See Jacob and Flink, *American Behavorial Scientist Supplement,* V, 15–16, and Perrucci, "Sociology," pp. 12–15.

others may be rather drastic and readily observed both by the individual and by those with whom he has contact. The rate of change within persons varies depending somewhat upon outward circumstances and age, but more upon inward dynamics. The recognition that modification of thinking and behavior is continuous within persons should cause differences in perceiving others. If an individual is constantly taking in new ideas, his rate of change will be more rapid than that of the person who leads a more inert life. Persons recognizing change in others will make judgments that are tentative and will realize that at a given moment enough information is not available to make a truly sound evaluation of another. Recognition of the ongoingness of personality also means tentativeness in judgments about persons, for one can never know when that one piece of information is lacking that might cause total revision of the image one has of another.

Recognition of the ongoingness of human nature means a willingness to relook at what may appear to be another's shortcomings or errors and to reevaluate one's thinking in light of new insights or information. Readiness to "unfreeze" perceptions of another is an important learning if one does not want to stand in the way of growth.

If the schools are successful in helping individuals maintain their risk taking qualities and their spontaneity, then they need to help individuals learn to deal with failure and discouragement. The more vigorous the person in his search for newness, the greater the likelihood that he will make mistakes. Therefore the individual has need for sustained encouragement if he is to maintain his buoyancy and potential for blazing new trails.

Respect for the Internalized Self of Others

The internalized self is the base point from which the person takes in new ideas, reacts to them, organizes and reorganizes his memories and perceptions, and plans courses of action. The churning and ferment of ideas is hidden from the view of other persons. Developing competency in helping another express even his most tentatively held viewpoints is a way of demonstrating respect for the internalized life of another. At the same time, persons need to understand the shared self may have elements of confusion and distortion which may not be perceived by even the most astute listener.

Self-Growth through Self-Giving

Self-growth is necessary if a person is to have the inner resources which enable him to make the contributions he desires to those in his world. Nonetheless, self-growth comes about in peculiar ways, for that individual who seeks only self-satisfaction may find self-growth eluding him. Growth oftentimes comes about through discriminate giving of self. Children and youth early need to become involved in activities which permit them to learn the contentment that may be theirs as they plan for the welfare of others.

Respect for the Various Fields of Human Endeavor

No man can live on this planet independent of his fellowmen. The complexity of modern life demands specialization and consequent interdependence such as we have never known before.

This means two things: (1) Man must learn to respect the development of fields of knowledge which demand expertise that a single individual may not possess; and (2) man must work in interdisciplinary approaches on problems needing such an approach.

As individuals overlap in their mutual endeavors and concerns and as this overlap is seen to be beneficial to all concerned, greater strides can be made in many fields which ultimately affect the wider population. Persons can work out what best can be done alone and what is best accomplished in groups of various sizes representing different competencies.

Interest in the Communication Process

The intricacies of the communication process have long intrigued thoughtful persons anxious that the factors of the process which can enable men to live together more harmoniously be continuously studied and hopefully understood. Such study involves verbal as well as nonverbal communication. It includes problems of inter-professional communication, inter-cultural communication, and inter-personal communication even among groups whose mutual sharing, participation, and caring are leading to productivity. Communicating is closely interwoven with values, for it is the communication process that causes values to be understood or misunderstood, even among well-intentioned persons. Attention to the communication process means more mores are explicit, less implicit; more points of view are aired, less hidden; more persons are involved in an issue concerning them, fewer left out or alienated.

Attention to the Individuality of the Person

Although anthropologists, sociologists, and other persons interested in man's collective behavior indicate that groups usually have common elements, there seems to be an overemphasis on the characteristics of groups of persons within a culture rather than upon individual traits and potentialities. We speak glibly of the "culturally deprived," the "suburbanite," and the "international student" as though the members of these groups had many qualities in common. In actuality, if we were to penetrate to the core of the personality and study modes of thinking, decision making, creative producing, and knowing, we probably would find our ways of categorizing persons very inadequate.

If we are to be wise in our judgments and helpful in our outreach to others, a need exists to focus upon the individual, what he believes, how he is changing, what he knows, and what he prizes. The impact of group mores, norms, standards upon the person is important. It is more critical, however, to ascertain the individual's perceptions of the group rather than to rely upon what the observer sees to be group norms, standards, or values.

Examined and Explicit Biases

Although persons often think that rationality and objectivity govern their behavior, in actuality actions are often dictated by unstated biases. Learning to bring assumptions into the open would enable persons to understand better the bases for their actions. Such openness is not easy but relates to the first guideline of integrity. Biases should be studied as facts since they often lead to facts.

The Establishment of Priorities

If an individual is to live harmoniously and productively, he prizes various elements of life which may seem to be incompatible. For example, he prizes opportunities for solitude, but also opportunities for togetherness. He prizes the precision of science and the freedom of much art. He can be filled with awe and wonder, but he can also seek to get at the causes of his awe. If brief, he realizes that life is composed of ingredients which might appear to be incompatible but which together give personality wholeness. These ingredients are varied, and the person has the right, obligation, and privilege to savor all of them—though not necessarily in equal quantities.

The establishment of priorities is the key to success in valuing and dealing with the ethical. It is not the "good" and the "bad" that will ordinarily come into conflict but rather "two goods" in a particular situation and at a particular point in time. The person who can handle conflict as he establishes priorities is well on his way to becoming a person who is enchanted with the ethical.

VALUING AND SCHOOL PRACTICES

To teach the concept of valuing is extremely difficult; for *values*, *valuing*, and related terms have such a multiplicity of meanings. The concept also varies in its potential impact depending upon the degree to which valuing is seen as an ongoing process. As schools plan for the teaching of valuing, how the term is used will be critical in the planning. Beliefs are taught in different ways from commitments which are more long lasting and deep seated. Teaching for establishing priorities which take into account good but competing values will involve a different kind of program from teaching values which are seen as absolute. The degree to which value decisions are seen as situationally related will also make a difference in how school programs are developed.[21]

The young often have been introduced in various ways to a myriad of values. Lacking time to sort them out and to weigh one against the other, children need the opportunity to clarify what their values are and to differentiate them from tentatively held beliefs. One of the tasks of schooling, therefore, is to help its youth *clarify* values.

At times clarification may indicate incompatibility between two different values held by the same individual. At such a point the task of the school may be to help the individual *change* his values.

Within some groups, a need may exist to create values not represented in the group or to provide children the opportunity to place their values in some type of hierarchy. Developing hierarchical orderings is a way of establishing priorities. In the process of arranging, new values may be created.

Hence, the task of the school may be to clarify, change, or create values depending upon the setting and a variety of factors involved. Let us briefly consider each of these tasks.

Clarifying Values

Until an individual has brought to the level of awareness the values he holds and how he arrives at them, he can do little to change or create values with intent. The process and components of ethical decision making are often elusive, but the better an individual understands them, the more apt he is to handle future ethical decisions in a way that is satisfying to himself. Consequently, it is important

---

[21] For one view of situationally-oriented ethics, see Joseph Fletcher, *Situation Ethics: The New Morality* (Philadelphia: The Westminster Press, 1966).

that the school provide children and youth with resources that will help them clarify their values.

One way to do this is to look for clues in a person's speech. According to Jacob and Flink, statements such as these are operational indices to values:

(1) "Ought" or "should" statements in rationalizations of actions.
(2) Statements indicating guilt, shame, or diffuse anxiety associations with specific actions.
(3) Statements indicating moral indignation or approbation of action on the one hand, and of esteem on the other.[22]

Raths suggests that values can be clarified through the use of questions such as the following:

1. Reflect back what the student has said and add, "Is that what you mean?"
2. Reflect back what the student has said with distortions and add, "Is that what you mean?"
3. "How long have you felt (acted) that way?"
4. "Are you glad you think (act) that way?"
5. "In what way is that a good idea?"
6. "What is the source of your idea?"
7. "Should everyone believe that?"
8. "Have you thought of some alternatives?"
9. "What are some things you have done that reflect this idea of yours?"
10. "Why do you think so?"
11. "Is this what you really think?"
12. "Did you do this on purpose?"
13. Ask for definitions of key words.
14. Ask for examples.
15. Ask if the position is consistent with a previous one he has taken.[23]

Clarifying values takes place oftentimes in conversation between the student and the teacher. Some teachers may wish to set aside daily a portion of time to work with an individual or a small group. Other

---

[22] Jacob and Flink, *American Behavioral Scientist Supplement*, V, 16.

[23] James Raths, "A Strategy for Developing Values," *Educational Leadership*, XXI (May, 1964), pp. 509–514, pp. 512–513. Reprinted with permission of the Association for Supervision and Curriculum Development and James Raths. Copyright © 1964 by the Association for Supervision and Curriculum Development. Also see Raths, Harmin, and Simon, *Values and Teaching*, for further specific suggestions for clarifying values.

teachers may give written assignments which elicit responses to which the teacher might raise questions such as those Raths suggests. Assignments might ask students to describe what they feel ought to be done in a value-laden situation. Students might be asked to establish a situation in which the chief character was engaging in a behavior which would gain the writer's approval (or disapproval) and tell why. Another task might be to ask the student to interpret an incident involving ethical behavior. Through the questions the teacher raises in his reading of the interpretation, he can help the student see the underlying values guiding his interpretation.

The clarification of values is particularly important to the secondary school student about to make a commitment to the work world. To find an occupation where the inherent values are similar to those of the individual is necessary if the individual is to achieve satisfaction as a result of compatibility of occupational and personal values.[24]

In summary, the teacher wishing to help children and youth clarify their values will provide many opportunities for the questioning and reconsideration of values. Arnstine says, "the more practice that is afforded in questioning what are held to be values, the more facile will be the transit between the learner's warehouse of values . . . and his choices in practical situations."[25]

Changing Values

After persons begin to become aware of their values and priorities, they may wish to make some changes. A person may sense the need for change through a variety of circumstances. For example, he may note that he does not perceive positively persons unlike himself. Or he may feel tense or uneasy in a situation where change on the part of either himself or the situation seems necessary.

Value change is a process which must give attention to both the rational and emotional qualities of the person. According to Sartre, "In the end, feeling is what counts. I ought to choose whichever pushes me in one direction."[26]

If feeling and the irrational enter into value decisions, children and youth need much involvement in planned direct experience. The

---

[24] See John F. Kinnane and Joseph R. Gaubinger, "Life Values and Work Values," *Journal of Counselling Psychology*, X, No. 4 (1963), 362–367, for a discussion of this topic.

[25] Donald G. Arnstine, "Some Problems in Teaching Values," *Educational Theory*, XI (1961), pp. 158–167, p. 163.

[26] Jean-Paul Sartre, *Existentialism and Human Emotions* (New York: The Wisdom Library, Philosophical Library, Inc., 1957), p. 26.

experience should be such that it involves thinking in the area where change is desired. The experience also should be of such intensity that strong feelings come to the fore.

Values can be changed too, when an individual becomes part of a new group and wishes to adopt some of their ways. Implications for school practices are that each child should have the opportunity to be part of a variety of groups so that he can see which values of the various groups are like and unlike his own. At what points an individual should attempt to change his values as a result of interacting with peers is a problem which the school should help individuals solve.

Creating Values

Values may be created in a number of ways. Through the years teachers and parents have lectured, preached, cajoled, moralized in attempts to create values. These attempts have been met with more or less success—probably less because most persons do not hear unless they are ready to hear. This readiness usually comes about through an active, dynamic process rather than a passive one.

Values can be created in several ways. First, a school can plan together for the handling of the ethical. Through developing simulated materials and providing real experiences which are designed to evoke responses dealing with the ethical, schools can assist in bringing to the level of awareness major value questions with which children and youth must deal.

For example, teachers can plan situations in which students cope with values in a specific rather than general way. In a situation in which a film was used to teach democratic values, the researchers point out, "In the future, perhaps there should be fewer books and films dealing with the total problem of prejudice facing all citizens in a democracy, and more material designed specifically to help a particular group realize its potential for accepting others."[27]

Second, students can be taught the difference between valuations or values and evaluations. Through many opportunities for evaluations, students come to create values. "A value or valuation differs from an evaluation because it is immediate—it is the direct feeling of liking or disliking, of approving or disapproving. Evaluation, on the other hand, is a conscious, intellectual, discursive process in which

---

[27] Gerald Engel and Harriet E. O'Shea, "Teaching Democratic Values: A Study of the Effect of Prejudice upon Learning," *Journal of Social Psychology,* LX, (1963), pp. 157–167, p. 167.

consequences of choice or actions are consciously weighed."[28] As students are given the chance for deliberate choice, when immediate response is necessary, more consistency of values will be evident than if students had not had the opportunity for evaluations.

A third way to create values is to provide the time, setting, and encouragement for children and youth to reflect upon life, its meaning, necessary changes, and what the individual can, wishes, or ought to do. Cantril says,

> We are dealing here with meditation, contemplation, and communion, with the sort of thing that took Jesus to the top of the mountain, that made Gandhi choose a day of silence each week, for which Abe Lincoln paced the White House halls in the early morning hours. These men were not thinking, they were meditating, they were working out some kind of value system or value priori, and I submit that this is something we have almost completely missed in our whole education system.[29]

Elementary and secondary school children are able to struggle with problems of the ethical and should be given the chance to feel what it is like to try to develop some coherence in their patterns of valuing.

Fifth, values can be developed through the example of the teacher. Children are known to be imitators and may copy not only the end product or value, but also the valuing process.

Teachers, therefore, may wish to examine their direct influence upon children. The teacher may invite a colleague to describe his verbal and nonverbal behavior so that he can see whether what he thinks he values and how he behaves coincide. This type of activity might also appeal to some more mature student who would like a colleague to provide feedback about his behavior and then to see if actions jive with the stated values. Through a comparison of records of intended and actual behavior, individuals can come to see whether practice and intent are congruent.

VALUING AND THE SCHOOL OF THE FUTURE

Children going through today's schools get a heavy dose of the techniques and ways of thinking of the scientist. At the same time,

---

[28] Arnstine, *Educational Theory*, XI, p. 161.
[29] Hadley Cantril, in a panel discussion, "The Organization of Freedom," in *Conflict and Creativity, Control of the Mind*, Part 2, eds. Seymour M. Farber and Roger H. L. Wilson (New York: McGraw-Hill Book Company, 1963), p. 231.

because of the tremendous power which the scientist has harnessed, he is turning with intense interest to value questions—questions of "should" and "ought."

As the schools look for new insights to many fields of human endeavor, including both the scientific and the humanistic, they will find themselves dealing increasingly with value questions. Man's relationship to man will be a dominant theme. What man has created will take a more subordinate role than it does now.

If man is to exist in a meaningful way with his fellows, schools will need to help individuals understand how they view the ethical. In simulated and real life situations, therefore, children and youth will have the opportunity to try on different ways of responding to problem-laden situations. Youth will role-play problems in which the solution is found in an analysis of the context of the situation. Then they will role-play the same episode using a solution based upon ethical principles formulated from a different base.

Because the classroom setting will invite ethical choice, much evaluation will take place as to how such choices are made. "When a learner, unaided, makes choices on the basis of certain values previously presented to him, then we shall say he has been taught these values. We shall not claim that those values have been taught if the learner has been enabled only to enunciate those values."[30]

The school of the future will design its curriculum in such a way that more students may demonstrate fairly coherent behavior patterns than is now the case. In unplanned situations, reasoned judgments will come about more spontaneously because of planned practice in dealing with ethical dilemmas.

Children and youth will spend time learning to resolve conflict. If children begin struggling at an early age with the complexities inherent in the valuing process, they will soon learn that conflict is unavoidable. "Our choices are never perfect."[31] The school of the future will help children adapt to conflict and subsequent guilt so that no matter where an ethical decision might lead, children and youth will not lose their enchantment with the ethical.

---

[30] Arnstine, *Educational Theory*, XI, p. 161.
[31] George F. Kneller, *Existentialism and Education* (New York: Science Editions, John Wiley & Sons, Inc., 1958), p. 114.

Hypotheses for Testing

If children and youth practice establishing priorities among "good things to do" in the classroom setting, they will establish priorities more satisfying to them in out-of-class activities.

If children have much practice in dealing with the ethical in planned activities, they are more apt to select to deal with value-laden problems in situations in which a choice of activity exists than if they have less help in dealing with ethical situations.

If children and youth learn about resolving conflict they will develop more complex solutions to problems than if they have not learned about conflict in relation to the ethical.

PART 3

Toward New Programs

ORGANIZING THE CURRICULUM FOR NEW EMPHASES

11

As new ideas emerge which should find their way into the school, there must be a transformation of the curriculum lest children be overloaded with concepts. A meshing of the old and the new necessitates creative exploration on the part of curriculum workers in order to find means for refining and teaching new priorities and emphases.

The purpose of this chapter is to suggest some possible ways of organizing broad areas within the curriculum so that children and youth have the opportunity to become process-oriented persons, as process has been described in the preceding pages. The writer is aware that it takes time to bring broad concepts to an operational level, to develop materials, and to prepare teachers to work with children differently. Nonetheless we must start with what is available and with the knowledge, problems, and questions we have if programs for children are to move beyond the *status quo.*

ORGANIZING SCHEMES

We shall discuss next six organizing schemes that allow for the development of process skills. Some of the constructs give major attention to process skills, others attempt to interrelate the concept of process with more traditional school subjects and methods. The assumption is made that within each of these constructs attention can and should be given to the pre-teaching aspects of curriculum, such as gathering material and studying children's records and written plans; to the interactive or actual teaching situation; and to the evaluative dimensions which follow teaching and instruction.

Since, as we have indicated in the discussion of knowing, new ideas cause a metamorphosis of the old, the organization constructs which suggest interweaving a process dimension with more traditional elements within the curriculum will probably culminate in a totally new curriculum design. The three examples which follow are cases in point.

Blending Process and Traditional Subjects

Through the years lists of curriculum objectives have enumerated process-related skills as being important in school learning. Yet, the examination of recommended content and method would indicate that the process skills either were lost in the implementation of the curriculum or were given inadequate attention. Therefore, in planning for the actual teaching situation the teaching of process skills should be given as much as or more attention than the teaching of the usual subjects under the traditional organizational pattern.

Within this scheme, in planning for the teaching of arithmetic or social studies the teacher would consciously provide for a process skill such as organizing or decision making. For example, in an English lesson, children might be asked to describe how they feel when they have made a poor decision. Teachers will constantly be looking for ways to link process skills to what they are teaching. Figure 4 illustrates the overlapping nature of this type of curriculum design.

Hypothesis for testing. *If curriculum developers were to examine curriculum guides to see whether proposed activities and content were related to process skills listed in the section on objectives, they would find suggested activities ordinarily did not give specific attention to the listed process skills.*

FIGURE 4

Blending Process and Traditional Subjects

TRADITIONAL SUBJECTS

	Mathematics	Social Studies	English	Art	Science
Organizing					
Decision Making					
Loving					
Knowing					
Communicating					
Creating					
Valuing					
Perceiving					

PROCESS SKILLS

Process, Content, and Methodology

This organizational scheme is similar to the previous one except that it gives heavier emphasis to classroom methodology. Many curriculum workers who give attention to methodology often think they are developing process skills. Although they may in subtle ways be providing children with the opportunity to be developing such skills, they often are not helping children bring their process learnings to a level of awareness.

For example, a teacher might attempt to teach the concept that different conditions stimulate different people to create. This might be linked to an art lesson. The methodology employed would be that students would be given an assignment involving creative production over a series of days. Each day, however, the setting would be different. One day students might work in individual carrels, a second day in groups within the classroom, a third day on a grassy hillside, etc. After having the opportunity to work in these various settings, children would be asked to describe which one caused them to feel

FIGURE 5

Process, Content, and Methodology

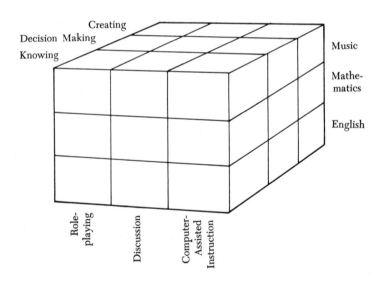

PROCESS   CONTENT

METHODOLOGY

most like creating. Figure 5 on the preceding page indicates what must be taken into account when process, content, and methodology are considered in curriculum planning.

> **Hypotheses for testing.** *If various methods which are used in teaching were to be analyzed in terms of their adaptability to teaching a range of process skills, then it would be found that some methods lend themselves to the development of a wider range of process skills than others.*
>
> *If the range of process skills which can be taught through programmed instruction were tabulated, the range would be smaller than the range developed through such methods as discussion, aids at the end of a chapter, or the development of an individual project.*

Combining One Process and the Traditional Subjects

Rather than try to deal with a variety of process skills during a year as well as the traditional school subjects, some curriculum workers might prefer to emphasize one process skill along with existing subjects. This mode of organization might have variations, in that one process skill might be stressed over a period of three or four years, one year, or months. For example, communicating might permeate a total school curriculum from kindergarten through grade eight, or a high school curriculum might emphasize the teaching of decision making as a central theme.

In this type of curriculum organization the process skill of organizing might enter into the teaching of all school subjects over a period of a year. Children might learn how a musician arranges musical notes to make a composition, how a scientist orders old concepts with a touch of ingenuity to invent something new, or how an historian reorders old data to make a new interpretation of an historical event. Figure 6 shows one way of organizing within this construct.

> **Hypothesis for testing.** *If children over a specified period of time, through the study of the traditional school subjects, have the opportunity to learn concepts related to one of the eight skills discussed in this book, then they will see more relevance of the traditional school subjects for everyday situations than if they have not been introduced in a planned way to the teaching of such concepts.*

FIGURE 6

One Process and Traditional Subjects

PRIMARY
SCHOOL

	Mathematics	Science	English	
Concepts the School Has Defined Relative to Communicating				

MIDDLE
SCHOOL

	Art	Physical Education	Social Studies	
Concepts the School Has Defined Relative to Valuing				

HIGH
SCHOOL

	History	Biology	Algebra	
Concepts the School Has Defined Relative to Knowing				

Emphasis on Individual Process

The next three constructs demand more major curriculum revision than the last three, for the concept of process determines the focus, content, and methodology.

Each process can be taught separately as a unit of work. Children would have the opportunity to experience as many aspects of the process as possible. In addition, much of the substance of the curriculum would have to do with the content of the process.

For example, creating might be taught as a unit of work. How man produces newness in various fields of human endeavor would receive major emphasis. What man does in the process of creating would receive more attention than what man has created. Students, too, would have the opportunity to look at themselves in the process of creating. They would begin early to ascertain and understand themselves as creators.

Figure 7 gives one set of components that might be used in developing a unit on creating. The concentric circles are drawn with broken lines to indicate the interplay among the various elements within the circle.

FIGURE 7

Emphasis on Individual Process

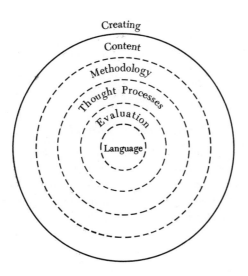

It should be noted that each process, such as creating, lends itself to the teaching of certain thought processes. Among areas needing study are techniques for evaluation and the language which fosters creativity.

> **Hypothesis for testing.** *If concepts such as creating, communicating, knowing, and organizing were spelled out in behavioral terms, then curriculum developers would be able to find sufficient content and methodology which related to the behavioral objectives to develop a curriculum directly related to human functions.*

Interrelatedness of Processes

As one spells out the components of the eight processes with which we have been concerned, one sees much overlap among them. Another construct, therefore, is one which gives specific attention to the common elements of the various processes.

For example, the concept of commitment is very important to valuing, to creating, and to loving. Personal knowledge, a component of knowing, is also a critical element in creating. Integrity has been pointed out as vital to worthwhile communicating, to creating, and to valuing. The list could become very extensive, and the idea is worthy of rather comprehensive study by those persons seeking to include process elements within the curriculum. Figure 8 shows one means of organizing in order to establish likenesses and differences among the processes.

> **Hypothesis for testing.** *If a list were compiled of behavioral components of each of the eight processes discussed in this book, then points of overlap and uniqueness of the various processes would be identified which would enable a clearer understanding of the relationships among processes.*

One Process Pervasive

In this scheme, one process such as perceiving or patterning is pervasive and comprehensive. In other words either a large block of time is devoted to the teaching of it, or it may recur as the child progresses through school. The process, however, is linked to the other processes when appropriate.

FIGURE 8

Interrelatedness of Processes

	Perceiving	Valuing	Loving	Knowing	Patterning	Creating	Decision Making	Communicating
Perceiving								
Valuing								
Loving								
Knowing								
Patterning								
Creating								
Decision Making								
Communicating								

For example, perceiving might be a process that permeates the curriculum in a middle school. Creating, knowing, loving, etc., are taught in relation to perceiving. Figure 9 illustrates roughly what we are saying.

FIGURE 9

One Process Pervasive

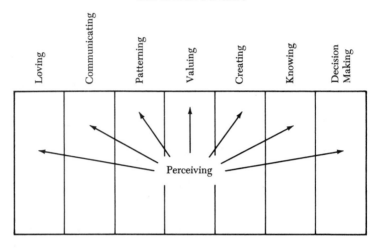

Hypothesis for testing. *If a student has the opportunity to learn well in a school situation one of the process skills, in an out-of-school setting the student will use the skill better than if he had not had planned teaching of it in school.*

CONSIDERATIONS IN ORGANIZING THE CURRICULUM

Many factors need to be considered as schools seek to organize or reorganize the curriculum. The preceding pages have dealt primarily with organizing around the substance of the curriculum. We chose to take this stance because it seemingly is not receiving the same emphasis in current curriculum study and writing as organizational problems of age or ability. We would, however, like to mention a few other considerations that enter into planning for teaching process.

Criteria for Developing an Organizing Construct

The criteria for developing an organizing construct around which the curriculum might be built are essentially two. One has to do with the curriculum worker's view of the culture, the other with his view of the individual. Obviously they are related.

If the culture is viewed as holding to the already created rather than to the emergent, then a process-oriented curriculum is unnecessary. Inherent in a process-oriented curriculum is the concept of fairly rapid change. If, however, the culture prizes, values, and initiates change, a process-oriented curriculum might accelerate the pace and enable more worthwhile changes. A process-oriented curriculum can provide the student with the skills for examining human institutions such as the home, church, or family, and for knowing when to maintain stability and when to seek innovation within these institutions.

Another factor important in deciding whether a process-oriented curriculum is appropriate is the view that is accorded the person. Is the person seen as an individual who must know a body of information? Or is he seen as one who is encouraged to develop personal meaning? Is the individual viewed as consuming what has already been created? Or is he seen as contributing to what is in the process of being created? If the school selects as its primary function the passing down of the wisdom of the ages, a process-oriented curriculum is not very important. If, however, the school sees as its responsibility equipping its young to be continuing creators, then a modification of the process-oriented curriculum should be developed.

Grouping of Students

A process-oriented curriculum lends itself to a variety of ways of grouping students. Our primary concern has not been with this problem, even though it is important. We would hope, however, that whatever the predominant mode of grouping is, two opportunities would be available to children.

The first is the chance to be with a perceptive adult some part of a day or week. Only as process skills are applied to the individual do they become really meaningful. Hopefully the adult would have studied for himself the concept of priorities we have discussed. Through the help of a teacher, the child can clarify his thinking and begin to change where necessary. The adult can help determine the nature of the activities for the child and provide enough support so that the child is comfortable in working alone or with his peers the major portion of the day.

Then children need the opportunity to work with peers like and unlike themselves—in age, in interests, in ways of thinking and behaving. Certain process skills necessitate the chance to handle one's self with a variety of persons. Such opportunities provide necessary practice.

Use of Materials

Hopefully teachers would use a variety of materials in teaching process skills. Individualized materials especially developed for a particular child should teach certain skills discussed more effectively than can mass-produced materials. To personalize is critical in teaching process skills. Commercial materials might serve as a source of ideas for teachers or might be used by children when predetermined sequence is important to learning certain concepts of the culture. But if children are to make something of their own lives, they need the opportunity for individualized assignments designed to help them make of themselves unique beings.

The Use of Time

Emphasis upon process-oriented persons could mean much more flexible use of time than is now common in school programs. Because of the need for attention to each child's pattern of development, schools will need to consider such questions as these: Can a particular subject or area be learned at home as well as at school? Can the subject be adapted to teaching during evening tutorial sessions held in various neighborhoods around the school? Can certain concepts be taught as well by television at home with provision being made for parents and children together to engage in some type of follow-up activity? What can be done to give adults skills so that the child receives help from a wide number of people during his years of schooling? How can the school insure that process skills are encouraged in the child throughout the day, whether or not he is involved in formal lessons?

Our concern is that parents and other adults who are responsible for children be helped to understand and foster within the child the processes which hopefully the school is taking the leadership in developing with children.

EPILOGUE

If the schools could but even faintly hear the beat of the drummer of twenty-five years hence, how different the march would be. Instead, the schools oftentimes respond loudly and clearly to the drummer of fifty years past. Not only is the beat of the music from the past, but the melodies appear to be only slightly changed variations on old themes. The sounds of the future come through, erratic in their beat and dissonant in sound.

It is the dissonance which must eventually make sense, be the sounds ever so new if education is to help provide opportunities for persons to become contented, contributing members of tomorrow's world. Our hypothesis is that as the school places priority upon developing a setting where children and youth have the opportunity to experience and verbalize the meanings of creating, loving, knowing, organizing, and other process skills, they will orchestrate more beautifully the components of tomorrow's world than if they did not have such new priorities established in the curriculum.

APPENDIX

SUGGESTED TASKS DESIGNED TO ASSIST IN DETERMINING
DISPOSITION TOWARD COMPLEXITY*

In attempting to determine an individual's or group's disposition toward complexity, some of the tasks listed below might be tried. In analyzing the student's reactions to the task, teachers may consider the complexity of the task the individual chooses, his ability to see detail in relation to the whole, his awareness of the nature of the ordering process. The suggestions which follow are merely suggestive and should be modified as appropriate.

---

* Appendix from Louise M. Berman, *Creativity in Education: A Guide to a Television Series* (Milwaukee: Milwaukee Public Schools, 1963), pp. 47–49. The total chapter on "Order-Disorder," pp. 42–50, contains pertinent practical suggestions for teaching patterning.

Make a Game. Ask individuals or groups to make up a game to play with another individual or group. Diagrams necessary to the playing or understanding of the game should be made. Rules should be written as clearly as possible.

> *Possible evaluative procedure.* Strike out irrelevant information. Count the number of steps in the game.

Group Planning. Directions are given to a group of children as follows: "We'll develop a school (a town, a classroom, etc.) of our own. What kind of school would we want?" Use tape recorder to get the information. Record about 15-20 minutes of the discussion.

> *Possible evaluative procedure.* Try to categorize responses. Give points for the number and variety of responses.

Make a Collage. Have a box of assorted materials available. In the box include different kinds of papers, cloth, metallic substances, strings, ropes, beads. etc. Ask the children to make something from the materials.

> *Possible evaluative procedure.* Count the number of materials used. Count the ways a given material is used. Total the score.

Description of Friend. Ask the child to write a description of his best friend (may also be a member of the family).

> *Possible evaluative procedure.* Note whether individual emphasizes scattered details or whether he attempts a synthesis of ideas, making detail subordinate to general impressions. Note the unusual features which are part of the synthesis. Give two scores, one for unusualness of detail, one for unusualness of organization.

Choice of Game. Have available three unfamiliar games (may be commercial ones). These games should vary in their complexity. Give children the opportunity to study the directions for each one. Individual then makes a choice of game.

> *Possible evaluative procedure.* Give different point values to games according to complexity. Individual is not asked to follow through on the game, but score is determined by the choice.

Describe a Vocational Choice. Give directions such as the following (probably to secondary school students): "Describe the kind of job you would like when you finish school. What kinds of preparation do you think you will need? Tell about some of the things you will do. What aspects of your work do you think you will like? What parts will you dislike?"

Possible evaluative procedure. Develop a scale ranging from one to five, one being a response representing simplicity, five representing complexity. Attempt to rate the responses in terms of the scale. Average the score.

The probable value of this task lies in the discussion it may evoke.

Paired Choices. Describe a series of pairs of jobs to be accomplished, one simple, the other complex, in each pair. Make sure the tasks are in the same areas or subject. Ask the individual to choose one task in each pair that he would prefer to carry out.

Possible evaluative procedure. Total the number of complex tasks the individual chooses.

Develop a Research Project. Give the following directions: "Prepare a research project in an area of your choice. Include in the design of your project means for communicating the findings to your classmates. Use as much ingenuity as possible in preparing your findings for sharing so that your classmates will understand and be interested in your project."

Possible evaluative procedure. In this assignment identify the kinds and quantity of procedures the individual used in communicating the findings. Were the procedures patterned in such a way that the order was unique but meaningful?

BIBLIOGRAPHY

GENERAL

Bell, Daniel, "Twelve Modes of Prediction," in *Penguin Survey of the Social Sciences 1965*, pp. 96–127. Baltimore: Penguin Books, Inc., 1965.

Brauner, Charles J., "The Evolution of American Educational Theory," USOE Cooperative Research Project No. 245. Stanford: Stanford University, 1962.

Edie, James M., ed., *An Invitation to Phenomenology: Studies in the Philosophy of Experience*. Chicago: Quadrangle Books, Inc., 1965.

Educational Policies Commission, *Education and the Spirit of Science*. Washington, D.C.: National Education Assn., 1966.

Educational Policies Commission, *The Central Purpose of American Education*. Washington, D.C.: National Education Assn., 1961.

197

Erikson, Erik H., *Insight and Responsibility*. New York: W. W. Norton & Company, Inc., 1964.

ESI Quarterly Report. Watertown, Mass.: Education Development Center, (Winter–Spring, 1964).

Frost, Joe L., and Glen R. Hawkes, eds., *The Disadvantaged Child: Issues and Innovations*. New York: Houghton Mifflin Company, 1966.

Heuscher, Julius E., "What Is Existential Psychotherapy?" *Review of Existential Psychology and Psychiatry*, IV (Spring, 1964), 158–167.

Hollister, William G., M. D., "Curriculum Development to Foster Mental Strength," *Educational Leadership*, XXIV (November, 1966), 161–171.

Inlow, Gail M., "Factors that Influence Curriculum Change," *Educational Leadership*, XXIII (October, 1965), 39–44.

Lauer, Quentin, *Phenomenology: Its Genesis and Prospect*. New York: Harper Torchbooks, Harper & Brothers, Publishers, 1958.

Nash, Paul, *Authority and Freedom in Education: An Introduction to the Philosophy of Education*. New York: John Wiley & Sons, Inc., 1966.

Nikelly, Arthur, "Existentialism and Education for Mental Health," *Journal of Existentialism*, V (Fall, 1964), 205–211.

Sigel, Irving, and Elinor Waters, "Child Development and Social Science Education, Part III: Abstracts of Relevant Literature," Publication No. 112 of the Social Science Education Consortium, USOE Cooperative Research Program. Lafayette, Indiana: Purdue University, 1966.

Webster, Staten W., ed., *The Disadvantaged Learner: Knowing, Understanding, Educating*. San Francisco: Chandler Publishing Co., 1966.

CHAPTER ONE
TOWARD PROCESS-ORIENTED PERSONS

Allport, Gordon, *The Nature of Prejudice*. Cambridge: Addison-Wesley Publishing Co., Inc., 1954.

Ambrose, Edna, and Alice Miel, *Children's Social Learning: Implications of Research and Expert Study*. Washington, D. C.: Association for Supervision and Curriculum Development, NEA, 1958.

Aschner, Mary Jane McCue, "Thinking and Meaning," in *Language and Meaning*, eds. James B. Macdonald and Robert K. Leeper. Washington, D. C.: Association for Supervision and Curriculum Development, NEA, 1966.

Association for Supervision and Curriculum Development, *Perceiving, Behaving, Becoming: A New Focus for Education*, 1962 Yearbook, ed. Arthur W. Combs. Washington, D. C.: The Association, NEA, 1962.

Berman, Louise, *From Thinking to Behaving: Assignments Reconsidered*. Practical Suggestions for Teaching, ed. Alice Miel. New York: Teachers College Press, Teachers College, Columbia University, 1967.

Bernier, Normand, "The Affective Domain in Teaching," The First Florence B. Stratemeyer Lecture. Cedar Falls, Iowa: Association for Student Teaching, Iowa State University, 1966.

Bartlett, Sir Frederick, *Thinking: An Experimental and Social Study.* New York: Basic Books, Inc., Publishers, 1958.

Biddle, W. Earl, *The Integration of Religion and Psychiatry.* New York: Collier Books, Collier-Macmillan Ltd., 1955.

Bloom, Benjamin S., ed., *Taxonomy of Educational Objectives: The Classification of Educational Goals. Handbook I: Cognitive Domain.* New York: David McKay Co., Inc., 1956.

Bower, Eli M., "The Achievement of Competency," in *Learning and Mental Health in the School,* 1966 Yearbook, eds. Walter B. Waetjen and Robert R. Leeper. Washington, D. C.: Association for Supervision and Curriculum Development, NEA, 1966.

Browver, Paul J., "The Power to See Ourselves," *Harvard Business Review,* XLII, No. 6 (1964), 156–165.

Bruner, Jerome, Jacqueline Goodnow, and George A. Austin, *A Study of Thinking.* New York: John Wiley & Sons, Inc., 1956.

Bruner, Jerome, Rose Olver, Patricia Greenfield, and Others, *Studies in Cognitive Growth.* New York: John Wiley & Sons, Inc., 1966.

Buytendijk, F. J. J., "The Phenomenological Approach to the Problem of Feelings and Emotions," in *Feelings and Emotions,* ed. Martin L. Reymert. New York: McGraw-Hill Book Company, 1950. Also in *Psychoanalysis and Existential Philosophy,* pp. 155–178, ed. Hendrik M. Ruitenbeek. New York: E. P. Dutton & Co., Inc., 1962.

Cantril, Hadley, *The Why of Man's Experience.* New York: The Macmillan Company, 1950.

Carpenter, Helen, ed., *Skill Development in Social Studies,* Thirty-third Yearbook of the National Council for the Social Studies. Washington, D. C.: National Education Assn., 1963.

Clive, Geoffrey, "The Inauthentic Self," *Journal of Existentialism,* V (Summer, 1964), 51–66.

Combs, Arthur W., and Donald Snygg, *Individual Behavior.* New York: Harper & Brothers, Publishers, 1959.

Dressel, Paul L., "Development of Critical Thinking," in *Current Issues in Higher Education,* 18th Annual Conference on Higher Education. Washington, D. C.: Association for Higher Education, NEA, 1963.

Ennis, Robert H., "A Concept of Critical Thinking," *Harvard Educational Review,* XXXII (Winter, 1962), 81–111.

Eisner, Elliott W., "Critical Thinking: Some Cognitive Components," *Teachers College Record,* LXVI (April, 1965), 624–634.

Emmerling, Frank C., and Kanawha Z. Chavis, *The Teacher Aide in North Carolina's Comprehensive School Improvement Project,* Publication No. 395. Raleigh: State Department of Public Instruction, 1966.

Fraser, J. T., ed., *The Voices of Time.* New York: George Braziller, Inc., 1966.

Gillham, Helen, *Helping Children Accept Themselves and Others.* Practical Suggestions for Teaching, ed. Alice Miel. New York: Bureau of Publications, Teachers College, Columbia University, 1959.

Gordon, Ira J., *Studying the Child in School.* New York: John Wiley & Sons, Inc., 1966.

Gotschalk, Richard, "Buber's Conception of Responsibility," *Journal of Existentialism,* VI (Fall, 1965), 1–8.

Gould, Samuel B., *Knowledge Is Not Enough.* Yellow Springs, Ohio: Antioch Press, 1959.

Gruber, Howard, E., Glenn Terrell, and Michael Wertheimer, eds., *Contemporary Approaches to Creative Thinking.* New York: Atherton Press, 1962.

Guilford, J. P., *Personality.* New York: McGraw-Hill Book Company, 1959.

Guilford, J. P., "The Three Faces of Intellect," *American Psychologist,* XIV (September, 1959), 469–479.

Hall, Edward T., *The Hidden Dimension.* Garden City, N. Y.: Doubleday & Company, Inc., 1966.

Hammarskjöld, Dag, *Markings.* New York: Alfred A. Knopf, Inc., 1964.

Harper, Robert J. C., and Others, *The Cognitive Processes: Readings.* Englewood Cliffs, New Jersey: Prentice-Hall, Inc., 1964.

Hollister, William G., M.D., "Preparing the Minds of the Future: Enhancing Ego Processes through Curriculum Development," in *Curriculum Change: Direction and Process,* ed. Robert R. Leeper. Washington, D. C.: Association for Supervision and Curriculum Development, NEA, 1966.

Hopkins, Thomas, *The Emerging Self.* New York: Harper & Brothers, Publishers, 1954.

Hullfish, H. Gordon, and Philip G. Smith, *Reflective Thinking: The Method of Education.* New York: Dodd, Mead & Co., 1962.

Johnson, Donald M., *The Psychology of Thought and Judgment.* New York: Harper & Brothers, Publishers, 1955.

Kastenbaum, Robert, "As the Clock Runs Out," *Mental Hygiene,* L (July, 1966), 332–336.

Kneller, George F., *Existentialism and Education.* New York: Science Editions, John Wiley & Sons, Inc., 1958.

Kubie, Lawrence, *Neurotic Distortion of the Creative Process.* Lawrence, Kansas: University of Kansas Press, 1958.

Langer, Susanne K., *Mind: An Essay on Human Feelings,* Vol. I. Baltimore, Md.: The Johns Hopkins Press, 1967.

Langer, Susanne K., *Philosophical Sketches.* Baltimore, Md.: The Johns Hopkins Press, 1962.

Langer Susanne K., *Philosophy in a New Key.* Cambridge: Harvard University Press, 1957.

Lehmann, Irvin J., and Stanley O. Ikenberry, "Critical Thinking, Attitudes, and Values in Higher Education," USOE Cooperative Research Project No. 372. East Lansing: Michigan State University, 1959.

McCully, Harold C., "Conceptions of Man and the Helping Professions," *The Personnel and Guidance Journal*, XLIV (May, 1966), 911–918.

Miel, Alice, and Peggy Brogan, *More than Social Studies*. Englewood Cliffs, New Jersey: Prentice-Hall, Inc., 1957.

Miles, Matthew B., "Education in the '70's: Some Predictions," *Teachers College Record*, LXV (February, 1964), 441–454.

Nicoll, Maurice, *Living Time and the Integration of Life*. London: Vincent Stuart, 1959.

Otto, Herbert A., ed., *Explorations on Human Potentialities*. Springfield, Illinois: Charles C. Thomas, Publisher, 1966.

Passow, A. Harry, ed., *Nurturing Individual Potential*. Washington, D. C.: Association for Supervision and Curriculum Development, NEA, 1964.

Passow, Harry, and Robert R. Leeper, eds., *Intellectual Development: Another Look*. Washington, D. C.: Association for Supervision and Curriculum Development, NEA, 1964.

Piaget, Jean, "Time Perception in Children," in *The Voices of Time*, pp. 202–216, ed. J. T. Fraser. New York: George Braziller, Inc., 1966.

Polanyi, Michael, *The Tacit Dimension*. New York: Doubleday & Company, Inc., 1966.

Prescott, Daniel, *Emotion and the Educative Process*. Washington, D. C.: The American Council on Education, 1938.

Raths, Louis E., and Others, *Teaching for Thinking: Theory and Application*. Columbus; Charles E. Merrill Publishing Company, 1967.

Reik, Theodore, *Listening with the Third Ear: The Inner Experience of a Psychoanalyst*. New York: Grove Press, Inc., 1948.

Ruitenbeek Hendrik M., ed., *Psychoanalysis and Existential Philosophy*. New York: E. P. Dutton & Co., Inc., 1962.

Russell, David, *Children's Thinking*. Waltham, Massachusetts: Blaisdell Publishing Company, a Division of Ginn and Company, 1956.

Sanders, Norris M., *Classroom Questions: What Kinds?* New York: Harper & Row, Publishers, 1966.

Sarason, Seymour B., and Kenneth S. Davidson, "A Study of Teacher Behavior in Relation to Children Differing in Anxiety Level," USOE Cooperative Research Project No. 624. New Haven: Yale University, 1965.

Sartre, Jean-Paul, *Existentialism and Human Emotions*. New York: The Wisdom Library, a Division of Philosophical Library, Inc. 1957.

Schrader, George A., "The Structure of Emotion," in *An Invitation to Phenomenology*, pp. 252–265, ed. James M. Edie. Chicago: Quadrangle Books, Inc., 1965.

Shirk, Evelyn, *The Ethical Dimension: An Approach to the Philosophy of Values and Valuing*. New York: Appleton-Century-Crofts, 1965.

Siegel, Sol, "A Note on Hypocrisy in the Counselling Process," *Review of Existential Psychology and Psychiatry*, IV (February, 1964), 47–51.

Simon, Sidney B., and Phyllis Lieberman, "Analyzing Advertising: An Approach to Critical Thinking," *The National Elementary Principal*, XLVI (September, 1966), 16–18.

Stein, Maurice, Arthur J. Vidich, and David M. White, eds., *Identity and Anxiety: Survival of the Person in Mass Society*. Glencoe, Illinois: The Free Press of Glencoe, 1960.

Taba, Hilda, Samuel Levine, and Freeman F. Elzey, "Thinking in Elementary School Children," USOE Cooperative Research Project No. 1574. San Francisco: San Francisco State College, 1964.

Tournier, Paul, *The Healing of Persons*, trans. Edwin Hudson. New York: Harper & Row, Publishers, 1965.

Usery, Mary Lou, "The Process of Critical Thinking: A Theory and Application to Children's Literature," Unpublished Master's Thesis. Milwaukee: University of Wisconsin–Milwaukee, 1965.

Vygotsky, Lev Semenovich, *Thought and Language*, trans. and ed. by Eugenia Hanfmann and Gertrude Vakar. Cambridge: The MIT Press, 1962.

Waetjen, Walter B., and Robert R. Leeper, eds., *Learning and Mental Health in the School*, 1966 Yearbook. Washington, D. C.: Association for Supervision and Curriculum Development, NEA, 1966.

Winthrop, Henry, "Empathy and Self-Identity Versus Role-Playing and Alienation," *Journal of Existentialism*, V (Summer, 1964), 37–50.

CHAPTER TWO
THE EMERGING EDUCATIONAL SCENE

Association for Supervision and Curriculum Development, *Educational Leadership*, XIX (December, 1961), major portion of issue devoted to "What is Teaching?" 146–186.

Beggs, David W., III, and Edward G. Buffie, *Independent Study: Bold New Venture*. Bloomington: Indiana University Press, 1965.

Bellack, Arno A., ed., *Theory and Research in Teaching*. New York: Bureau of Publications, Teachers College, Columbia University, 1963.

Berman, Louise M., "New Curriculum Designs for Children," in *The New Elementary School*, ed. Alexander Frazier. Washington, D. C.: Association for Supervision and Curriculum Development, NEA, 1968.

Berman, Louise M., ed., *The Nature of Teaching: Implications for the Education of Teachers*, Edward A. and Rosa Uhrig Memorial Lectures. Milwaukee: School of Education, University of Wisconsin–Milwaukee, 1963.

Berman, Louise M., and Mary Lou Usery, *Personalized Supervision: Sources and Insights.* Washington, D. C.: Association for Supervision and Curriculum Development, NEA, 1966.

Biddle, Bruce J., and William J. Ellena, eds., *Contemporary Research on Teacher Effectiveness.* New York: Holt, Rinehart & Winston, Inc., 1964.

Bruner, Jerome S., "Needed: A Theory of Instruction," *Educational Leadership,* XX (May, 1963), 523–532.

Burnham, Brian, ed., *New Designs for Learning,* Highlights of the Reports of the Ontario Curriculum Institute, 1963–1966. Published for the Ontario Institute for Studies in Education. Toronto: University of Toronto Press, 1967.

Byrnes, Robert F., "Our First Need: Improved Teaching," *Bulletin of the National Association of Secondary School Principals,* LI (May, 1967), 132–143.

Department of Elementary School Principals, *The National Elementary Principal,* XLIV (January, 1965), entire issue devoted to "Cooperative Teaching."

Diack, Hunter, *Language for Teaching.* New York: Philosophical Library, Inc., 1966.

Drews, Elizabeth Monroe, "Student Abilities, Grouping Patterns, and Classroom Interaction," USOE Cooperative Research Project No. 608. East Lansing: Office of Research and Publications, College of Education, Michigan State University, 1963.

Eisner, Elliott, "Instruction, Teaching, and Learning: An Attempt at Differentiation," *The Elementary School Journal,* LXV (December, 1964), 115–119. Reprinted in *Professional Reprints in Education,* No. 8610. Columbus: Charles E. Merrill Publishing Company.

Fleming, Robert S., ed., *Curriculum for Today's Boys and Girls.* Columbus: Charles E. Merrill Publishing Company, 1963.

Gage, N. L., ed., *Handbook of Research on Teaching,* A Project of the American Educational Research Association, NEA. Chicago: Rand McNally & Co., 1963.

Goodlad, John I., ed., *The Changing American School,* Sixty-fifth Yearbook of the National Society for the Study of Education. Chicago: University of Chicago Press, 1966.

Goodman, Paul, "Discussion: The Education Industries," *Harvard Educational Review,* XXXVII, No. 1 (1967), 107–110.

Green, Thomas F., "Teaching, Acting, Behaving," *Harvard Educational Review,* XXXIV, No. 4 (1964), 507–524.

Hughes, Marie M., "What Is Teaching? One Viewpoint," *Educational Leadership,* XIX (January, 1962), 251–259.

Jackson, Philip W., "The Way Teaching Is," in *The Way Teaching Is,* Report of the Seminar on Teaching. Washington, D. C.: Association for Supervision and Curriculum Development and the Center for the Study of Instruction, NEA, 1966.

King, Arthur R., and John A. Brownell, *The Curriculum and the Disciplines of Knowledge: A Theory of Curriculum Practice.* New York: John Wiley & Sons, Inc., 1966.

Kneller, George F., *Logic and Language of Education.* New York: John Wiley & Sons, Inc., 1966.

Macdonald, James, Dan W. Andersen, and Frank B. May, *Strategies of Curriculum Development: Selected Writings of the Late Virgil E. Herrick.* Columbus: Charles E. Merrill Publishing Company, 1965.

Macdonald, James B., and Robert R. Leeper, *Theories of Instruction.* Washington, D. C.: Association for Supervision and Curriculum Development, NEA, 1965.

Mahan, Thomas W., Jr., "The Teacher as Provocative Adventurer," *Teachers College Record,* LXVII (February, 1966), 330–337.

McLendon, Jonathan C., *Social Foundations of Education: Current Readings from the Behavioral Sciences.* New York: The Macmillan Company, 1966.

McLuhan, Marshall, and George B. Leonard, "The Future of Sex," *Look,* XXXI (July 25, 1967), 56–63.

Miel, Alice, ed., *Creativity in Teaching: Invitations and Instances,* Belmont, Cal.: Wadsworth Publishing Co., Inc., 1961.

National Commission on Teacher Education and Professions Standards, *Auxiliary School Personnel.* Washington, D. C.: National Education Assn., 1967.

Oliver, Donald W., "Discussion: The Education Industries," *Harvard Educational Review,* XXXVII, No. 1 (1967), 110–113.

Peter, Laurence J., *Prescriptive Teaching.* New York: McGraw-Hill Book Company, 1965.

Phenix, Philip H., *Realms of Meaning: A Philosophy of the Curriculum for General Education.* New York: McGraw-Hill Book Company, 1964.

Raths, James, John R. Pancella, and James S. Van Ness, eds., *Studying Teaching.* Englewood Cliffs, New Jersey: Prentice-Hall, Inc., 1967.

Raths, Louis E., and Others, *Teaching for Thinking:* Theory and Application. Columbus: Charles E. Merrill Publishing Company, 1967.

Robison, Helen F., ed., *Precedents and Promise in the Curriculum Field.* New York: Teachers College Press, Columbia University, 1966.

Sanders, Norris M., *Classroom Questions: What Kinds?* New York: Harper & Row, Publishers, 1966.

Scheffler, Israel, "Philosophical Modes of Teaching," *Harvard Educational Review,* XXXV, No. 2 (1965), 131–143.

Sizer, Theodore R., "Some Problems in Curriculum Development," *ESI Quarterly Report,* pp. 192–196. Watertown, Mass.: Education Development Center, Summer–Fall, 1965.

Smith, B. Othanel, and Milton O. Meux, "A Study of the Logic of Teaching," USOE Cooperative Research Project No. 258. Urbana: University of Illinois, 1963.

Soltis, Jonas F., and Others, "Discussion: Teaching, Acting, and Behaving," *Harvard Educational Review*, XXXV, No. 2 (1965), 191–209.

Taba, Hilda, and Freeman F. Elzey, "Teaching Strategies and Thought Processes," *Teachers College Record*, LXV (March, 1964), 524–534.

Taylor, Calvin W., and Others, "Development of a Theory of Education from Psychological and other Basic Research Findings," USOE Cooperative Research Project No. 621. Salt Lake City: University of Utah, 1964.

Thelen, Herbert A., *Classroom Grouping for Teachability*. New York: John Wiley & Sons, Inc., 1967.

Winthrop, Henry, "What Can We Expect from the Unprogramed Teacher?" *Teachers College Record*, LXVII (February, 1966), 315–329.

Yates, Alfred, ed., *Grouping in Education*, A Report Sponsored by the UNESCO Institute for Education, Hamburg. New York: John Wiley & Sons, Inc., 1966.

CHAPTER THREE
PERCEIVING: THE STIMULUS FOR MAN'S BEHAVIOR

Allport, Gordon W., *Personality and Social Encounter: Selected Essays*. Boston: Beacon Press, 1960.

Bach, Marcus, *The Power of Perception*. Garden City, N.Y.: Doubleday & Company, Inc., 1966.

Bandura, A., "Observational Learning as a Function of Symbolization and Incentive Set," *Child Development*, XXXVII (September, 1966), 499–506.

Brookover, Wilbut B., Ann Paterson, and Shailer Thomas, "The Relationship of Self-Images to Achievement in Junior High School Subjects," USOE Cooperative Research Project No. 845. East Lansing: Office of Research and Publications, Michigan State University, 1962.

Bruner, Jerome S., *On Knowing: Essays for the Left Hand*. Cambridge: Harvard University Press, 1962.

Bruner, Jerome S., "On Perceptual Readiness," in *The Cognitive Processes: Readings*, pp. 223–256, eds. Robert J. C. Harper and Others. Englewood Cliffs, New Jersey: Prentice-Hall, Inc., 1964.

Bruner, Jerome S., "Social Psychology, and Perception," in *Readings in Social Psychology*, Third Edition, pp. 85–94, eds. Eleanor E. Maccoby, Theodore M. Newcomb, and Eugene L. Hartley. New York: Henry Holt and Company, 1958.

Campbell, Paul B., "School and Self-Concept," *Educational Leadership*, XXIV (March, 1967), 510–515.

Church, Joseph, *Language and the Discovery of Reality: A Developmental Psychology of Cognition*. New York: Random House, Inc., 1961.

Ciardi, John, "The Curriculum of Perception," in *Strength Through Reappraisal*, pp. 113–125, Sixteenth Yearbook of the American Association of Colleges for Teacher Education. Washington, D. C.: National Education Assn., 1963.

Combs, Arthur W., *The Professional Education of Teachers: A Perceptual View of Teacher Preparation*. Boston: Allyn & Bacon, Inc., 1965.

Combs, Arthur W., ed., *Perceiving, Behaving, Becoming: A New Focus for Education*, 1962 Yearbook. Washington, D. C.: Association for Supervision and Curriculum Development, NEA, 1962.

Combs, Arthur W., and Donald Snygg, *Individual Behavior: A Perceptual Approach to Behavior*. New York: Harper & Brothers, Publishers, 1959.

Combs, Arthur W., and Daniel W. Soper, "The Relationship of Child Perceptions to Achievement and Behavior in the Early School Years," USOE Cooperative Research Project No. 814. Gainesville: University of Florida, 1963.

Edie, James M., *An Invitation to Phenomenology*. Chicago: Quadrangle Books, Inc., 1965.

Foshay, Arthur, "The Creative Process Described," in *Creativity in Teaching*, pp. 22–40, ed. Alice Miel. Belmont, California: Wadsworth Publishing Co., Inc., 1961.

Frazier, Alexander, ed., *Learning More About Learning*. Washington, D. C.: Association for Supervision and Curriculum Development, NEA, 1959.

Gordon, Ira J., and William D. Spears, "Interpersonal Perception: The Effect of Training in Perceptual Theory, Observations and Analysis of Behavior Upon Accuracy of Prediction of Children's Self Reports," USOE Cooperative Research Project No. 813. Gainesville: University of Florida, 1962.

Hall, Everett W., *Our Knowledge of Fact and Value*. Chapel Hill: The University of North Carolina Press, 1961.

Heider, Fritz, "On Social Cognition," *The American Psychologist*, XXII, No. 1 (1967), 25–31.

Kephart, Newell C., *The Slow Learner in the Classroom*. Columbus: Charles E. Merrill Publishing Company, 1960.

Koestler, Arthur, "Perception and Memory," in *The Act of Creation*, Book II, Chapter X, pp. 513–543. New York: The Macmillan Company, 1964.

Kubie, Lawrence S., "Research in Protecting Preconscious Functions in Education," in *Nurturing Individual Potential*, pp. 28–42, ed. Harry Passow. Washington, D. C.: Association for Supervision and Curriculum Development, NEA, 1964.

Langer, Susanne K., *Mind: An Essay on Human Feeling*, Vol. I. Baltimore: The Johns Hopkins Press, 1967.

Matson, Floyd, *The Broken Image: Man, Science, and Society*. New York: George Braziller, Inc., 1964.

Merleau-Ponty, Maurice, *The Primacy of Perception and Other Essays*, ed. James M. Edie. Evanston: Northwestern University Press, 1964.

Nash, Shirlyn, "Young Children's Perceptions of Decision Making in the Classroom." Milwaukee: School of Education, University of Wisconsin —Milwaukee, 1964 (mimeographed).

Oakeshott, Michael, *Experience and its Modes*. London: Cambridge University Press, 1933.

Phenix, Philip H., *Realms of Meaning*. New York: McGraw-Hill Book Company, 1964.

Polanyi, Michael, *The Tacit Dimension*. Garden City, N.Y.: Doubleday & Company, Inc., 1966.

Russell, David H., *Children's Thinking*. Waltham, Massachusetts: Blaisdell Publishing Company, a Division of Ginn and Company, 1956.

Sartre, Jean-Paul, *The Words*, trans. from the French by Bernard Frechtman. New York: George Braziller, Inc., and Librairie Gallimard, 1964.

Schachtel, Ernest, *Metamorphosis: On the Development of Affect, Perception, Attention, and Memory*. New York: Basic Books, Inc., Publishers, 1959.

Signell, K. A. "Cognitive Complexity in Person Perception and Nation Perception—A Developmental Approach," *Journal of Personality*, XXXIV (December, 1966), 517–537.

Singer, Jerome L., "Exploring Man's Imaginative World," *Teachers College Record*, LXVI (November, 1964), 165–179.

Stock, Dorothy, "Group Effects on Perceptual Behavior," Research Reprint Series of the National Training Laboratories, No. 7. Washington, D. C.: NEA (mimeographed).

Thomas, William I., and Florian Znaniecki, "Three Types of Personality," in *Images of Man*, pp. 405–436, ed. C. Wright Mills. New York: George Braziller, Inc., 1960. From "The Introduction" of "Life Record of an Immigrant," Vol. II, part IV, in *The Polish Peasant in Europe and America*, pp. 1831, 1837–38, 1850–1903. New York: Dover Publications, Inc., 1958.

Vernon, M. D., *The Psychology of Perception*. Baltimore: Penguin Books, Inc., 1962.

Wattenberg, William W., and Clare Clifford, "Relationship of the Self-Concept to Beginning Achievement in Reading," USOE Cooperative Research Project No. 377. Detroit: Wayne State University, 1962.

Whiteman, Marvin, "Children's Conceptions of Psychological Causality," *Child Development*, XXXVIII (March, 1967), 143–156.

Wolfson, Bernice J., and Shirlyn Nash, "Who Decides What in the Classroom?" *The Elementary School Journal*, LXV (July, 1965), 436–438.

"The Worlds of Perception," in *The World of Psychology*, Vol. I, part I, 3–229, ed. G. B. Levitas. New York: George Braziller, Inc., 1963.

Zalkind, Sheldon S., and Timothy W. Costello, "Perception: Some Recent Research and Implications for Administration," *Administrative Science Quarterly*, VII (September, 1962), 218–235.

CHAPTER FOUR
COMMUNICATING: THE SHARING OF PERSONAL MEANING

American Educational Research Association, *Review of Educational Research*, XXXVII (April,1967). Entire issue devoted to discussion of "Language Arts and Fine Arts," 105–214.

Anderson, James A., "Equivalence of Meaning Among Statements Presented Through Various Media," *AV Communication Review*, XIV, No. 4 (1966), 499.

Aschner, Mary Jane McCue, "Meaning and Thinking," in *Language and Meaning*, pp. 74–92, eds. James B. Macdonald and Robert R. Leeper. Washington, D. C.: Association for Supervision and Curriculum Development, NEA, 1966.

Bales, Robert, *Interaction Process Analysis*. Cambridge: Addison Wesley Publishing Co., Inc., 1961.

Barbara, Dominick A., "Nonverbal Communication," *Journal of Communication*, XIII (September, 1963), 166–173.

Barbara, Dominick A., *The Art of Listening*. Springfield, Illinois: Charles C. Thomas, Publisher, 1958.

Barnlund, Dean C., "Toward a Meaning-Centered Philosophy of Communication," *ETC*, XX (December, 1963), 454–469.

Baumgartel, Howard, "Some Human Problems in Interprofessional Communication," *Journal of Communication*, XIV (September, 1964), 172–182.

Bellack, Arno, ed., *Theory and Research in Teaching*. New York: Bureau of Publications, Teachers College, Columbia University, 1963.

Bellack, Arno A., and Joel R. Davitz, *The Language of the Classroom*. New York: Institute of Psychological Research; Bureau of Publications, Teachers College, Columbia University, 1963.

Benda, Clemens E., *The Image of Love. Modern Trends in Psychiatric Thinking*. New York: The Free Press of Glencoe, Inc., a Division of the Crowell-Collier Publishing Company, 1961.

Bereiter, Carl, and Siegfried Engelmann, *Teaching Disadvantaged Children in the Preschool*. Englewood Cliffs, N.J.: Prentice-Hall, Inc., 1966.

Berlo, David, *The Process of Communication*. New York: Holt, Rinehart & Winston, Inc., 1960.

Berman, Louise M., *From Thinking to Behaving: Assignments Reconsidered*, Practical Suggestions for Teaching, ed. Alice Miel. New York: Teachers College Press, Columbia University, 1967.

Broadbent, D. E., *Perception and Communication*. Oxford, N.Y.: Pergamon Press, Inc., 1958.

Cady, Edwin Laird, *Creative Communication*. New York: Reinhold Publishing Corp., 1956.

Carroll, Lewis (Charles Dodgson), *Alice's Adventures in Wonderland, Through the Looking Glass, and the Hunting of the Snark*. New York:

The Modern Library, Random House, Inc., 1925. Reprinted in David Berlo, *The Process of Communication.*

Carterette, Edward C., and Margaret Hubbard Jones, "Contextual Constraints in the Language of the Child," USOE Cooperative Research Project No. 1877. Los Angeles: University of California, 1965.

Cherry, Colin, *On Human Communication.* Cambridge: Massachusetts Institute of Technology, 1957.

Church, Joseph, *Language and the Discovery of Reality.* New York: Random House, Inc., 1961.

Communication and the Communication Arts. New York: Bureau of Publications, Teachers College, Columbia University, 1955.

Corbin, Richard, and Muriel Crosby, Co-chairmen, *Language Programs for the Disadvantaged,* The Report of the NCTE Task Force on Teaching English to the Disadvantaged. Champaign, Illinois: National Council of Teachers of English, 1965.

Dale, Edgar, "Instructional Resources," in *The Changing American School,* Chapter IV, pp. 84–109, ed. John Goodlad; The Sixty-fifth Yearbook of the National Society for the Study of Education, Part II. Chicago: University of Chicago Press, 1966.

Deeves, Evelyn, "Inundation by Media," *Educational Leadership,* XXIV (March, 1967), 540–545.

Department of Elementary School Principals, *The National Elementary Principal,* XXXVII (February, 1958), Special Section on "Communication," 12–36.

Deutsch, Martin, and Others, "Communication of Information in the Elementary School Classroom," USOE Cooperative Research Project No. 908. New York: Institute for Developmental Studies, Department of Psychiatry, New York Medical College, 1964.

Devine, Thomas G., "Chapter IV: Listening," *Review of Educational Research,* XXXVII (April, 1967), 152–158.

Dimitrovsky, Lilly, "The Ability to Identify the Emotional Meaning of Vocal Expressions at Successive Age Levels," in *The Communication of Emotional Meaning,* pp. 69–86, eds. Joel R. Davitz and Others. New York: McGraw-Hill Book Company, 1964.

Educational Policies Commission, *Mass Communication and Education.* Washington, D. C.: National Education Assn., 1958.

Eisenson, Jon, J. Jeffery Auer, and John V. Irwin, *The Psychology of Communication.* New York: Appleton-Century-Crofts, 1963.

Fry, C. L., "Training Children to Communicate to Listeners," *Child Development,* XXXVII (September, 1966), 675–685.

Gage, N. L., ed., *Handbook of Research on Teaching.* Chicago: Rand McNally & Co., 1963.

Galloway, Charles M., "Teacher Nonverbal Communication," *Educational Leadership,* XXIV (October, 1966), 55–63.

Gerbner, George, "A Theory of Communication and its Implications for Teaching," in *The Nature of Teaching: Implications for the Education of Teachers*, ed. Louise M. Berman. Milwaukee: University of Wisconsin—Milwaukee, 1963.

Goodlad, John, ed., *The Changing American School*, Part II, The Sixty-fifth Yearbook of the National Society for the Study of Education. Chicago: University of Chicago Press, 1966.

Gropper, George L., "Does 'Programmed' Television Need Active Responding?" *AV Communication Review*, XV, No. 1 (1967), 5–22.

Hall, Edward T., *The Silent Language*. New York: Premier Books, Fawcett Publications, Inc., 1959.

Hall, Edward T., and William Foote Whyte, "Intercultural Communication: A Guide to Men of Action," *Practical Anthropology*, X, No. 5 (1963), 216–232.

Halpin, Andrew W., "Muted Language," *The School Review*, LXVIII (September, 1960), 85–104.

Hammarskjöld, Dag, *Markings*. New York: Alfred A. Knopf, Inc., 1964.

Hayakawa, S. I. "Communication: Interracial and International," *ETC*, XX (December, 1963), 395–410.

Hayakawa, S. I., *Language in Thought and Action*. New York: Harcourt, Brace & World, Inc., 1949.

Hornstein, Marion G., "Accuracy of Emotional Communication and Interpersonal Compatibility," *Journal of Personality*, XXXV (March, 1967), 20–30.

Hovland, Carl I., Irving L. Janis, and Harold H. Kelley, *Communication and Persuasion*. New Haven: Yale University Press, 1953.

Howe, Reuel L., *The Miracle of Dialogue*. New York: The Seabury Press, Inc., 1963.

Hulett, J. Edward, Jr., "A Symbolic Interactionist Model of Human Communication, Part One: The General Model of Social Behavior; The Message-Generating Process," *AV Communication Review*, XIV, No. 1 (1966), 5–33.

Hulett, J. Edward, Jr., "A Symbolic Interactionist Model of Human Communication, Part Two: The Receiver's Function; Pathology of Communication; Noncommunication," *AV Communication Review*, XIV, No. 2 (1966), 203–220.

Hunter, Ernest L., "Articulation . . . for Continuity in the School Program," *The National Elementary Principal*, XLVI (January, 1967), 58–60.

Johnson, Craig, and Georg R. Klare, "General Models of Communication Research," *Journal of Communication*, XI (March, 1961), 13–26.

Kean, John M., "Schools, Children and Communication," *Educational Leadership*, XXIV (April, 1967), 618–623.

Kloman, William, "Aspects of Existential Communication," *Journal of Existentialism*, VI (Fall, 1965), 59–68.

Langer, Susanne K., *Philosophy in a New Key*. New York: Mentor Books, The New American Library, Inc., 1951.

Loban, Walter, "Language Ability in the Middle Grades of the Elementary School," USOE Cooperative Research Project No. 324. Berkeley: Department of Education, University of California, 1961.

Loban, Walter D., *The Language of Elementary School Children*. Champaign, Illinois: National Council of Teachers of English, 1963.

Mackintosh, Helen, ed., *Children and Oral Language*. Association for Childhood Education, International; Association for Supervision and Curriculum Development; International Reading Association; and National Council of Teachers of English, 1964.

MacLeod, Robert B., "Preface" to *Language and the Discovery of Reality*, by Joseph Church. New York: Random House, Inc., 1961.

Matson, Floyd, and Ashley Montagu, eds., *The Human Dialogue: Perspectives on Communication*. New York: The Free Press, 1967.

McLuhan, Herbert Marshall, *Understanding Media: The Extensions of Man*. New York: McGraw-Hill Book Company, 1964.

Mehling, Reuben, "The Lost Magic of Communication," *The Journal of Communication*, XIII (December, 1963), 215–216.

Miel, Alice, with Edwin Kiester, Jr., *The Shortchanged Children of Suburbia: What Schools Don't Teach About Human Differences and What Can Be Done About It*, Institute of Human Relations, Pamphlet Series No. 8. New York: The American Jewish Committee, 1967.

Mooney, Ross L. "Creation: Contemporary Culture and Renaissance," *The Journal of Creative Behavior*, I (July, 1967), 259–281.

Munkres, Alberta, *Helping Children in Oral Communication*. Practical Suggestions for Teaching, ed. Alice Miel. Bureau of Publications, Teachers College, Columbia University, 1959.

National Association of Secondary School Principals, *The Bulletin* of the NASSP, LI (April, 1967). Major portion of issue devoted to "The English Curriculum in the Secondary School," 2–126.

Oliver, Robert T., and Dominick A. Barbara, *The Healthy Mind in Communion and Communication*. Springfield, Illinois: Charles C. Thomas, Publisher, 1962.

Orten, Samuel Torrey, *Reading, Writing, and Speech Problems in Children*. New York: W. W. Norton & Company, Inc., 1937.

Pei, Mario, *The Story of Language*. New York: Mentor Books, The New American Library, Inc., 1949.

Raths, Louis E., "Clarifying Values," in *Curriculum for Today's Boys and Girls*, pp. 315–342, ed. Robert Fleming. Columbus: Charles E. Merrill Publishing Company, 1963.

Raths, Louis E., and Others, *Teaching for Thinking: Theory and Application*. Columbus: Charles E. Merrill Publishing Company, 1967.

Raths, Louis E., Merrill Harmin, and Sidney B. Simon, *Values and Teaching*. Columbus: Charles E. Merrill Publishing Company, 1966.

Riling, Mildred E., "Oral and Written Language of Children in Grades 4 and 6 Compared with the Language of Their Textbooks," USOE Cooperative Research Project No. 2410. Durant, Oklahoma: Southeastern State College, 1965.

Rubens, Jack L., moderator, "Distorted Communication in the Psychoneurotic: A Round Table Discussion," *The American Journal of Psychoanalysis*, XXII, No. 1 (1962), 89–104.

Ruesch, Jurgen, "The Role of Communication in Therapeutic Transactions," *The Journal of Communication*, XIII (September, 1963), 132–139.

Ruesch, Jurgen, *Therapeutic Communication*. New York: W. W. Norton & Company, Inc., 1961.

Ruesch, Jurgen, and Weldon Kees, *Nonverbal Communication: Notes on the Visual Perception of Human Relations*. Berkeley: University of California Press, 1959.

Sanders, Norris M., *Classroom Questions: What Kinds?* New York: Harper & Row, Publishers, 1966.

Sapir, Edward, *Language: An Introduction to the Study of Speech*. New York: Harvest Books, Harcourt, Brace & World, Inc., 1921 and 1949.

Sartre, Jean-Paul, *The Words*, trans. from the French by Bernard Frechtman. New York: George Braziller, Inc., and Librairie Gallimard, 1964.

Schramm, Wilbur Lang, *Mass Communications. A Book of Readings*. Urbana: University of Illinois, 1960.

Schramm, Wilbur Lang, *The Science of Human Communication*. New York: Basic Books, Inc., Publishers, 1963.

Shuy, Roger W., ed., "Social Dialects and Language Learning," A Report of a Conference Sponsored by Illinois Institute of Technology and the National Council of Teachers of English, USOE Cooperative Research Project No. F-059. Champaign: NCTE, 1964.

Smith, Dora V., *Communication: The Miracle of Shared Living*. New York: The Macmillan Company, 1955.

Staats, Arthur W., Carolyn K. Staats, and Richard E. Schutz, "The Development of Textual Behavior and its Function in Communication," USOE Cooperative Research Project No. 1048. Tempe, Arizona: Arizona State University, 1962.

Steinberg, Erwin R., ed., "Curriculum Development and Evaluation in English and Social Studies," A Report on the Research Development Conference for Personnel of USOE Curriculum Study Centers in English and Social Studies, USOE Cooperative Research Project No. F-041. Pittsburgh: Carnegie Institute of Technology, 1964.

Strickland, Ruth G., "Some Important Research Gaps in the Teaching of Elementary School Language Arts," in "Needed Research in the Teaching of English," pp. 10–13, ed. Erwin R. Steinberg, USOE Cooperative Research Project No. F-0007. Pittsburgh: Proceedings of a Conference Held at Carnegie Institute of Technology, May, 1962.

Virtue, Clark F., "Creativity and Symbolism," in *Creativity and Psychological Health*, pp. 55–73, ed., Michael F. Andrews. Syracuse: Syracuse University Press, 1961.

Vygotsky, Lev Semenovich, *Thought and Language*. trans. and ed. by Eugenia Hanfmann and Gertrude Vakar. Cambridge: The MIT Press, 1962.

Wagner, Robert W., "Machines, Media and Meaning," *Educational Leadership*, XXIII (March, 1966), 491–497.

Whatmough, Joshua, *Language: A Modern Synthesis*. New York: Mentor Books, The New American Library, Inc., 1956.

Work, William, "Developments in Speech," *The Bulletin of the National Association of Secondary School Principals*, LI (April, 1967), 39–46.

CHAPTER FIVE
LOVING: HUMAN EXPERIENCE AS CO-RESPONDING

Allport, Gordon W., *Personality and Social Encounter*. Boston: Beacon Press, 1960.

Ashley-Montagu, Montague F., *The Meaning of Love*. New York: Julian Press, Inc., 1953.

Bayley, John, *The Character of Love: A Study in the Literature of Personality*. New York: Collier Books, 1960.

Benda, Clemens E., *The Image of Love: Modern Trends in Psychiatric Thinking*. New York: The Free Press of Glencoe, Inc., a Division of the Crowell-Collier Publishing Company, 1961.

Berl, Emmanuel, *The Nature of Love*. New York: The Macmillan Company, 1924.

Berlin, I., "Love and Mastery in the Educational Process," *Educational Forum*, XXX (November, 1966), 43–49.

Berman, Louise M., ed., *The Humanities and the Curriculum*. Washington, D. C.: Association for Supervision and Curriculum Development, NEA, 1967.

Bion, Michael Sherwood, "Experiences in Groups: A Critical Evaluation," in *Human Relations: Studies Toward the Integration of the Social Studies*, XVII, No. 2 (May, 1964), 113–20. London: Tavistock Publications, 1964.

Bower, Eli M., "The Achievement of Competency," in *Learning and Mental Health in the School*, 1966 Yearbook of the Association for Supervision and Curriculum Development, eds. Walter B. Waetjen and Robert R. Leeper. Washington, D. C.: The Association, NEA, 1966.

Bowers, Norman D., and Robert S. Soar, "Studies of Human Relations in the Teaching-Learning Process, V, Final Report: Evaluation of Laboratory Human Relations Training for Classroom Teachers," USOE Coop-

erative Research Project No. 469. Columbia: University of South Carolina, and Chapel Hill: University of North Carolina, 1961.

Brunner, Emil, *Faith, Hope, and Love.* Philadelphia: The Westminster
Press, 1956.

Buber, Martin, *I and Thou,* Second Edition. New York: Charles Scribner's
Sons, 1958.

D'Arcy, M. C., S. J., *The Mind and Heart of Love.* Cleveland: Meridian
Books, The World Publishing Company, 1956.

Davitz, Joel R., and Others, *The Communication of Emotional Meaning.*
New York: McGraw-Hill Book Company, 1964.

Ferreira, Antonio, "Loneliness and Psychopathology," *The American Journal
of Psychoanalysis,* XXII, No. 2 (1962), 201–207.

Fletcher, Joseph, *Situation Ethics: The New Morality.* Philadelphia: The
Westminster Press, 1966.

Fromm, Eric, *The Art of Loving.* New York: Harper & Row, Publishers,
1956.

Fromme, Allan, *The Ability to Love.* New York: Farrar, Straus & Giroux,
Inc.; also Pocket Cardinal Edition, Pocket Books, 1965.

Great Religions of Modern Man, 6 Volumes. New York: George Braziller,
Inc., 1961.

Hammarskjöld, Dag, *Markings.* New York: Alfred A. Knopf, Inc., 1964.

Heider, Fritz, *The Psychology of Interpersonal Relations.* New York: John
Wiley & Sons, Inc., 1958.

Hora, Thomas, "The Epistemology of Love," *Journal of Existential Psychiatry,* now *Journal of Existentialism,* II (Winter, 1962), 303–312.

Jensen, Everett, "How Can I Learn to Love," in National Education Association, *Addresses and Proceedings of the One-Hundred-and-Second Annual Meeting Held at Seattle, Washington, June 28–July 3,* Vol. 102,
pp. 29–34. Washington, D. C.: NEA, 1964.

Katz, Robert L., *Empathy: Its Nature and Uses.* New York: The Free
Press of Glencoe, 1963.

Kierkegaard, Søren, *Works of Love.* New York: Harper Torchbooks, Harper
& Row, Publishers, 1962.

Lewis, C. S., *The Four Loves.* New York: Harcourt, Brace & World, Inc.,
1960.

Machotka, Otakar, *The Unconscious in Social Relations.* New York: Philosophical Library, Inc., 1964.

Maslow, Abraham H., *Eupsychian Management: A Journal.* Homewood,
Illinois: Richard D. Irwin, Inc., and the Dorsey Press, 1965.

Menninger, Karl A., *Love Against Hate.* New York: Harcourt Brace &
World, Inc., 1942.

Menninger, Karl A., *The Vital Balance.* New York: The Viking Press, Inc.,
1963.

Miles, Matthew B., "Human Relations Training and Current Status," in
Selected Reading Series, Five: Issues in Training, pp. 3–13, eds.

Irving R. Wechsler and Edgar H. Schein. Washington, D. C.: National Training Laboratories, NEA, 1962. Revised version of paper read at the 14th International Congress of Applied Psychology, Copenhagen, August, 1961.

Morgan, Douglas N., *Love: Plato, The Bible, and Freud.* Englewood Cliffs, N. J.: Spectrum Books, Prentice-Hall, Inc., 1964.

Moustakas, Clark E., *Loneliness.* Englewood Cliffs, N. J.: Prentice-Hall, Inc., 1961.

Otto, Herbert A., ed., *Explorations in Human Potentialities.* Springfield, Illinois: Charles C. Thomas, Publisher, 1966.

Pfuetze, Paul E., *Self, Society, Existence.* New York: Harper Torchbooks, Harper & Brothers, Publishers, 1954.

Phillips, Derek L., "Social Participation and Happiness," *The American Journal of Sociology,* LXXII, No. 5 (March, 1967), 479.

Reik, Theodor, *The Need to be Loved.* New York: Farrar, Straus & Giroux, Inc., 1963.

Rogers, Carl R., "The Loneliness of Contemporary Man," *Review of Existential Psychology and Psychiatry,* I (May, 1961), 94–101.

Rogers, Vincent, "Developing Sensitivity and Concern in Children," *Social Education,* XXXI (April, 1967), 299.

Rogers, Vincent, "Exploratory Study of the Development of Sociological Sensitivity in Elementary School Children," *Journal of Educational Research,* LIX (May, 1966), 392–394.

Rubins, Jack L., "On the Psychopathology of Loneliness," *The American Journal of Psychoanalysis,* XXIV, No. 2 (1964), 153–166.

Scheler, M., *The Nature of Sympathy,* trans. by P. Heath. London: Routledge and Kegan Paul, 1954.

Schneider, Isidor, *The World of Love,* 2 Volumes. New York: George Braziller, Inc., 1964.

Scoppettone, Sandra, *The Wonderful Adventures of Suzuki Beane.* New York: Macfadden Books, 1961.

Tewskbury, John L., *Nongrading in the Elementary School.* Columbus: Charles E. Merrill Publishing Company, 1967.

Tillich, Paul, *Love, Power, and Justice.* New York: Oxford University Press, 1954.

Ward, Hiley H., *Creative Giving.* New York: The Macmillan Company, 1958.

Weigert, Edith, "The Role of Sympathy in the Psychotherapeutic Process," *The American Journal of Psychoanalysis,* XXII, No. 1 (1962), 3–14.

Wood, Margaret Mary, *Paths of Loneliness.* New York: Columbia University Press, 1953.

Zander, Alvin, and Elmer Van Egmond, "Effects of Children's Social Power and Intelligence on their Interpersonal Relations," USOE Cooperative Research Project No. 99. Ann Arbor, Michigan: Research Center for Group Dynamics, Institute for Social Research, The University of

Michigan, September, 1957. Summarized in the *Journal of Educational Psychology*, XLIX, No. 5 (1950), 257–268.

CHAPTER SIX

KNOWING: THE METAMORPHOSIS OF IDEAS

Almy, Millie, "Intellectual Mastery and Mental Health," *Teachers College Record*, Perspectives 1961–1962, pp. 54–64.

Association for Supervision and Curriculum Development, *What Are the Sources of the Curriculum?: A Symposium*. Washington, D. C.: The Association, NEA, 1962.

Banerjee, Nikunja Vihari, *Language, Meaning, and Persons*. London: G. Allen and Unwin, 1963.

Beberman, Max, and Herbert E. Vaughan, "Mathematics Text Makes News," Course I, Announcement of *High School Mathematics*. Boston: D. C. Heath & Company, 1964.

Bellack, Arno A., "What Knowledge Is of Most Worth?" *The High School Journal*, XLVIII (February, 1965), 315–363.

Berelson, Bernard, ed., *The Behavioral Sciences Today*. New York: Harper Torchbooks, Harper & Row, Publishers, 1963.

Berlyne, D. E., and F. D. Frommer, "Some Determinants of the Incidence and Content of Children's Questions," *Child Development*, XXXVII (March, 1966), 177–190.

Bohanan, Paul, "Anthropology," Publication No. 106 of the Social Science Education Consortium, USOE Cooperative Research Program. Lafayette, Indiana: Purdue University, 1966.

Broudy, Harry S., "Contemporary Art and Aesthetic Education," *The School Review*, LXXII (Autumn, 1964), 394–411. Reprinted in *Professional Reprints in Education*, No. 8005. Columbus: Charles E. Merrill Publishing Company.

Broudy, Harry S., "Knowledge and the Curriculum," Lecture II. Washington, D. C.: National Education Assn., 1964 (mimeographed).

Broudy, Harry S., "The Nature of Knowledge and the Uses of Schooling," Lecture I. Washington, D. C.: National Education Assn., 1964 (mimeographed).

Broudy, Harry S., "The Teacher as the Mediator of Knowledge," Washington, D. C.: National Education Assn., 1964 (mimeographed).

Bruner, Jerome S., "Man: A Course of Study," in *ESI Quarterly Report*, pp. 85–95. Watertown, Mass.: Education Development Center, Summer–Fall, 1965.

Bruner, Jerome S., *On Knowing: Essays for the Left Hand*. Cambridge: Harvard University Press, 1962.

Bruner, Jerome S., *The Process of Education*. Cambridge: Harvard University Press, 1961.

Carin, Arthur, and Robert B. Sund, *Discovery Teaching in Science.* Columbus: Charles E. Merrill Publishing Company, 1966.

Carroll, John B., "Words, Meanings and Concepts," *Harvard Educational Review,* XXXIV, No. 2 (1964), 178–202.

Clark, James V., *Education for the Use of Behavioral Science.* Los Angeles: University of California, 1962.

Denemark, George W., "Concept Learning: Some Implications for Teaching," *Liberal Education* (March, 1965), 54–69. Reprinted in *Professional Reprints in Education,* No. 8821. Columbus: Charles E. Merrill Publishing Company.

Denemark, George W., "The Curriculum Challenge of Our Times," *NEA Journal,* L (December, 1961), 12–14. Reprinted in *Professional Reprints in Education.* Columbus: Charles E. Merrill Publishing Company.

Deutsch, Martin, "Some Psychosocial Aspects of Learning in the Disadvantaged," *Teachers College Record,* LXVII (January, 1966), 260–266.

Dewey, John, *Nature and Experience,* quoted in *Intelligence in the Modern World,* ed. Joseph Ratner. New York: Random House, Inc., 1939.

Elam, Stanley, ed., *Education and the Structure of Knowledge.* Chicago: Rand McNally & Co., 1964.

Elkins, Keith, and Martha Porter, "Classroom Research on Subgroup Experiences in a U.S. History Class," Publication No. 114 of the Social Science Education Consortium, USOE Cooperative Research Program. Lafayette, Indiana: Purdue University, 1966.

ESI Quarterly. Watertown, Mass.: Education Development Center, Summer–Fall, 1965.

Ford, G. W., and Lawrence Pugno, eds., *The Structure of Knowledge and the Curriculum.* Chicago: Rand McNally & Co., 1964.

Foshay, Arthur W., "A Modest Proposal for the Improvement of Education," in *What Are the Sources of the Curriculum? A Symposium,* pp. 1–13, Washington, D. C.: Association for Supervision and Curriculum Development, NEA, 1962.

Fox, Robert S., Ronald Lippitt, and John E. Lohman, "Teaching of Social Science Material in the Elementary School," USOE Cooperative Research Project No. E-011. Ann Arbor: The University of Michigan, 1964.

Frazier, Alexander, ed., *New Insights and the Curriculum,* 1963 Yearbook. Washington, D. C.: Association for Supervision and Curriculum Development, NEA, 1963.

Friedlander, B. Z, "A Psychologist's Second Thoughts on Concepts, Curiosity, and Discovery in Teaching and Learning," *Harvard Educational Review,* XXXV (Winter, 1965), 18–37.

Goodlad, John I., Renata von Stoephasius, and M. Frances Klein, *The Changing School Curriculum.* New York: The Fund for the Advancement of Education, 1966.

Greco, Peter, "Geography," Publication No. 102 of the Social Science Education Consortium, USOE Cooperative Research Program. Lafayette, Indiana: Purdue University, 1966.

Haber-Schaim, Uri, "Objectives and Content of the Course," in *Introductory Physical Science: A Brief Description of a New Course.* Watertown, Mass.: Education Development Center, 1964 (Preliminary Edition).

Hall, Everett Wesley, *Our Knowledge of Fact and Value.* Chapel Hill: University of North Carolina Press, 1961.

Hartland-Swann, John, *An Analysis of Knowing.* London: G. Allen and Unwin, 1958.

Heath, Robert W., ed., *New Curricula.* New York: Harper & Row, Publishers, 1964.

Henle, Robert J., *A Meditation about Knowing,* Bode Memorial Lectures, 1964. Columbus: The College of Education, Ohio State University, 1966.

Hill, Thomas English, *Contemporary Theories of Knowledge.* New York: The Ronald Press Company, 1961.

Hintikka, Kaarlo Jaakko Juhani, *Knowledge and Belief.* Ithaca, N. Y.: Cornell University Press, 1962.

Huebner, Dwayne, ed., *A Reassessment of the Curriculum.* New York: Bureau of Publications, Teachers College, Columbia University, 1964.

Innovation and Experiment in Education, Panel on Educational Research and Development. Washington, D. C.: United States Government Printing Office, 1964.

Jarolimek, John, and Huber M. Walsh, eds., *Readings for Social Studies in Elementary Education.* New York: The Macmillan Company, 1965.

Jenkins, William A., ed., *The Nature of Knowledge: Implications for the Education of Teachers.* Milwaukee: University of Wisconsin—Milwaukee, 1962.

Johnson, Donald M., "Cognitive Structures and Intellectual Processes," in *Intellectual Development: Another Look,* pp. 27–39, eds. A. Harry Passow and Robert R. Leeper. Washington, D. C.: Association for Supervision and Curriculum Development, NEA, 1964.

Johnson, Earl S., "Ways of Knowing," in *The Nature of Knowledge: Implications for the Education of Teachers,* pp. 16–26, William Jenkins. Milwaukee: School of Education, University of Wisconsin—Milwaukee, 1962. Reprinted in *Professional Reprints in Education,* No. 8000. Columbus: Charles E. Merrill Publishing Company.

Jones, Philip Chapin, *The Nature of Knowledge.* New York: Scarecrow Press, Inc., 1964.

Jung, Charles, and Others, "Retrieving Social Science Knowledge for Secondary Curriculum Development," Publication No. 109 of the Social Science Education Consortium, USOE Cooperative Research Program. Lafayette, Indiana: Purdue University, 1966.

King, Arthur R., Jr., and John A. Brownell, *The Curriculum and the Disciplines of Knowledge: A Theory of Curriculum Practice.* New York: John Wiley & Sons, Inc., 1966.

Kliebard, Herbert, "Structure of the Disciplines: A New Slogan," *Teachers College Record,* LXVI (April, 1965), 598–603.

Kollins, C. D., ed., *Knowledge and Experience,* Oberlin Colloquium in Philosophy. Pittsburgh: University of Pittsburgh Press, 1962.

Krippner, Stanley, "Reading Instruction and Existential Philosophy," *Review of Existential Psychology and Psychiatry,* V (Winter, 1965), 60–79.

Loretan, Joseph O., and Shelley Umans, *Teaching the Disadvantaged: New Curriculum Approaches.* New York: Teachers College Press, Teachers College, Columbia University, 1966.

Maccia, Elizabeth Steiner, "The Nature of a Discipline-Centered Curricular Approach," Occasional Paper 64–166. Part of USOE Cooperative Research Program, Project HS-082. n.p., n.d.

Mackinnon, D. W., "The Nature of Creativity," in *Creativity and College Teaching.* Lexington, Kentucky: College of Education, University of Kentucky, 1963.

Malcolm, Norman, *Knowledge and Certainty.* Englewood Cliffs, N. J.: Prentice-Hall, Inc., 1963.

Maritain, Jacques, *The Degrees of Knowledge.* New York: Charles Scribner's Sons, 1938.

Massialas, Byron G., and C. Benjamin Cox, *Inquiry in Social Studies.* New York: McGraw-Hill Book Company, 1966.

Matson, Floyd W., *The Broken Image: Man, Science, and Society.* New York: George Braziller, Inc., 1964.

"Men and Ideas: ESI's Social Studies and Humanities Program," A Conversation with Elting Morison in *ESI Quarterly Report,* p. 37. Watertown, Mass.: Education Development Center, Winter, 1962–1963.

Morrissett, Irving, ed., *Concepts and Structure in the New Social Science Curricula.* West Lafayette, Indiana: Social Science Education Consortium, Inc., 1966.

Mumford, Lewis, "The Automation of Knowledge," *AV Communication Review,* XII (Fall, 1964), 261–276. Reprinted in *Professional Reprints in Education,* No. 8011. Columbus: Charles E. Merrill Publishing Company.

National Education Association, *Current Curriculum Studies in Academic Subjects,* The Project on the Instructional Program of the Public Schools. Washington, D. C.: The Association, 1962.

National Education Association, *Deciding What to Teach,* The Project on the Instructional Program of the Public Schools. Washington, D. C.: The Association, 1963.

National Education Association, *The Scholars Look at the Schools,* The Project on the Instructional Program of the Public Schools. Washington, D. C.: The Association, 1962.

Nietz, John A., *The Evolution of American Secondary School Textbooks.* Rutland, Vermont: Charles E. Tuttle Co., Inc., 1966.

Noll, James, "Humanism as a Method," *Educational Forum* (May, 1964), pp. 489–495. Reprinted in *Professional Reprints in Education,* No. 8819. Columbus: Charles E. Merrill Publishing Company.

Oakeshott, Michael, *Experience and Its Modes.* London: Cambridge University Press, 1933 and 1966.

Oliver, Donald W., and James P. Shaver, *Teaching Public Issues in the High School.* Boston: Houghton Mifflin Company, 1966.

Passow, Harry A., ed., *Curriculum Crossroads,* Bureau of Publications, Teachers College, Columbia University, 1962.

Patterson, Franklin K., *Man and Politics: Curriculum Models for Junior High School Social Studies,* Occasional Paper No. 4. Watertown, Mass.: Education Development Center, 1965.

Perrucci, Robert, "Sociology," Publication No. 101 of the Social Science Education Consortium, USOE Cooperative Research Program. Lafayette, Indiana: Purdue University, 1966.

Phenix, Philip H., *Realms of Meaning: A Philosophy of the Curriculum for General Education.* New York: McGraw-Hill Book Company, 1964.

Polanyi, Michael, *Personal Knowledge: Towards a Post-Critical Philosophy.* Chicago: The University of Chicago Press, 1958.

Ratner, Joseph, ed., *Intelligence in the Modern World: John Dewey's Philosophy.* New York: Random House, Inc., 1939.

Reid, Louis Arnaud, *Ways of Knowledge and Experience.* London: G. Allen and Unwin, 1961.

Rosenbloom, Paul C., ed., *Modern Viewpoints in the Curriculum.* New York: McGraw-Hill Book Company, 1964.

Ryle, Gilbert, *The Concept of Mind.* New York: Barnes & Noble, Inc., 1949.

Samler, Joseph, "The School and Self-Understanding," *Harvard Educational Review,* XXXV, No. 1 (1965), 55–70.

Schwab, Joseph J., "The Concept of the Structure of Discipline," *The Educational Record,* XLIII (July, 1962), 197–205. Reprinted in *Professional Reprints in Education,* No. 8001. Columbus: Charles E. Merrill Publishing Company.

Senesh, Lawrence, "Economics," Publication No. 105 of the Social Science Education Consortium, USOE Cooperative Research Program. Lafayette, Indiana: Purdue University, 1966.

Senesh, Lawrence, *Our Working World. Families at Work.* Chicago: Resource Unit, Science Research Associates, Inc., 1964.

Shulman, Lee S., and Evan R. Keislar, *Learning by Discovery: A Critical Appraisal.* Chicago: Rand McNally & Co., 1966.

Soderquist, Harold O., *The Person and Education.* Columbus: Charles E. Merrill Publishing Company, 1964.

Steinberg, Erwin R., ed., "Curriculum Development and Evaluation in English and Social Studies," A report on the Research and Development

Conference for Personnel of USOE Curriculum Study Centers in English and Social Studies, USOE Cooperative Research Project No. F-041. Pittsburgh: Carnegie Institute of Technology, 1964.

Steinberg, Erwin R., ed., "Needed Research in the Teaching of English," USOE Cooperative Research Project No. F-007. Pittsburgh: Carnegie Institute of Technology, 1962.

Stern, Carolyn, and Evan R. Keislar, "Acquisition of Problem Solving Strategies by Young Children, and Its Relation to Mental Age," *American Educational Research Journal*, IV (January, 1967), 1–12.

The Structure of Knowledge and the Nature of Inquiry, State Department of Education. Salem, Oregon: Division of Education Development, 1965.

Suchman, Richard, "Inquiry Training: Building Skills for Autonomous Discovery," *Merrill Palmer Quarterly*, VII (July, 1961), 147–169.

Suchman, Richard, "Inquiry Training in the Elementary School," *The Science Teacher*, XXVII (November, 1960), 42–47.

Taulmin, S., *Philosophy of Science*, p. 13. London: Hutchinson University Library, 1953.

Thelen, Herbert A., *Education and the Human Quest*. New York: Harper & Brothers, Publishers, 1960.

Thelen, Herbert A., "Insights for Teaching from a Theory of Interaction," in *The Nature of Teaching: Implications for the Education of Teachers*, pp. 19–31, ed. Louise M. Berman. Milwaukee: University of Wisconsin—Milwaukee, 1963.

Thelen, Herbert A., "Pupil Self-Direction," *Bulletin of the National Association of Secondary School Principals*, L (April, 1966), 99–109.

Tykociner, Joseph T., "Zetetics and Areas of Knowledge," in *Education and the Structure of Knowledge*, pp. 121–147, ed. Stanley Elam, Fifth Annual Phi Delta Kappa Symposium on Educational Research. Chicago: Rand McNally & Co., 1964.

Tyler, Ralph W., "The Interrelationship of Knowledge," *The National Elementary Principal*, XLIII (February, 1964), 13–21. Reprinted in *Professional Reprints in Education*, No. 8004. Columbus: Charles E. Merrill Publishing Company.

Tyler, Ralph W., "The Knowledge Explosion: Implications for Secondary Education," *The Educational Forum*, XXIX (January, 1965), 145–153.

Unruh, Glenys, ed., *New Curriculum Developments*. Washington, D. C.: Association for Supervision and Curriculum Development, NEA, 1965.

Weigel, Gustave, S. J., and Arthur G. Madden, *Knowledge: Its Values and Limits*. Englewood Cliffs, New Jersey: Prentice-Hall, Inc., 1961.

CHAPTER SEVEN

DECISION MAKING: THE PRESENT AS TURNING POINT BETWEEN PAST AND FUTURE

Berman, Louise M., *From Thinking to Behaving: Assignments Reconsidered*, Practical Suggestions for Teachers, ed., Alice Miel. New York: Teachers College Press, Teachers College, Columbia University, 1967.

Blake, Robert R., and Leland P. Bradford, "Decisions . . . Decisions . . . Decisions!" in *Selected Reading Series, One: Group Development*, pp. 69–72, ed. Leland P. Bradford. Washington, D. C.: National Training Laboratories, NEA, 1961. Reprinted from *Adult Leadership*, II, No. 7 (1963).

Boelen, Bernard J., "Martin Heidegger's Approach to Will, Decision, and Responsibility," *Review of Existential Psychology and Psychiatry*, I (November, 1961), 197–204.

Braybrooke, David, and Charles E. Lindblom, *A Strategy of Decision: Policy Evaluation as a Social Process*. Glencoe: The Free Press of Glencoe, 1963.

Brim, Orville G., and Others, *Personality and Decision Processes*. Stanford: Stanford University Press, 1962.

Cabot, Hugh, and Joseph A. Kahl, *Human Relations: Concepts and Cases in Concrete Social Science*, Part I. Cambridge: Harvard University Press, 1956.

Child, I. L., and Whiting, J. W. M., "Determinants of Level of Aspiration: Evidence from Everyday Life," in *The Study of Personality*, pp. 495–508, ed. H. Brand. New York: John Wiley & Sons, Inc., 1954.

Cooper, Joseph D., *The Art of Decision Making*. Garden City: Doubleday & Company, Inc., 1961.

Dill, William K., "Decision Making," in *Behavioral Science and Educational Administration*, pp. 199–222, ed. Daniel E. Griffiths. Sixty-third Yearbook of the National Society for the Study of Education, Part II. Chicago: University of Chicago Press, 1964.

Dilley, Josiah S., "Decision Making Ability and Vocational Maturity," *The Personnel and Guidance Journal*, XLIV (December, 1967), 423–427.

Doll, Ronald C., *Curriculum Improvement: Decision-Making and Process*. Boston: Allyn & Bacon, Inc., 1964.

Engle, Shirley H., "Decision-Making: The Heart of Social Studies Instruction," in *Readings for Social Studies in Elementary Education*, pp. 195–202, eds. John Jarolimek and Huber M. Walsh. New York: The Macmillan Company, 1965. Reprinted from *Social Education*, XXIV (November, 1960), 301–304.

Fletcher, Joseph, *Situation Ethics: The New Morality*. Philadelphia: The Westminster Press, 1966.

Friedman, Maurice, "Will, Decision, and Responsibility in the Thought of Martin Buber," *Review of Existential Psychology and Psychiatry*, I (November, 1961), 217–227.

Gelatt, H. B., "Decision-Making: A Conceptual Frame of Reference for Counselling," *Journal of Counselling Psychology*, IX, No. 3 (1962), 246–251.

Gerard, H. B., "Choice Difficulty, Dissonance, and the Decision Sequence," *Journal of Personality*, XXXV (March, 1967), 91–108.

Griffiths, Daniel E., *Administrative Theory*. New York: Appleton-Century-Crofts, 1959.

Hack, Walter G., and Others, eds., *Educational Administration: Selected Readings*. Boston: Allyn & Bacon, Inc., 1965.

Herrick, Virgil E., "Teaching as Curriculum Decision Making," in *The Nature of Teaching: Implications for the Education of Teachers*, pp. 66–80, ed., Louise M. Berman. Milwaukee: School of Education, University of Wisconsin–Milwaukee, 1963.

Hilton, Thomas L., Chief Investigator, "Cognitive Processes in Career Decision-Making," USOE Cooperative Research Study No. 1046. Pittsburgh: Carnegie Institute of Technology, 1962.

Hood, Bruce L., "Human Nature, Existentialism, and Education," *The University of Kansas Bulletin of Education*, XX (May, 1966), 99–109.

Jacob, Philip E., and James J. Flink, "Values and Their Function in Decision Making," *American Behavioral Scientist Supplement*, V (May, 1962), 5–34.

Keller, Paul, W., "The Study of Face to Face International Decision-Making," *Journal of Communication*, XIII, No. 2 (1963), 67–75.

Kimbrough, Ralph B., *Political Power and Educational Decision-Making*, Chicago: Rand McNally & Co., 1964.

Lewin, Kurt, "Group Decision and Social Change," *Readings in Social Psychology*, Third Edition, pp. 197-211, eds. Eleanor E. Maccoby, Theodore M. Newcomb, and Eugene L. Hartley. New York: Henry Holt and Company, 1958.

Lippitt, Gordon L., "Improving Decision Making with Groups," in *Selected Reading Series, One: Group Development*, pp. 90–93, ed. L. P. Bradford. Washington, D. C.: National Training Laboratories, NEA, 1961. Reprinted from *Y Work with Youth* (April, 1958).

Litchfield, Edward H., "Notes on a General Theory of Administration," in *Educational Administration: Selected Readings*, pp. 313–337, eds. Walter G. Hack and Others. Boston: Allyn & Bacon, Inc., 1965. Originally in *Administration Science Quarterly*, I (June, 1956), 3–29.

May, Rollo, "Will, Decision, and Responsibility: Summary Remarks," *Review of Existential Psychology and Psychiatry*, I (November, 1961), 249–259.

Messick, Samuel, and Arthur H. Brayfield, eds., *Decision and Choice: Contributions of Sidney Siegel*. New York: McGraw-Hill Book Company, 1964.

Miel, Alice, "Knowledge and the Curriculum," in *New Insights and the Curriculum*, pp. 71–104, ed. Alexander Frazier, 1963 Yearbook. Washington, D. C.: Association for Supervision and Curriculum Development, NEA, 1963.

Miller, Van, "Inner Direction and the Decision Maker," in *Educational Administration: Selected Readings*, eds. Walter G. Hack and Others. Boston: Allyn & Bacon, Inc., 1965.

Mills, Judson, and Richard Snyder, "Avoidance of Commitment: Need for Closure, and the Expression of Choice," *Journal of Psychology*, XXX (March–December, 1962), 458ff.

Nash, Paul, *Authority and Freedom in Education: An Introduction to the Philosophy of Education*. New York: John Wiley & Sons, Inc., 1966.

Nash, Shirlyn, "Young Children's Perceptions of Decision-Making in the Classroom." Milwaukee: School of Education, University of Wisconsin–Milwaukee, 1964 (mimeographed).

Oliver, Donald W., and James P. Shaver, *Teaching Public Issues in the High School*. Boston: Houghton Mifflin Company, 1966.

Parsons, Talcott, "Suggestions for a Sociological Approach to the Theory of Organizations: I," *Administrative Science Quarterly*, I, No. 1 (June, 1956), 63–85.

Pelz, Edith Bennett, "Some Factors in 'Group Decision,' " in *Readings in Social Psychology*, Third Edition, pp. 212–219, eds. Eleanor E. Maccoby, Theodore M. Newcomb, and Eugene L. Hartley. New York: Henry Holt and Company, 1958.

Salfield, D. J., "Decision," *Journal of Existential Psychiatry*, IV (Fall, 1963), 151–158.

Seymour, Melman, *Decision Making and Productivity*. New York: John Wiley & Sons, Inc., 1958.

Shackle, George Lennox Sharman, *Decision, Order, and Time in Human Affairs*. London: Cambridge University Press, 1961.

Simon, Herbert, *Administrative Behavior*. New York: The Macmillan Company, 1950.

Sutherland, Richard L., "Choosing—as Therapeutic Aim, Method, and Philosophy," *Journal of Existential Psychiatry*, now *Journal of Existentialism*, II (Spring, 1962), 371–392.

Thrall, Robert McDowell, ed., *Decision Processes*. New York: John Wiley & Sons, Inc., 1966.

Trueblood, D. Elton, "Deciding for the Difficult," in *Education for Decision*, pp. 31–42, eds. Frank E. Gaebelein, Earl G. Harrison, Jr., and William L. Swing. New York: The Seabury Press, Inc., 1963.

Wasserman P., and F. S. Silander. *Decision-Making: An Annotated Bibliography.* Ithaca, New York: Cornell University Press, 1958.

Willner, Dorothy, *Decisions, Values and Groups.* Oxford, N.Y.: Symposium Publications Division, Pergamon Press, Inc., 1960.

Wolfson, Bernice J., and Shirlyn Nash, "Who Decides What in the Classroom?" *The Elementary School Journal,* LXV (May, 1965), 436–438.

CHAPTER EIGHT
PATTERNING: SYSTEMATIZING OF HUMAN EXPERIENCE

Barron, Frank, "Creative Vision and Expression," in *New Insights and the Curriculum,* 1963 Yearbook, pp. 285–305, ed. Alexander Frazier. Washington, D. C.: Association for Supervision and Curriculum Development, NEA, 1963.

Barron, Frank, "The Needs for Order and for Disorder as Motives in Creative Activity," in *Scientific Creativity: Its Recognition and Development,* pp. 155–160, eds. Calvin W. Taylor and Frank Barron. New York: John Wiley & Sons, Inc., 1963.

Barron, Frank, "The Psychology of Imagination," *Scientific American,* IX (September, 1958), 150–166. Reprinted in *A Source Book for Creative Thinking,* pp. 227–237, eds. Sidney J. Parnes and Harold F. Harding. New York: Charles Scribner's Sons, 1962.

Berlyne, D. E., "Recent Developments in Piaget's Work," in *The Cognitive Processes: Readings,* pp. 311–323, eds. Robert J. C. Harper and Others. Englewood Cliffs, N. J.: Prentice-Hall, Inc., 1964.

Berman, Harold J., and William R. Greiner, *The Nature and Functions of Law.* Brooklyn: The Foundation Press, Inc., 1966.

Berman, Louise M., *Creativity in Education: A Guide to a Television Series.* Milwaukee: Milwaukee Public Schools, 1963.

Bower, Eli M., "Personality and Individual Social Maladjustment," in Social Deviancy among Youth, Sixty-fifth Yearbook of the National Society for the Study of Education, Part I. Chicago: The University of Chicago Press, 1966.

Bruner, Jerome S., Jacqueline J. Goodnow, and George A. Austin, *A Study of Thinking.* New York: Science Editions, Inc., 1962. Also, New York: John Wiley & Sons, Inc., 1956.

Bruner, Jerome S., and Helen J. Kenney, "On Multiple Ordering," in *Studies in Cognitive Growth,* pp. 154–167, eds. Jerome S. Bruner, Rose R. Olver, and Patricia M. Greenfield. New York: John Wiley & Sons, Inc., 1966.

Center for the Study of Instruction, *Rational Planning in Curriculum and Instruction.* Washington, D. C.: National Education Assn., 1967.

Collier, David, "The Political System," Publication No. 103 of the Social Science Education Consortium, USOE Cooperative Research Program. Lafayette, Indiana: Purdue University, 1966.

Darrow, Helen Fisher, and R. Van Allen, *Independent Activities for Creative Learning*, Practical Suggestions for Teachers, Number, 21, ed. Alice Miel. New York: Bureau of Publications, Teachers College, Columbia University, 1961.

De Carlo, Charles, "Educational Technology and Value Systems," *Motive*, XXVII (March/April, 1967), 19–25.

Dewey, John, *The Child and the Curriculum and the School and Society*. Chicago: The University of Chicago Press, 1902.

Easton, David, "A Systems Approach to Political Life," Publication No. 104 of the Social Science Education Consortium, USOE Cooperative Research Program. Lafayette, Indiana: Purdue University, 1966.

Eikenberry, Alice, and Ruth Ellsworth, "Organizing and Evaluating Information," in *Skill Development in Social Studies*, ed. Helen McCracken Carpenter, Thirty-third Yearbook of the National Council for the Social Studies. Washington, D. C.: National Education Assn., 1963.

Freund, Paul A., "The Law and the Schools," *Harvard Educational Review*, XXXVI, No. 4 (1966), 470–476.

Frymier, Jack R., *The Nature of Educational Method*. Columbus: Charles E. Merrill Publishing Company, 1965.

Ghiselin, Brewster, ed., *The Creative Process: A Symposium*. New York: A Mentor Book, by arrangement with the University of California Press, 1952.

Ghiselin, Brewster, Roger Rompel, and Calvin W. Taylor, "A Creative Process Check List: Its Development and Validation," in *Widening Horizons in Creativity*, pp. 19–23, ed. Calvin Taylor. New York: John Wiley & Sons, Inc., 1964.

Gordon, Ira J., "New Conceptions of Children's Learning and Development," in *Learning and Mental Health in the School*, 1966 Yearbook, pp. 49–73, eds. Walter B. Waetjen and Robert R. Leeper. Washington, D. C.: Association for Supervision and Curriculum Development, NEA, 1966.

Hollister, William G., M.D., "Preparing the Minds of the Future: Enhancing Ego Processes through Curriculum Development," in *Curriculum Change: Direction and Process*, pp. 27–42, ed. Robert R. Leeper. Washington, D. C.: Association for Supervision and Curriculum Development, NEA, 1966.

Humphrey, Doris, *The Art of Making Dances*. New York: Rinehart & Company, Inc., 1959.

Jennings, Frank G., "Jean Piaget: Notes on Learning," *Saturday Review*, L (May 20, 1967), 81–83.

Kamii, Constance K., and Norma L. Radin, "A Framework for a Preschool

Curriculum Based on Some Piagetian Concepts," *The Journal of Creative Behavior*, I (July, 1967), 314–324.

Krathwohl, David R., Benjamin S. Bloom, and Bertram B. Masia, *Taxonomy of Educational Objectives, The Classification of Educational Goals, Handbook II: Affective Domain.* New York: David McKay Company, Inc., 1964.

Mednick, Sarnoff A., and Martha T. Mednick, "An Associative Interpretation of the Creative Process," in *Widening Horizons in Creativity*, pp. 54–68, ed. Calvin W. Taylor. New York: John Wiley & Sons, Inc., 1964.

Menninger, Karl, *The Vital Balance.* New York: The Viking Press, Inc., 1963.

Mooney, Ross L., "Creation: Contemporary Culture and Renaissance," *The Journal of Creative Behavior*, I (July, 1967), 259–281.

Perrucci, Robert, "Sociology," Publication No. 101 of the Social Science Education Consortium, USOE Cooperative Research Program. Lafayette, Indiana: Purdue University, 1966.

Piaget, Jean, *The Language and Thought of the Child*, Chapter 5, trans. M. Gabain. New York: Humanities Press, 1926. Reprinted in *New Classics in Psychology*, pp. 994–1031, ed. Thorne Shipley. New York: Philosophical Library, Inc., 1961.

Polanyi, Michael, *The Tacit Dimension.* Garden City, N. Y.: Doubleday & Company, Inc., 1966.

Read, Sir Herbert, *The Forms of Things Unknown.* New York: Horizon Press, 1960.

Sigel, Irving, "Child Development and Social Science Education, Part II: The Conference Report," Publication No. 111 of the Social Science Education Consortium, USOE Cooperative Research Program. Lafayette, Indiana: Purdue University, 1966.

Sigel, Irving, "Child Development and Social Science Education. Part IV: A Teaching Concept Derived from Some Piagetian Concepts," Publication No. 113 of the Social Science Education Consortium, USOE Cooperative Research Project. Lafayette, Indiana: Purdue University, 1966.

"The Spectre of a Leisure-Ridden World," *The Futurist*, I (June, 1967), 36–37.

Taylor, Calvin W., ed., *Widening Horizons in Creativity.* New York: John Wiley & Sons, Inc., 1964.

Vygotsky, Lev Semenovich, *Thought and Language*, trans. and ed. Eugenia Hanfmann and Gertrude Vakar. Cambridge: The MIT Press, 1962.

CHAPTER NINE
CREATING: REACHING FOR THE UNPRECEDENTED

Alexander, Franz, "Neurosis and Creativity," *The American Journal of Psychoanalysis*, XXIV, No. 2 (1964), 116–130.

Anderson, Harold H., ed., *Creativity and Its Cultivation*. New York: Harper & Brothers, Publishers, 1959.

Andrews, Michael F., ed., *Creativity and Psychological Health*. Syracuse: Syracuse University Press, 1961.

Arnstine, Donald, "Curiosity," *Teachers College Record*, LXVII (May, 1966), 595–602.

Barron, Frank, "The Psychology of Imagination," *Scientific American*, IX (September, 1958), 150–166. Reprinted in *A Source Book for Creative Thinking*, pp. 227–237, eds. Sidney J. Parnes and Harold F. Harding. New York: Charles Scribner's Sons, 1962.

Bartlett, Phyllis, *Poems in Process*. New York: Oxford University Press, 1951.

Berman, Louise M., *Creativity in Education: A Guide to a Television Series*. Milwaukee: Milwaukee Public Schools, 1963.

Berman, Louise M., *From Thinking to Behaving: Assignments Reconsidered*. Practical Suggestions for Teaching, ed. Alice Miel. New York: Teachers College Press, Columbia University, 1967.

Broderick, Mary, "Creativity in the Classroom; Some Case Studies," *The National Elementary Principal*, XLVI (November, 1966), 18–24.

Brooks, Van Wyck, intro., *Writers at Work; The Paris Review Interviews*, Second Series. New York: The Viking Press, Inc., 1963.

Brown, George I., "A Second Study in the Teaching of Creativity," *Harvard Educational Review*, XXXV, No. 1 (1965), 39–54.

Buber, Martin, "Productivity and Existence," in *Identity and Anxiety, Survival of the Person in Mass Society*, pp. 628–632, eds. Maurice R. Stein, Arthur J. Vidich, and David Manning White. Glencoe: The Free Press of Glencoe, 1960.

Buel, William D., "The Validity of Behavioral Rating Scale: Items for the Assessment of Individual Creativity," *Journal of Applied Psychology*, XLIV, No. 6 (1960), 407–412.

Carnegie Corporation of New York Quarterly, *Creativity*, IX, No. 3 (July 1961).

Caulfield, Henry P., "Creative Federalism in Water and Related Land Resources Planning," Typewritten paper read at Cornell Conference on State Planning. New York: Cornell University, 1966.

Clive, Geoffrey, "A Phenomenology of Boredom," *Journal of Existentialism*, V (Summer, 1965), 359–370.

Combs, Arthur, and Donald Snygg, *Individual Behavior: A Perceptual Approach to Behavior*. New York: Harper & Brothers, Publishers, 1959.

Cooper, Russell M., ed., *The Two Ends of the Log: Learning and Teaching in Today's College*. Minneapolis: University of Minnesota Press, 1958.

Cross, K. Patricia, "On Creativity," *The Research Reporter*, II, No. 2 (1967), 1–4. Berkeley: The Center for Research and Development in Higher Education, University of California.

Darrow, Helen Fisher, and R. Van Allen, *Independent Activities for Creative Learning*. Practical Suggestions for Teaching, ed. Alice Miel. New York: Bureau of Publications, Teachers College, Columbia University, 1961.

Drevdahl, John E., "A Study of the Etiology and Development of the Creative Personality," USOE Cooperative Research Project No. 664. Coral Gables: University of Miami, 1962.

Fleming, Robert S., ed., *Curriculum for Today's Boys and Girls*. Columbus: Charles E. Merrill Publishing Company, 1963.

Freidlander, Bernard Z., "A Psychologist's Second Thoughts on Concepts, Curiosity, and Discovery in Teaching and Learning," *Harvard Educational Review*, XXV, No. 1 (1965), 18–38.

Gallagher, James J., "Research on Enhancing Productive Thinking," in *Nurturing Individual Potential*, pp. 43–56, ed. A. Harry Passow. Washington, D. C.: Association for Supervision and Curriculum Development, NEA, 1964.

Gardner, John, *Self-Renewal: The Individual and the Innovative Society*. New York: Harper & Row, Publishers, 1964.

Getzels, Jacob W., and Philip W. Jackson, *Creativity and Intelligence: Explorations with Gifted Students*. New York: John Wiley & Sons, Inc., 1962.

Ghiselin, Brewster, ed., *The Creative Process*. New York: Mentor Books, The New American Library, Inc., 1952.

Gibb, Jack R., "The Effects of Group Size and of Threat Reduction upon Creativity," Research Reprint Series of the National Training Laboratories, No. 4. Washington, D. C.: National Education Assn. (mimeographed).

Gordon, William J. J., *Synectics: The Development of Creative Capacity*. New York: Harper & Row, Publishers, 1961.

Gruber, Howard E., Glenn Terrell, and Michael Wertheimer, eds., *Contemporary Approaches to Creative Thinking*. New York: Atherton Press, Prentice-Hall, Inc., 1962.

Guilford, J. P., "Creativity: Its Measurement and Development," in *A Source Book for Creative Thinking*, pp. 151–168, eds. Sidney J. Parnes and Harold F. Harding. New York: Charles Scribner's Sons, 1962.

Guilford, J. P., "Factors that Aid and Hinder Creativity," *Teachers College Record*, Perspectives 1961–62, pp. 41–53.

Guilford, J. P., "The Three Faces of Intellect," *American Psychologist*, XIV (September, 1959), 469–479.

Hallman, Ralph J., "Creativity and Educational Philosophy," *Educational Theory*, XVII (January, 1967), 3–13.

Hallman, Ralph J., "Principles of Creative Teaching," *Educational Theory*, XV, No. 4 (October, 1965), 306–316.

Harper, Robert S., "Variability, Conformity, and Teaching," *Teachers College Record*, LXIII (May, 1962), 642–648.

Hyman, Ray, *Creativity and the Prepared Mind*, Research Monograph, No. 1. Washington, D. C.: National Art Education Association, NEA, 1965.

The Journal of Creative Behavior. Buffalo: The Creative Education Foundation.

Kelman, Harold, "Oriental Psychological Processes and Creativity," *The American Journal of Psychoanalysis*, XXIII, No. 1 (1963), 67–84.

Kneller, George F., *The Art and Science of Creativity*. New York: Holt, Rinehart & Winston, Inc., 1965.

Koestler, Arthur, *The Act of Creation*. New York: The Macmillan Company, 1964.

Keniston, Kenneth, "Alienation and the Decline of Utopia," *The American Scholar*, XXIX (Spring, 1960), 161–200.

Kris, Ernst, "Psychoanalysis and the Study of Creative Imagination," in *The World of Psychoanalysis*, I, pp. 41–58, ed. G. B. Levitas. New York: George Braziller, Inc., 1965.

Kubie, Lawrence S., M.D., *Neurotic Distortion of the Creative Process*, Porter Lecture Series 22. Lawrence: University of Kansas Press, 1958.

Langer, Susanne K., *Mind: An Essay on Human Feeling*, Vol. I. Baltimore: The Johns Hopkins Press, 1967.

Lowenfeld, Viktor, *Creative and Mental Growth*, Third Edition. New York: The Macmillan Company, 1957.

Marksberry, Mary Lee, *Foundation of Creativity*. New York: Harper & Row, Publishers, 1963.

Maw, Wallcice H., and Ethel W. Maw, "An Exploratory Investigation into the Measurement of Curiosity in Elementary School Children" USOE Cooperative Research Project No. 801. Newark: University of Delaware, 1964.

Mearns, Hughes, *Creative Power: The Education of Youth in the Creative Arts*, Second Edition. New York: Dover Publications, Inc., 1958.

Merleau-Ponty, Maurice, *The Primacy of Perception and Other Essays*, ed. James M. Edie. Chicago: Northwestern University, 1964.

Miel, Alice, ed., *Creativity in Teaching: Invitations and Instances*. Belmont, California: Wadsworth Publishing Company, Inc., 1961.

Munro, Thomas, and Herbert Read, *The Creative Arts in American Education*. Cambridge: Harvard University Press, 1960.

Murphy, Gardner, *Human Potentialities*. New York: Basic Books, Inc., Publishers, 1958.

Myers, R. E., and E. Paul Torrance, "Can Teachers Encourage Creative Thinking?" *Educational Leadership*, XIX (December, 1961), 156–159.

Myers, R. E., and E. Paul Torrance, *Can you Imagine?* A Book of Ideas for Children in the Primary Grades. Boston: Ginn and Company, 1965. Teachers' Guide available.

Myers, R. E., and E. Paul Torrance, *For Those Who Wonder.* Boston: Ginn and Company, 1966. Teachers' Guide available.

Myers, R. E., and E. Paul Torrance, *Invitations to Speaking and Writing Creatively.* Boston: Ginn and Company, 1965. Teachers' Guide available.

Myers, R. E., and E. Paul Torrance, *Invitations to Thinking and Doing.* Boston: Ginn and Company, 1964. Teachers' Guide available.

Myers, R. E., and E. Paul Torrance, *Plots, Puzzles, and Ploys. Adventures in Self-expression.* Boston: Ginn and Company, 1966. Teachers' Guide available.

National Education Association, *News of the NEA's Project on the Academically Talented*, Vol. II. Washington, D. C.: NEA, February, 1961.

Nelson, L. N., "Maximizing Creativity in the Classroom," *Young Children*, XXI (January, 1966), 130–136.

Parnes, Sidney J., and Harold F. Harding, *A Source Book for Creative Thinking.* New York: Charles Scribner's Sons, 1962.

Patrick, Catherine, *What Is Creative Thinking?* New York: Philosophical Library, Inc., 1955.

"Psychoanalysis as Creative Process: A Symposium, Part I," *The American Journal of Psychoanalysis*, XXIII, No. 2 (1963), 133–204.

Read, Sir Herbert, *The Forms of Things Unknown: Essays Towards an Aesthetic Philosophy.* New York: Horizon Press, 1960.

Reiss, Albert J., and Albert Lewis Rhodes, "A Socio-psychological Study of Conforming and Deviating Behavior among Adolescents," USOE Cooperative Research Project No. 507 (8133). Iowa City: The State University of Iowa, 1959.

Robertson, Malcolm, "A Method of Stimulating Original Thinking in College Students," USOE Cooperative Research Project No. 2235. Kalamazoo: Western Michigan University, 1964.

Rogers, Carl R., "Toward a Theory of Creativity," in *Creativity and Its Cultivation*, p. 76, ed. Harold A. Anderson. New York: Harper & Brothers, Publishers, 1959.

Rubin, Louis J., ed., *Nurturing Classroom Creativity.* Ventura, California: Ventura County Secondary Schools, 1960.

Rugg, Harold, *Imagination.* New York: Harper & Row, Publishers, 1963.

Samples, Robert E., "Kari's Handicap—The Impediment of Creativity," *Saturday Review*, L (July 15, 1967), 56–57.

Schachtel, Ernest, *Metamorphosis.* New York: Basic Books, Inc., Publishers, 1959.

Schulman, D., "Openness of Perception as a Condition for Creativity," *Exceptional Child*, XXXIII (October, 1966), 89–94.

Smith, Paul, ed., *Creativity: An Examination of the Creative Process*, A Report on the Third Communications Conference of the Art Directors Club of New York. New York: Hastings House Publishers, 1959.

"The Spectre of a Leisure-Ridden World," *The Futurist*, I (June, 1967), 36–37.

Stein, Morris I., and Shirley J. Heinze, *Creativity and the Individual: Summaries of Selected Literature in Psychology and Psychiatry*. Glencoe: The Free Press of Glencoe, 1960.

Steiner, Gary, A., ed., *The Creative Organization*. Chicago: The University of Chicago Press, 1965.

Taylor, Calvin W., *Creativity: Progress and Potential*. New York: McGraw-Hill Book Company, 1964.

Taylor, Calvin W., "Cultivating Creativity Within the New Curriculum," *National Association of Secondary School Principals Bulletin*, L (April, 1966), 110–131.

Taylor, Calvin W., "Effects of Instructional Media on Creativity," *Educational Leadership*, XIX (April, 1962), 453–458.

Taylor, Calvin W., "Questioning and Creating; A Model for Curriculum Reform," *Journal of Creative Behavior*, I, No. 1 (1967), 22–33.

Taylor, Calvin W., and Frank Barron, eds., *Scientific Creativity: Its Recognition and Development*. New York: John Wiley & Sons, Inc., 1963.

Taylor, Calvin W., and Frank E. Williams, eds., *Instructional Media and Creativity*. New York: John Wiley & Sons, Inc., 1966.

Thomas, William I., and Florian Znaniecki, "Three Types of Personality," in *Images of Man*, pp. 405–436, ed. C. Wright Mills. New York: George Braziller, Inc., 1960.

Torrance, E. Paul, *Creativity*. Washington, D. C.: Department of Classroom Teachers, NEA, 1963.

Torrance, E. Paul, *Guiding Creative Talent*. Englewood Cliffs, New Jersey: Prentice-Hall, Inc., 1962.

Torrance, E. Paul, "The Minnesota Studies of Creative Behavior: National and International Extensions," *The Journal of Creative Behavior*, I (Spring, 1967), 137–154.

Torrance, E. Paul, "Testing and Creative Talent," *Educational Leadership*, XX (October, 1962), 7–10.

Torrance, E. Paul, "Uniqueness and Creativeness: The School's Role," *Educational Leadership*, XXIV (March, 1967), 493–496.

Vygotsky, Lev Semenovich, *Thought and Language*, trans. and ed. by Eugenia Hanfmann and Gertrude Vakar. Cambridge: The MIT Press, 1962.

Waetjen, Walter B., "Curiosity and Exploration: Roles in Intellectual Development and Learning," in *Intellectual Development: Another Look*, pp. 40–58, eds. A. Harry Passow and Robert R. Leeper.

Washington, D. C.: Association for Supervision and Curriculum Development, NEA, 1964.

Weigert, Edith, "The Goal of Creativity in Psychotherapy," *The American Journal of Psychoanalysis*, XXIV, No. 2 (1964), 3–16.

Westcott, Malcolm R., "Inference, Guesswork and Creativity," USOE Cooperative Research Project No. 684. Poughkeepsie, N. Y.: Vassar College, 1962.

Williams, Frank E., "Chapter 13: Conference Overview with Models and Summary Lists of Tenable Ideas and Research Areas," in *Instructional Media and Creativity*, pp. 353–379, eds. Calvin W. Taylor and Frank E. Williams. New York: John Wiley & Sons, Inc., 1966.

Williams, Frank E., "Intellectual Creativity and the Teacher," *Journal of Creative Behavior*, I (Spring, 1967), 173–180.

Wyschograd, Michael, "The Cult of Creativity," *Teachers College Record*, LXVII (May, 1966), 618–622.

Yamamoto, K., "Creativity: A Blind Man's Report on the Elephant," *Journal of Counselling Psychology*, XII (Winter, 1965), 428–434.

CHAPTER TEN

VALUING: ENCHANTMENT WITH THE ETHICAL

Adorno, T. W., and Others, *The Authoritarian Personality*. New York: Harper & Row, Publishers, 1950.

Allport, Gordon W., "Values and Our Youth," *Teachers College Record*, LXIII (December, 1961), 211–219. Reprinted in *Professional Reprints in Education*, No. 8400. Columbus: Charles E. Merrill Publishing Company.

Argyris, Chris, "T-Groups for Organizational Effectiveness," *Harvard Business Review*, XLII, No. 2 (March–April, 1964), 60–74.

Arnstine, Donald G., "Some Problems in Teaching Values," *Educational Theory*, XI (1961), 158–167.

Association for Supervision and Curriculum Development, *Educational Leadership*, XXI (May, 1964), major portion of issue devoted to "Personal and Social Values," 483–526.

Association for Supervision and Curriculum Development, *Educational Leadership*, XXII (October, 1964), major portion of issue devoted to "Commitment: To What and Why?" 3–34.

Averill, Lloyd J., "The Climate of Valuing," *Current Issues in Higher Education*, 1963 Yearbook of the Association for Higher Education, Washington, D. C.: Association for Higher Education, NEA, 1963, pp. 67–73.

Beasley, G. Spencer, "Commitment Is a Personal Quality," *Educational Leadership*, XXII (October, 1964), 21–23.

Becker, Howard S., "Notes on the Concept of Commitment," *American Journal of Sociology*, LXVI (July, 1960–May, 1961), 32–40.

Cabot, Hugh, and Joseph A. Kahl, *Human Relations*. Cambridge: Harvard University Press, 1956.

Cantril, Hadley, in a panel discussion, "The Organization of Freedom," in *Conflict and Creativity, Control of the Mind*, Part 2, pp. 229–237, eds. Seymour M. Farber and Roger H. L. Wilson. New York: McGraw-Hill Book Company, 1963.

Cohen, Yehudi, *The Transition from Childhood to Adolescence*. Chicago: Aldine Publishing Company, 1964.

Combs, Arthur, ed., *Perceiving, Behaving, Becoming*, 1962 Yearbook. Washington, D. C.: Association for Supervision and Curriculum Development, NEA, 1962.

Crawford, Claud C., "Commitment," *The Personnel and Guidance Journal*, XLIV (May, 1966), 904–909.

Dean, John P., and Alex Rosen, *A Manual of Intergroup Relations*. Chicago: Phoenix Books, University of Chicago Press, 1955.

De Beauvoir, Simone, *The Ethics of Ambiguity*. New York: Philosophical Library, Inc., 1966.

Dreeben, Robert, "The Contribution of Schooling to the Learning of Norms," *Harvard Educational Review*, XXXVII (Spring, 1967), 211–237.

Engel, Gerald, and Harriet E. O'Shea, "Teaching Democratic Values: A Study of the Effect of Prejudice upon Learning," *Journal of Social Psychology*, LX (1963), 157–167.

Ezer, Melvin, "Value-teaching in Middle and Upper Grades: A Rationale for Teaching but not Transmitting Values," *Social Education*, XXXI (January, 1967), 34–40.

Fletcher, Joseph, *Situation Ethics: The New Morality*. Philadelphia: The Westminster Press, 1966.

Foster, Julian, Richard Stanek, and Witold Krassowski, "The Impact of a Value-Oriented University on Student Attitudes and Thinking," USOE Cooperative Research Project No. 729. Santa Clara, California: University of Santa Clara, 1961.

Gage, N. L., ed., *Handbook of Research on Teaching*. Chicago: Rand McNally & Co., 1963.

Gardner, John W., *Self-Renewal: The Individual and the Innovative Society*. New York: Harper & Row, Publishers, 1964.

Getzels, Jacob W., and Philip W. Jackson, *Creativity and Intelligence: Explorations with Gifted Students*. New York: John Wiley & Sons, Inc., 1962.

Goodykoontz, Bess, *Basic Values for Childhood Education*. Washington, D. C.: Association for Childhood Education International, NEA, 1963.

Graham, Angus Charles, *The Problem of Value*. London: Hutchinson University Library, 1961.

Greenberg, Bradley S., "On Relating Attitude Change and Information Gain," *Journal of Communication,* XIV (September, 1964), 157–171.

Harmin, Merrill, and Sidney B. Simon, "Values and Teaching: A Humane Process," *Educational Leadership,* XXIV (March, 1967), 517–525.

Harris, Dale B., "Changing Values I," *Young Children,* XX (March, 1965), 230–248.

Hartley, Ruth E., "Relationships Between Perceived Values and Acceptance of a New Reference Group," *The Journal of Social Psychology,* LI (February, 1960), 181–190.

Hill, Winifred F., "Learning Theory and the Acquisition of Values," *Psychological Review,* LXVII, No. 5 (1960), 317–331.

Jacob, Philip E., and James J. Flink, "Values and Their Function in Decision Making: Toward an Operational Definition for Use in Public Affairs Research," *American Behavioral Scientist Supplement,* V (May, 1962), 5–34.

Jenkins, David H., "Ethics and Responsibility in Human Relations Training," in *Selected Reading Series, Five: Issues in Training,* pp. 108–113, eds. Irving R. Wechsler and Edgar H. Schein. Washington, D. C.: National Training Laboratories, NEA, 1962.

Johnson, Earl, *Theory and Practice of the Social Studies.* New York: The Macmillan Company, 1956.

Kaufman, Walter, "Educational Development from the Point of View of a Normative Philosophy," *Harvard Educational Review,* XXXVI, No. 3 (1966), 247–264.

Keniston, Kenneth, *The Uncommitted: Alienated Youth in American Society.* New York: Harcourt, Brace & World, Inc., 1966.

Kimball, Solon T., "Individualism and the Formation of Values," *Journal of Applied Behavioral Science,* II, No. 4 (1966), 465–480.

Kinnane, John F., and Joseph R. Gaubinger, "Life Values and Work Values," *Journal of Counselling Psychology,* X, No. 4 (1963), 362–372.

Kluckhohn, Clyde, and Others, "Value and Value-Orientations in the Theory of Action," in *Toward a General Theory of Action,* pp. 388–433, eds. Talcott C. Parsons and Edward A. Shils. New York: Harper Torchbooks, Harper & Row, Publishers, 1962. Originally published by Harvard University Press, 1951.

Kneller, George F., *Existentialism and Education.* New York: Science Editions, John Wiley & Sons, Inc., 1958.

Kohlberg, Lawrence, "Moral Education in the Schools: A Developmental View," *The School Review,* LXXIV (Spring, 1966), 1–30.

Krathwohl, David R., Benjamin S. Bloom, and Bertram B. Masia, *Taxonomy of Educational Objectives. The Classification of Educational Goals, Handbook II: Affective Domain.* New York: David McKay Co., Inc., 1964.

Krutch, Joseph Wood, "The Conditioned Man," in *The Fate of Man*, pp. 242–254, ed. Crane Brinton. New York: George Braziller, Inc., 1961. From *Human Nature and the Human Condition*, pp. 169–190. New York: Random House, Inc., 1957.

Lichtenberg, Philip, "Comparative Valuation and Individual Action," *The Journal of Social Psychology*, LVI (February, 1962), 97–105.

Lieberman, Phyllis, and Sidney Simon, "Values and Student Writing," *Educational Leadership*, XXII (March, 1965), 414–421f.

Machotka, Otakar, *The Unconscious in Social Relations*. New York: Philosophical Library, Inc., 1964.

Metraux, Rhoda, "Gaining Freedom of Value Choice," in *New Insights and the Curriculum*, 1963 Yearbook, pp. 190–220, ed. Alexander Frazier. Washington, D. C.: Association for Supervision and Curriculum Development, NEA, 1963.

Miel, Alice, and Peggy Brogan, *More Than Social Studies: A View of Social Learning in the Elementary School*. Englewood Cliffs, N. J.: Prentice-Hall, Inc., 1957.

Montefiore, Alan, "Moral Philosophy and the Teaching of Morality," *Harvard Educational Review*, XXXV (Fall, 1965), 435–449.

Myrdal, Gunnar, *An American Dilemma*. New York: Harper & Row, Publishers, 1944 and 1962.

Oliver, Donald W., and James P. Shaver, *Teaching Public Issues in the High Schools*. Boston: Houghton Mifflin Company, 1966.

Parsons, Talcott, and Edward A. Shils, eds., *Toward a General Theory of Action*. New York: Harper Torchbooks, Harper & Brothers, Publishers, 1951.

Parsons, Theodore, "Attitudes and Values: Tools or Chains?" *Educational Leadership*, XXI (March, 1964), 343–346f.

Peattie, Lisa R., "Anthropology and the Search for Values," *The Journal of Applied Behavioral Science*, I, No. 4 (1965), 361–372.

Perrucci, Robert, "Sociology," Publication No. 101 of the Social Science Education Consortium, USOE Cooperative Research Program. Lafayette, Indiana: Purdue University, 1966.

Persky, Blanche, "Changing Values II," *Young Children*, XX (March, 1965), 249–258.

Pfuetze, Paul, *Self, Society, and Existence*. New York: Harper Torchbooks, Harper & Brothers, Publishers, 1954.

Phenix, Philip, *Realms of Meaning: A Philosophy of the Curriculum for General Education*. New York: McGraw-Hill Book Company, 1964.

Raths, James, "A Strategy for Developing Values," *Educational Leadership*, XXI (May, 1964), 509–514.

Raths, James, "Values and the Involvement of Children in Learning," Research Bulletin 62-1. Milwaukee: Campus School, School of Education, University of Wisconsin—Milwaukee, 1962 (mimeographed).

Raths, Louis E., "Clarifying Values," in *Curriculum for Today's Boys and Girls*, pp. 315–342, ed. Robert S. Fleming. Columbus: Charles E. Merrill Publishing Company, 1963.

Raths, Louis E., Merrill Harmin, and Sidney B. Simon, *Values and Teaching*. Columbus: Charles E. Merrill Publishing Company, 1966.

Ruesch, Jurgen, moderator, "The Organization of Freedom," in *Conflict and Creativity. Control of the Mind*, Part II, pp. 229–237, eds. Seymour M. Farber and Roger H. L. Wilson. New York: McGraw-Hill Book Company, 1963.

Sartre, Jean-Paul, *Existentialism and Human Emotions*. New York: The Wisdom Library, Philosophical Library, Inc., 1957.

Scriven, Michael, "The Methodology of Evaluation," Publication No. 110 of the Social Science Education Consortium, USOE Cooperative Research Program with Charles F. Kettering Foundation. Lafayette, Indiana: Purdue University, 1966.

Scriven, Michael, "Morality," Publication No. 122 of the Social Science Education Consortium, USOE Cooperative Research Program. Lafayette, Indiana: Purdue University, 1966.

Scriven, Michael, "Student Values as Educational Objectives," Publication No. 124 of the Social Science Education Consortium, USOE Cooperative Research Program. Lafayette, Indiana: Purdue University, 1966.

Scriven, Michael, "Value Claims in the Social Sciences," Publication No. 123 of the Social Science Education Consortium, USOE Cooperative Research Program. Lafayette, Indiana, Purdue University, 1966.

Shirk, Evelyn, *The Ethical Dimension: An Approach to the Philosophy of Values and Valuing*. New York: Appleton-Century-Crofts, 1965.

Shoben, Edward, Jr., "Texts and Values: The Irrelevance of Literary Education," *Liberal Education*, LIII, No. 2 (1967), 244.

Siegel, Alberta E., and Sidney Siegel, "Reference Groups, Membership Groups, and Attitude Change," in *Readings in the Social Psychology of Education*, pp. 264–268, eds. W. W. Charters, Jr., and H. L. Gage. Boston: Allyn & Bacon, Inc., 1963.

Snyder, Eldon E., "Implications of Changing Cultural Values," *Educational Leadership*, XXIV (February, 1967), 437–443.

Sparshott, F. E., "The Concept of Purpose," *Ethics: An International Journal of Social, Political, and Legal Philosophy*, LXXII (April, 1962), 157–170.

Spaulding, Irving A., "Of Human Values," *Sociology and Social Research*, XLVII (October, 1962–July, 1962), 169–177.

Taba, Hilda, "Education for Independent Valuing," in *New Insights and the Curriculum*, 1963 Yearbook, pp. 221–240, ed. Alexander Frazier. Washington, D.C.: Association for Supervision and Curriculum Development, NEA, 1963.

UNESCO, *Humanism and Education in East and West*. New York: United Nations, 1953.

Virtue, Charles F., "Creativity and Symbolism," in *Creativity and Psycholog-ical Health*, pp. 55–75, ed. Michael F. Andrews. Syracuse, N. Y.: Syracuse University Press, 1961.

von Bertalanffy, Ludwig, "The World of Science and the World of Values," *Teachers College Record*, LXV (March, 1964), 496–507.

Winthrop, Henry, "Some Neglected Considerations Concerning the Problem of Value in Psychology," *The Journal of General Psychology*, LXVI (January, 1961), 37–59.

Wolff, Robert Paul, "Reflections on Game Theory and the Nature of Value," *Ethics: An International Journal of Social, Political, and Legal Philosophy*, LXXII (April, 1962), 171–179.

Wonderley, William L., and Eugene A. Nida, "Cultural Differences and the Communication of Christian Values," *Practical Anthropology*, X, No. 6 (1963), 241–258.

Index